SEVENTEEN MILES FROM PARADISE

Saints v Pompey

Passion, Pride and Prejudice

DESERT ISLAND FOOTBALL HISTORIES

Club Histories	ISBN
Aberdeen: A Centenary History 1903-2003	1-874287-57-0
Aberdeen: Champions of Scotland 1954-55	1-874287-65-1
Aberdeen: The European Era – A Complete Record	1-874287-11-2
Bristol City: The Modern Era – A Complete Record	1-874287-28-7
Bristol City: The Early Years 1894-1915	1-874287-74-0
Cambridge United: The League Era – A Complete Record	1-874287-32-5
Cambridge United: 101 Golden Greats	1-874287-58-9
The Story of the Celtic 1888-1938	1-874287-15-5
Chelsea: Champions of England 1954-55	1-874287-77-5
Colchester United: Graham to Whitton – A Complete Record	1-874287-27-9
Coventry City: The Elite Era – A Complete Record	1-874287-83-X
Coventry City: An Illustrated History	1-874287-59-7
Dundee: Champions of Scotland 1961-62	1-874287-86-4
Dundee United: Champions of Scotland 1982-83	1-874287-71-6
History of the Everton Football Club 1878-1928	1-874287-14-7
Halifax Town: From Ball to Lillis – A Complete Record	1-874287-26-0
Hereford United: The League Era – A Complete Record	1-874287-18-X
Huddersfield Town: Champions of England 1923-1926	1-874287-88-0
Ipswich Town: The Modern Era – A Complete Record	1-874287-43-0
Ipswich Town: Champions of England 1961-62	1-874287-63-5
Kilmarnock: Champions of Scotland 1964-65	1-874287-87-2
Luton Town: The Modern Era – A Complete Record	1-874287-90-2
Luton Town: An Illustrated History	1-874287-79-1
Manchester United's Golden Age 1903-1914: Dick Duckworth	1-874287-80-5
The Matt Busby Chronicles: Manchester United 1946-69	1-874287-53-8
Motherwell: Champions of Scotland 1931-32	1-874287-73-2
Norwich City: The Modern Era – A Complete Record	1-874287-67-8
Peterborough United: The Modern Era – A Complete Record	1-874287-33-3
Peterborough United: Who's Who?	1-874287-48-1
Plymouth Argyle: The Modern Era – A Complete Record	1-874287-54-6
Plymouth Argyle: 101 Golden Greats	1-874287-64-3
Plymouth Argyle: Snakes & Ladders – Promotions and Relegations	1-874287-82-1
Portsmouth: From Tindall to Ball – A Complete Record	1-874287-25-2
Portsmouth: Champions of England – 1948-49 & 1949-50	1-874287-50-3
The Story of the Rangers 1873-1923	1-874287-16-3
The Romance of the Wednesday 1867-1926	1-874287-17-1
Seventeen Miles from Paradise – Saints v Pompey	1-874287-89-9
Stoke City: The Modern Era – A Complete Record	1-874287-76-7
Stoke City: 101 Golden Greats	1-874287-55-4
Potters at War: Stoke City 1939-47	1-874287-78-3
Tottenham Hotspur: Champions of England 1950-51, 1960-61	1-874287-84-8
West Ham: From Greenwood to Redknapp	1-874287-19-8
West Ham: The Elite Era – A Complete Record	1-874287-31-7
Wimbledon: From Southern League to Premiership	1-874287-09-0
Wimbledon: From Wembley to Selhurst	1-874287-20-1
Wimbledon: The Premiership Years	1-874287-40-6
Wrexham: The European Era – A Complete Record	1-874287-52-X
World Cup Histories	
England's Quest for the World Cup – A Complete Record	1-874287-61-9
Scotland: The Quest for the World Cup – A Complete Record	1-897850-50-6
Ireland: The Quest for the World Cup – A Complete Record	1-897850-80-8
Miscellaneous	
Red Dragons in Europe – A Complete Record	1-874287-01-5
The Book of Football: A History to 1905-06	1-874287-13-9
Football's War & Peace: The Tumultuous Season of 1946-47	1-874287-70-8

SEVENTEEN MILES FROM PARADISE

SAINTS V POMPEY

Passion, Pride and Prejudice

Series Editor: Clive Leatherdale

Colin Farmery

DESERT ISLAND BOOKS

First published in 2004
by
DESERT ISLAND BOOKS LIMITED
89 Park Street, Westcliff-on-Sea, Essex SS0 7PD
United Kingdom
www.desertislandbooks.com

British Library Cataloguing-in-Publication Data
A catalogue record for this book is available from the British Library

ISBN 1-874287-89-9

Printed in Great Britain
by
Biddles Ltd, King's Lynn

Photographs courtesy of the Southampton *Echo* and the Portsmouth Evening *News*

~ Contents ~

~ AUTHOR'S NOTE ~

The first professional football match I attended at the age of seven was at Fratton Park, in September 1970. My second, two months later, was at The Dell. In the early 1970s I was a semi-regular at both grounds and my memories of Saints and its shoehorned stadium are affectionate still. It's just that I was always taken by someone supporting the other side, and it's a habit I've never quite kicked. So, I've laid my cards on the table. I am a Pompey fan. However, like many followers of both clubs, I have always taken a healthy interest in what the other lot are up to. And I have a confession. I actually supported Saints in the 1976 FA Cup final, after my Auntie Jen suggested it would be 'nice' if a south coast team won the trophy. What her Manchester United-supporting husband, Roger, thought of the idea, I don't recall.

I am grateful for the comments and suggestions on my initial drafts made by my long-standing friend and writing partner, Peter Jeffs. On the Saints side, Nick Illingsworth, of the Rivals website the Ugly Inside, gave me several profitable leads to pursue, and Tim Mumford was a sterling supporter of the project. In particular, I cannot thank Chris Newman enough. Chris gave freely of his enthusiasm, knowledge and above all time, researching and photocopying archive material for me in Southampton Library, as well as correcting my errors on Saints' history. My ever-supportive wife, Di Lloyd, proved a meticulous proofreader. I owe her more than she could ever imagine, but a stress free summer next year (and perhaps the year after too) is the minimum. My editor-cum-sparring partner, Clive Leatherdale, proposed this project to me and buffed my tarnished text here and there to, I hope, make it shine. I am a better writer because of him. Steve Bone, Chris Gibbs, Chris Johnson, Roger Holmes, Richard Owen, Mick Cooper and the staff of Portsmouth City Library also helped me in various ways.

I pay tribute to the generations of journalists on the Southampton *Echo* and the Portsmouth *News* and *Sports Mail*. Without their professionalism in pursuing what can be a thankless task at times, this book would not be as complete as it is. I also thank the respective communities of the POMPEY-FANS.COM and THEUGLYINSIDE.COM message boards, who continue to provide a fascinating insight into the psychology underpinning this fractious derby.

Finally, I thank my colleague at St Vincent College, Gosport, Rob Hind. Recently moved to the area and bemused by my parochial passion, he supplied me with the quote from the satirical news source 'The Onion' which prefaces this book; a reminder that although this rivalry is a serious business, we take it too seriously at our peril.

COLIN FARMERY, October 2004

'If you need a reason why the sporting franchise representing my area is superior, look no further than the supporters of the two sides. Not only are the supporters of the team from my region more spirited, but they are also more intelligent and of finer breeding than of your ilk.'

THE ONION, 19th-25th April, 2001

BIBLIOGRAPHY:

Association Football and the Men Who Made It (Vol 4), Gibson A and Pickford W, Caxton, 1906
Southampton: The Complete History of the Club, East P, Wensum Books 1979
Pompey, Neasom M, Robinson D, Cooper M, Milestone Publishing, 1984
Saints: The Complete Record, Chalk G, Holley D, Breedon Books, 1987
The Alphabet of the Saints, Holley D, Chalk G, ACL and Polar Publishing, 1992
The Football Grounds of Great Britain, Inglis S, Collins Willow, 1987
The Football League and the Men Who Made It, Inglis S, Collins Willow, 1988
One Hump or Two, Worthington F, Polar Print, 1994
Dell Diamond, Bull D, Hagiology Publishing, 1998
Portsmouth FC: The Official Centenary History, Farmery C, Jeffs P, Owen R, Bishops Printers, 1998
CB Fry: An English Hero, Wilton I, Metro Publishing, 1999
Glory Gunners, Smith K, KS Publications, 1999
Portsmouth: From Tindall to Ball, Farmery C, Desert Island Books, 1999
Portsmouth: Champions of England, Farmery C, Desert Island Books, 2000
Match of the Millennium, Bull D, Brunskell B (eds), Hagiology Publishing, 2000
Pompey Players 1920-2001, Holmes R, Bishops Printers, 2001
Legend, Knight A (with Farmery C and Jeffs P) Legendary Publishing, 2003
In That Number, Chalk G, Holley D, Hagiology Publishing, 2003

~ INTRODUCTION ~

As the results filtered through on the last day of the 2003-04 Premiership season – finalising the League placings in a season dominated by Arsenal, Chelsea and Manchester United – in the red and blue halves of southern Hampshire two sets of supporters were digesting the fact that, to all intents, Southampton and Portsmouth were now roughly back on a par. While Pompey were thrashing Middlesbrough 5-1, Saints were succumbing 1-2 at Charlton. That left the two bitter rivals almost locked together. Pompey fans could claim that, but for a spat between manager Harry Redknapp and chairman Milan Mandaric hours before the visit of already-doomed Leicester a week earlier – which brought a shock 1-3 defeat – Pompey would have finished above Southampton for the first time since 1960. Saints fans would scoff that the final table never lies. Their team finished twelfth, two points better off than Pompey, who were one place lower. But no matter, the clear blue water (or should that be Red Sea?) – which in the late 1970s was as wide as the Solent – had all but dried up.

That the two clubs should have finished side by side in what was only Portsmouth's second top-flight season in 45 years is ironic. They boast urban areas of similar population, with a more rural hinterland beyond (centred on Salisbury, Winchester and Andover for Saints, Chichester, Petersfield and Bognor for Pompey). One might have expected the respective football clubs to have gone toe-to-toe over the decades, rather like East Anglian foes Norwich City and Ipswich Town, or the East Midlands' triumvirate of Leicester City, Derby County and Nottingham Forest. Perhaps a better analogy lies with the Tyne-Wear derby. If one takes a longer view, Pompey's two League titles and Saints' FA Cup offer a better post-War domestic return than that from football's supposed 'hot bed'. The south-coast derby, by rights, should have become an integral and enduring element in the fabric of Hampshire sporting culture.

In reality, the story of Saints and Pompey is nothing of the sort. Since the formation of Portsmouth FC in April 1898 – thirteen years after the birth of Southampton FC – the two clubs have met just 28 times in Football League combat, following the creation of the Third Division in 1920. Even if we throw in four cup-ties, we are still left with a rivalry which, although dating back more than a century, is largely immature. By a quirk of history, the two rivals have seemingly done everything possible to avoid each other. Each club has enjoyed a lengthy spell of divisional dominance over the other, during which their paths rarely crossed, save for the end-of-season testimonial or occasional 'friendly'.

Pompey were the first to impose themselves when gaining promotion to the First Division in 1927, establishing a period of superiority which would endure more than 30 years. In that time, they won the FA Cup in 1939 and, a decade later were crowned Champions of England two seasons running. They regularly played in front of 40,000 crowds in a Fratton Park ground regarded as one of the best in the land. In those days, Saints, in the quaint 'chocolate-boxed' confines of The Dell, were barely a blip on Pompey's radar. In 1949, as Pompey clinched the League title for the first time, Saints blew what seemed to be their big chance to challenge Pompey's ascendancy, by throwing away promotion. Having finished third in 1948 – in those days only two teams went up – the Saints looked certainties by Easter 1949 to make the top flight for the first time. Victory over Tottenham had lifted them eight points clear of the pack. They needed just four points from their final eight games (only two points for a win back then) to finish the task. However, an injury to centre-forward Charlie Wayman – 32 goals in 35 games – after scoring the winner against Spurs, wrecked their hopes. Saints ended up third, two points behind Fulham and one adrift of West Brom.

As Pompey claimed their second successive Championship twelve months later, Saints went closer still, but needing to beat West Ham 3-0 in their final game, they could only manage 3-2 and missed out on goal-average. It was the tightest ever climax to a promotion race. The two Sheffield clubs tied on points with Saints for the second promotion spot, behind runaway Second Division champions Spurs. The Owls made it by 0.063 of a goal.

As Pompey's powers waned in the 1950s, Saints too were on an ebb tide, sinking into the Third Division (South) in 1953. But Portsmouth, by this time, were starting to show the cracks that would lead to almost terminal collapse. A third place in 1955 could not paper over the problems which culminated in relegation from the top flight in 1959, under the catastrophic management of Freddie Cox, followed two seasons later by the drop into the Third Division.

Saints, meanwhile, were back in Division Two – Champions of the Third Division in 1960. Driven on by the ruthless ambition of manager Ted Bates, the south-coast pendulum was beginning to swing. Ends of eras are never clear cut, but 5th February 1966 can be seen, in retrospect, as a defining moment in this tale of two cities – Southampton could call itself such having been granted that elevated municipal status two years beforehand. For her part, Portsmouth, its cathedral city status dating back to 1194 and a Royal Charter granted by Richard I, had been a municipal city since 1925. Bates had moulded an exceptional Southampton team which married the twinkle-toed skills of inside-forward Jimmy Melia, the wily wing-play of England international Terry Paine – at a time when Second

Division status did not terminate a player's international prospects – and the rugged and uncompromising 'ale house' (to use Bill Shankly's colourful description) qualities of defender and captain Tony Knapp. By contrast Pompey, albeit rehabilitated in the Second Division under the sergeant-major routine of George Smith, were strapped for cash. In a desperate attempt to cut costs, the youth policy and reserve side had been scrapped and the team was a pale shadow of that which had been the best in the land barely fifteen years before.

Anyway, on 5th February 1966 Saints came to Fratton Park on the fringes of the Second Division promotion race. Their 5-2 win that day sparked a storming end to the season which saw Saints promoted behind champions Manchester City. Pompey would be left playing catch up for almost 40 years.

Saints set about establishing themselves among the elite – much as Pompey had done 40 years previously – under the steady chairmanship of George Reader, whose claims to fame included refereeing the concluding match of the 1950 World Cup in Brazil, as well as officiating (and sending off Jimmy Scoular) during Pompey's South American tour a year later. In 1969 Saints finished seventh and qualified for the Inter Cities Fairs' Cup – forerunner of the UEFA Cup – a feat they repeated in 1971. The impressive nurturing of the talent at their disposal, including future England internationals Mick Channon and Steve Williams, saw Saints eclipse Pompey on the field. This was despite the fanciful promises of big-spending property magnate John Deacon, who became Portsmouth chairman in May 1973. His earlier overtures to invest in Southampton had been rebuffed, and the next five years at Fratton would show how wise the board at The Dell had been to do so.

When Southampton slipped back into Division Two for four seasons under Bates' replacement, Lawrie McMenemy, it did not mean the gap with Pompey narrowed. Instead it opened wider. Pompey slipped into Division Three in 1976, Saints' last-minute 1-0 win at Fratton in April sealing their fate. The salt was rubbed in when Paulsgrove-born Pompey boy Bobby Stokes scored the goal which took the FA Cup to the south coast, as Second Division Saints defied the odds to topple Manchester United. The folly of George Smith's decision to axe Pompey's youth policy eleven years earlier was underlined by the fact that in the mid-1970s Southampton had no fewer than four Portsmouth-born professionals on their books. Two of these – the aforesaid Stokes and goalkeeper Steve Middleton – would in due course play for Pompey, but they were past their best by the time they arrived at Fratton and were bedevilled by having to live down their Dell 'origins'.

From the turn of the twentieth century, players had been crossing the Saints-Pompey divide. England centre-half Arthur Chadwick signed for

Pompey from Saints as early as 1901. Charles Burgess 'CB' Fry, who had played in Saints' two recent FA Cup final defeats, also swapped sides, although injury would cut short his Pompey career.

In general, however, movement between the two clubs has been limited, especially since the Second World War. As might be expected, given the long years of dominance by one club or the other, the weaker club usually picked up the other's cast-offs. This met with varying degrees of success, as poor Stokes and Middleton – not to mention their contemporary, Paul Gilchrist – would attest. More successful was full-back Bill Rochford, who starred in Pompey's 1939 FA Cup final victory and went on to give sterling service post-War at The Dell.

The two really significant moves – one each way – were unqualified successes. Barry Horne had established his reputation as a tough-tackling midfielder in Pompey's one season back in the old First Division in 1987-88, before a £650,000 transfer deadline-day move to Southampton in March 1989. At The Dell, Horne consolidated his Wales international career and went on to play for Everton. Meanwhile, Alan McLoughlin found a ready escape from being sidelined by Saints boss Ian Branfoot, who allowed the playmaker to join Pompey in March 1992 for £440,000. The Republic of Ireland international midfielder served Pompey with distinction for nine seasons and became the first player from the club to go to the World Cup finals since Northern Ireland's Norman Uprichard in 1958. McLoughlin scored the goal which sealed the Republic's qualification for USA 1994, although he wouldn't get off the bench during the tournament itself.

John Beresford and Mick Channon are two others who have arguably gained the respect of both sets of fans, although possibly the only man given equal billing by both sets of supporters is Alan Ball, a McMenemy signing for Saints, who went on to manage Portsmouth and guide them back to the old First Division in his third season, 1986-87. After a spell as Exeter City boss, Ball replaced the hapless Branfoot at The Dell in January 1994 and somehow guided Saints to Premiership salvation and respectability the following season. Only a dispute over a contract extension in the summer of 1995, which led to him leaving to take the vacant Manchester City job, blotted an otherwise perfect copybook on both sides of the Hampshire divide.

To return for a moment to the late 1970s, McMenemy was fast proving himself to be a canny operator at The Dell. He gave youth its head, while coaxing the likes of veterans Ball, Ted MacDougall and Phil Boyer – discarded by their previous clubs – to show they still had what it takes. By 1979 Pompey's abortive attempt to climb out of the Fourth Division at the first attempt, coupled with Saints' impressive return to the top flight – ninth place and another Wembley appearance (they lost 2-3 to Nottingham

Forest in the League Cup final) – meant the Hampshire rivals now stood 63 League places apart. Five years previously they had been within four places of each other.

Saints' sound husbandry, coupled with the voodoo economics of the Pompey madhouse, had combined to leave Southampton far more dominant over their near neighbours than Portsmouth had ever been, not even in their Championship pomp. In February 1980 McMenemy pulled off the transfer coup of the year, if not the decade, in persuading Kevin Keegan to sign for the Saints, ending his three years at SV Hamburg. There was no denying it, Saints were now a glamour side and in the spring of 1982 they topped the old First Division for six weeks, genuine title contenders, while Pompey scuffled along nowhere in the Third Division.

In fact, even to call the two teams 'rivals' was open to question, certainly on the Saints side. With Brighton and Hove Albion enjoying their three-season sojourn in the top flight, the Seagulls became the principal 'rivals' for many Southampton fans, for whom Pompey were now an irrelevance, in sporting terms at least. This was rubbed in by BBC DJ Keith Chegwin in the early 1980s. At the traditional 'Radio One roadshow' at Southsea – so urban legend has it – he enquired of a local contestant his interests, and on being told 'football' Cheggers replied: 'Yes, it must be great to have Southampton on your doorstep.' Quite.

The events of the late 1960s and 70s provided the catalyst for the supporters' mutual antipathy which emerged over the next twenty years. A potent cocktail of jealousy on the one side and disdain on the other – the reader can guess which was which – was exacerbated by fixtures between the clubs becoming as rare as a red and white car sticker in Somers Town or a blue and white scarf on the Bar Gate. A vicious sub-culture was also developing around the rivalry; an unfortunate by-product of the scourge of football hooliganism which had poisoned the English game since the mid-1960s. Saints were now 'Scummers' and Pompey 'Skates'.

The former term of abuse has been embellished in recent times by urban myth and apocrypha. It is now held to derive from an acronym associated with the breaking of a Portsmouth dock strike in the 1940s (or in some versions the 1920s) by 'Southampton Company Union Men'. The contradiction in this improbable linking of capital and labour in the name is conveniently ignored, as is the fact that the city of Southampton has a proud radical tradition. The city returned the only Labour MP south of London in the Conservative General Election landslide of 1983 and its dockworkers have proved to be inherently militant over the years. To finally nail the misconception, it should be remembered too that 'unionised' dock labour did not exist pre-1950, when the National Dock Labour Board was established. Previously, work was allocated on a daily basis by a tally system, leaving workers at the whim of the employer. In an ironic twist to this tale, the Portsmouth commercial port, which expanded rapidly in the early 1970s, was able to do so in part because it was not bound by the restrictive practices of the NDLB, enabling it to poach Southampton's lucrative cross-channel ferry business.

By the same token, 'skates' – a reference to the alleged sexual proclivities of sailors, who inevitably frequent Portsmouth given that it is home to the Senior Service – ignores that fact that the term is also used by Portsmouth folk to disparage those very same sailors. Using the principle that my enemy's enemy must be my friend, the Southampton fanzine 'Ugly Inside' claims credit for coining the 'Skate' term in the late 1980s. As we all know, the first casualty of war is truth.

In essence the 'problem' boils down to a question of perception. How do we measure the status and stature of a club? For Portsmouth fans, Saints can never match Pompey's glorious past. This is probably true, but it is equally true that Portsmouth FC will never match Pompey's past. Those of the Blue persuasion measure the stature of their club in fading titles past; a sepia-tinted justification of perpetual hegemony. Seventeen miles up the by-now completed M27, Saints charted a steady course for the brave new football world which would emerge post-Hillsborough on the back of Rupert Murdoch's Sky TV millions. Pompey fans never shared the grudging admiration the rest of the football world bestowed on Southampton as they clung limpet-like to top-flight football, inspired by the loyalty (or lack of ambition?) of Matthew Le Tissier, and in spite of The Dell having a capacity of less than 16,000. 'Where are their titles?' chimed the response. But the football world was moving on and Pompey and their fans were increasingly being left behind. They were becoming as anachronistic as, well, a provincial club winning the Premier League.

As a symbol of modern football, St Mary's Stadium shines brightly. Its completion in August 2001 at a cost of £30 million is a tribute to the foresight of Saints Chairman Rupert Lowe. Whatever his overall legacy to Southampton Football Club, the delivery of this 32,000-capacity arena, with all the essential add-ons – restaurants, conference centre and executive boxes – has given Saints a possibly decisive advantage in this battle for south-coast supremacy. For not only has Lowe built it, he has filled it. Poor old Pompey can only look on, green with envy, as tatty old Fratton Park – once one of the better grounds in the country, but like its occupants that was 50 years ago – leaves the club looking distinctly economy class in the revenue stakes. Until Pompey can upgrade their facilities – and by the time you read this book a 'new' Fratton Park could be taking shape – they will continue to play second fiddle to the Saints, whatever the results on the pitch might say.

Portsmouth fans may claim, with an eye to history, that their club could match, nay better, Saints' gates, but that will remain untested until a planned revamp of Fratton is completed. As a result of Pompey's current lack of spare capacity – virtually every League game at Fratton since January 2003 has been a 20,000 sell-out – Saints' move from The Dell, coupled with some canny marketing, has enabled them to vacuum up the pool of floating support for top-grade football in south Hampshire and beyond. And those floating fans are becoming regulars, establishing the self-same habits which in the 1950s gave Pompey a support base it continued to mine until well into the 1980s.

Given the right conditions, that is to say a decent team, the conventional wisdom says the crowds would flock back to Fratton. Certainly in the 1970s gates in excess of 20,000, and even the odd one topping 30,000, were common enough, even as Pompey plummeted from the Second to the Fourth Division. In the 1979-80 season, Pompey actually showed several attendances bigger than Saints', despite the huge gulf in League status. However, that 'potential' has long-since dispersed, eroded by a combination of Old Father Time, endemic mismanagement at the club, and the changing demographics of the region. An increasingly affluent population makes 'leisure choices'. Grimsby at home on a January afternoon at windswept Fratton was never going to be one of them.

Conversely, Saints' current average attendance of 30,000 is difficult to reconcile with past performance. Throughout their First Division years at The Dell, even in the halcyon early 1980s when Lawrie McMenemy was assembling his dream team, its then capacity of around 24,000 was rarely put to the test. In the late 1960s and early 70s, as Saints established themselves among the elite, the record attendance at The Dell of 31,044 – set in October 1969 against Manchester United – was only occasionally challenged and then, usually, when United came to town. The numbers that turn up to watch Southampton regularly these days, historically speaking, are unprecedented, but have added a fascinating twist to the arguments for regional supremacy.

The story of Saints-Pompey rivalry extends far beyond football. From the control exercised over the commercial port at Portsmouth by its Southampton counterpart from the twelfth century, through to the snatching of the lucrative cross-channel ferry routes by the very same port from Southampton, this is a story where football, civic pride, commercial interest and even royal patronage intertwine. Who will be the 'winner' in this battle for south-coast supremacy? (Sorry Brighton and Bournemouth, but your role is that of bit players in this dispute.) That's for you to decide, but the mere fact that this book is having the debate suggests the result after all these years, as in season 2003-04, may be too tight to call and ultimately pose as many questions as answers.

Chapter 1

~ The Origins of a Bitter Rivalry ~

'How long football has been played in Hampshire no man knows … Football in Hants and Dorset is an indigenous game; it carries tradition back to the dawn of civilisation.' So wrote Alfred Gibson and William Pickford – who was himself to have a profound influence on the development of the sport in the county – in their seminal four-volume work, *Association Football and the Men Who Made It*, back in 1906. For 'football' is a sport whose roots burrow deep beyond the development of the 'modern' game in the mid-nineteenth century. The renowned Eton College Wall Game – a traditional form of football played to this day at the public school – was imported from Winchester, when the new public school 'borrowed' a master from the Hampshire college, who brought with him his love of football. In those days, 22-a-side was the norm and the sport was more akin to rugby, as the players indulged in one long 'hot maul' up and down a pitch that was only 27 yards wide. The county of Hampshire endorses the claim to be at the heart of the sport we know and love today. The first 'professional' south of London to be registered with the Football Association was one William Winkworth, a half-back with the Winchester Town club.

Modern football in Hampshire, strangely, had rural rather than urban roots, with the New Forest village of Fordingbridge and its team known as the Turks, being formed in 1868. Two years later, independent of the Turks, a club was founded in Southampton at Portswood Park, although the rules of their game were more akin to rugby football. A 'goal' was registered when the ball was kicked over the bar and the rules allowed for players to indulge in 'kicking and charging', although, to show regard for scruple, 'attempts to throttle or strangle are totally opposed to all principles of the game'.

Pickford and Gibson note that the game grew slowly in Southampton. Most clubs were inclined to adopt the 'rugby' model, with the Trojans club – who still play the union code to this day – to the fore. It was in the Wessex hinterlands that Association rules flourished, with clubs being established in Ringwood, Bournemouth (then in Hampshire, as it was until 1974), and Downton, and over the Dorset border at Sturminster and Wimborne. The game was rapidly gaining ground in the north of the county too, with Captain (latterly Colonel) May from Basingstoke providing a county 'Challenge Cup' in 1879. The original competition had seven entrants and was won by Fordingbridge Turks, who beat Basingstoke 1-0. Two additional clubs entered the fray in 1880, including the marvellously named Basingstoke Total Abstinence, but their dedicated sacrifice failed to have an effect on the field. The Turks retained the trophy, beating Queen's School, Basingstoke, in the final watched by a record crowd numbering more than 1,000. Then, in a bizarre twist, the Turks declined to put up the Cup for competition. Predictably, without the spur of regular cup matches, the popularity of Association Football slowly evaporated.

Rugby continued its rise, especially in Portsmouth and Southampton, but the spark for the rejuvenation of 'soccer' in the county arrived in 1883. Journalist-cum-author William Pickford arrived in Bournemouth. He had played Association Football in the hotbed of Lancashire, but discovered the organisation of the sport to be fairly haphazard in his newly adopted county. It didn't stay that way for long as Pickford threw himself into galvanising the structure of the local game, demonstrating in the process the organisational skills that would one day make him Secretary of the Football Association. By the following year he had established the South Hants and Dorset Football Association and re-established a senior and junior cup.

Pickford was also behind the development of Bournemouth FC – not to be confused with the Football League club – which was founded in 1875. Commonly known as the Poppies, the club still ply their trade in the Wessex League to this day. It is a curious footnote to this tale of Hampshire footballing pride that in soccer's early years on the south coast it was the Bournemouth area which was the driving force. Pickford and Gibson recount Bournemouth 'Veterans' playing an Association fixture against Southampton 'Rangers' in 1879 and winning by double figures. Spurred by Pickford and his brother, interest spread like 'wildfire' and within three years the new association had incorporated clubs from Portsmouth, Winchester and Woolston.

Clearly the geographical area administered by the association was prohibitive – these were the days before motorised transport – and it was decided to split the organisation. The Hampshire Football Association was founded in 1887 with seventeen clubs under its auspices and Pickford its honorary secretary. By the turn of the century he would be dividing his time between the south coast and London, as his work with the FA developed. Contemporary accounts have him using a penny-farthing as his preferred means of transport for the trip!

The respective formations of the modern Southampton and Portsmouth clubs, although different in many respects, share one characteristic – the sport was popularised in each town by other clubs. Although the St Mary's Club, acknowledged as the direct descendant of the present-day 'Saints', was founded in 1885, in the mid-1880s the power in Southampton football circles was Woolston Works – the club of the shipyard on the banks of the River Itchen – which rose to prominence after the takeover of the yard by Oswald Mordaunt & Co. The company expanded the business with Scottish labour, devotees of the round-ball game. In 1887 the club won the Hants and Dorset Cup and over the next three years they flourished, attracting high-profile London clubs such as Clapton and – appropriately enough – Caledonians, to the south coast for fixtures.

Just as Woolston looked set to dominate the game in Southampton, the failure of the shipyard stymied its ambitions. The Scots were forced to find pastures new and left St Mary's, at the time only a junior club, to build on the undoubted passion for the sport the people of Southampton had demonstrated.

It was to prove a similar story seventeen miles or so along the coast, where the development of the game was also racing ahead. Football, or at least the Association version, was first recorded in Portsmouth in the early 1880s when a team called Harlequins, who played at Grosvenor Green, played the occasional game of soccer, although their fixtures were primarily against rugby-playing teams. R Hemingsly, a correspondent for the *Portsmouth Times*, aided by J McDonald, formed the first real 'football' club in Portsmouth in 1884. Together with A E Kindersley they demonstrated their commitment to the sport by purchasing a cup and putting it up for competition in south-east Hampshire. There was even a hint of inter-city rivalry as Woolston Works lost 0-1 to the Portsmouth Club in the final of the inaugural Portsmouth FA Cup of 1887.

The development of a Portsmouth branch of the Hants FA in the late 1880s was helped in part by Southsea resident Dr (latterly Sir) Arthur Conan Doyle, creator of Sherlock Holmes. According to Gibson and Pickford, Doyle 'used his splendid athletic frame at the back' for the Portsmouth Sunflowers, a team composed primarily of former public schoolboys. A local cup final between Portsmouth Town and the Oxford Light Infantry in 1891 caused much local interest, records Kevin Smith in *Glory Gunners: The history of Royal Artillery (Portsmouth) FC* (1999). It was eventually won by the town side following a third replay, but the lack of a central ground meant the club fell into decline, allowing a military club to fill the breach and provide the calibre of team the Portsmouth public craved.

Although Portsmouth was ostensibly a naval town, regiments of soldiers – often Scots, who shared the Woolston shipworkers' enthusiasm for football – would be barracked in and around the town from time to time. It was their passion which was the driving force behind the growth of the Association code during the early 1890s. Naval clubs existed but the Army had the advantage in establishing the game for the simple reason that sailors spent much of their time at sea, leaving their clubs to the whim of the Admiralty draft.

What lay behind the birth of Portsmouth FC was the success of the Royal Artillery club – which was itself the product of the 1894 merger between the clubs of the 15th Company Royal Artillery, based at Fareham, and their bitter rivals, the Gosport-based Depot RA. The previous season both these sides had played Southampton St Mary's, 15th Co winning 3-1 at the Antelope Ground in what the *Evening News* described as a 'fantastic game' in January 1894 and RA Depot forcing a goalless draw a couple of weeks later (Smith 1999).

Under the 'vigorous management and zeal' of Sergeant Major Fred Windrum and Sergeant Richard 'Dick' Bonney, the new club were without peer in the Hampshire amateur game, winning the Army Cup in 1895 and 1897, the Hampshire Senior Cup in 1896 – beating St Mary's reserves – and the Portsmouth FA Cup in 1897. However, it was RA's exploits in the FA Amateur Cup which were to become the pride of Hampshire football. In 1896 they reached the final of the competition, only to lose by the odd goal to Bishop Auckland at Leicester. Three years later they were favourites to take the trophy, having reached the final again. With the game against Harwich and Parkstone due to be played in Middlesbrough, the players 'withdrew' to the east coast to prepare. It was to be a huge misjudgment. The inevitable 'expenses' detailed in Mike Neasom's *Pompey: The History of Portsmouth Football Club* (1984) as 'carriages £6 6s; wines £2 19s; billiards £2 4s and cigars £1 11s 3d' proved too much for the FA to sanction. The club was deemed to have breached amateur regulations and was disqualified.

By this time, the 'Gunners', as they were popularly known, had joined the Southern League – ironically filling a vacancy left by the resignation of Southampton-based Freemantle – and they stormed to the second division title in 1898, having won nineteen of their 22 matches. They also met Southampton in a benefit for the Hampshire FA in December 1897, but the game was marred by controversy. RA's goalkeeper, Gunner Matt Reilly, leant idly against a post, refusing to guard his goal, after a controversial penalty was awarded early in the second half. The kick was duly converted and Saints won the game late on, but the 'gate' of £40 from the 'large crowd' at the United Services' Men's Ground (Smith 1999), indicated the growing enthusiasm for football in Portsmouth.

Incidentally, Reilly played twice for Saints in the Southern League in December 1895, having been loaned to them with the permission of the Army, according to Holley and Chalk in their *A-Z of the Saints* (1992). The local press described his performances in those games as 'brilliant'.

Having gained promotion by winning a series of 'Test' matches against the teams finishing bottom of the first division, the following season RA would find the going tougher. At last they came up against professional outfits, including the Southampton club, who were the defending champions. The fixtures caused considerable interest in both towns, with the

Saints storming to a 4-1 victory at home on 8th October, while the RA salvaged some pride in the return on 17th December, drawing 1-1 with the champions-elect. According to Smith (1999) a crowd of more than 8,000 assembled at the USMG. Both the goals came in the first half, with Watty Keay giving Saints the lead. Corporal Walsh then reached a bouncing through ball ahead of Saints' England goalkeeper Jack Robinson. The effort hit the post, crept over the line, and 'the tremendous number of spectators gave out a mighty roar'. In the second half Saints pressed, but thanks to a clearance off his line by Gunner Turner, RA clung on to their draw.

However, a miserable return of just four wins throughout the season meant the Portsmouth-based side was condemned to the lottery of a 'Test' series to try to maintain their place. With the RA embroiled in a protracted appeal with the Football Association over their alleged professionalism, they were forced to field their reserve side and their relegation was confirmed by a 1-4 defeat against old rivals Cowes in the first 'Test'. RA withdrew from the Southern League, their battle with the FA lost. A brief revival in 1900-01 apart, their time had passed. Plans for professional football in Portsmouth were now well advanced, but the influence of the RA's success – coupled with the runaway success of professionalism at the St Mary's club – in the development of Portsmouth Football Club cannot be underestimated.

As St Mary's had been formed by the Young Men's Christian Association, aided by the parish curate, the Reverend A B Sole, there was at first much debate as to which code of football should be adopted by the fledgling club. According to Peter East in his history of *Southampton FC* (1979) 'He [the Rev Sole] wasn't sure whether soccer or rugby football would best suit the young men of his parish'. But once put to the vote, the Association game prevailed and the rest, as they say, was history. St Mary's YMCA had enjoyed considerable early success as a junior club, winning the Hampshire Junior Cup at the first attempt in 1887. Until then they had only played friendly matches, but their success was repeated in subsequent years and in 1890 they claimed the Cup as their own.

St Mary's were attracting significant public interest, obliging the club to appropriate the Antelope Cricket Ground to cope with the 'thousands' who wanted to see the team in action. In those days local 'rivalry' was a more parochial affair. The 'Saints', as they were now dubbed, played fractious matches against the suburban Freemantle Club, otherwise dubbed the Magpies. The first game was on 21st November 1885, when St Mary's gave early notice of their intention to become the town's top club. Establishing a four-goal lead by half time, the upstarts ran out 5-1 winners against the well-established Magpies. According to the *Southampton Independent* newspaper (cited in East), 'St Mary's showed that they have, among their members, the materials with which to form a fairly strong club.'

Gibson and Pickford state that the regular clashes between the Saints and the Magpies 'convulsed Southampton to the core' but in the end it was the Saints who emerged the stronger, largely because their ground was situated in the town centre, close to the homes of the workers who would form its support base. The Saints' success continued unabated: the Hampshire Senior Cup came their way in 1891 and 1892 and gate receipts frequently topped £200, especially for the 'derby' with the Magpies.

By this time St Mary's had established themselves as regular entrants in the English FA Cup, a role which would eventually catapult them to national prominence. As the undisputed premier club in Hampshire, their first foray into the Cup saw them win 4-1 at Warmley, a village close to Bristol, in October 1891. The honour of scoring the club's first Cup goal went to debutant Ernie Nicholls, who would become a stalwart until 1894, scoring 40 goals for the club before his retirement. He was also a fine cricketer and by 1902 was captain of the Deanery Club. Nicholls died, aged 99, in February 1971, having continued his support for the Saints as a season-ticket holder for more than 60 years (Holley and Chalk 1992).

In the next round of the Cup, St Mary's were drawn to play Reading and won 7-0 in front of more than 4,000 people at the Antelope Ground, only to see an FA committee uphold the visitors' claim that the home side had fielded two ineligible players. Forward John Fleming and centre-half Sandy McMillan had recently signed for St Mary's after impressing in a friendly against their regiment, the 93rd Highlanders, just a week after the victory against Warmley. Saints' protestation of innocence fell on deaf ears. It wasn't until the following 1892-93 season, which brought a 0-4 home defeat to Maidenhead, that St Mary's finally knew what it was like to lose a Cup-tie on the field of play.

St Mary's local ascendancy was challenged in 1893 when Freemantle 'stole' the Hampshire Senior Cup. The final turned on a suspect penalty converted by the Magpies. It was to prove a turning point in the club's fortunes, for in the aftermath Southampton St Mary's – as they were now called – decided it was time to exploit their superior resources and turn professional. Their ambition to become top dogs in the town was underlined when a visiting Stoke side trounced them 8-0 and saw four of their best players poached in the aftermath. Over the next few months, Stoke forward Charlie Baker, full-back 'Lachie' Thompson, centre-half Alf Littlehales, and outside-right William 'Chippy' Naughton – not to mention trainer Billy Dawson – would all find their way to the south.

Faced with such competition, the Freemantle club eventually folded – after they dropped out of the Southern League – leaving the Saints as the undisputed pride of Southampton. The club's links with the church were by now becoming increasingly tenuous. The formation of the Southern League in 1894 was as a direct consequence of the success of the Football League, established seven years earlier. The Football League was overwhelmingly populated by clubs from the North and Midlands, which left a vacuum for ambitious clubs south of Birmingham.

Strangely, Pickford had been dismissive of the Football League, befitting his amateur roots and his loyalty to the Football Association: 'We, in the south, did not take much interest in it. Twelve clubs struggling under the handicap of having to pay players' wages, as a consequence of their success in securing professionalism, bound themselves by three simple rules; to meet home and away, to keep fixtures as arranged and to play their best available teams. That was about all' (quoted in Inglis 1988).

Pickford could not have been more misguided about the enduring appeal of league football, although in fairness in 1938 he subsequently acknowledged its success in his commemorative 75th anniversary history of the FA. The rising tide of professionalism in the south was about to engulf him, but it might have been different. The Saints' hopes were dealt a potentially fatal blow when they were refused entry to the new league. However, some of the original clubs got cold feet and dropped out, leaving Saints one of the beneficiaries.

In their first season Saints felt vindicated, finishing third, eight points behind champions Millwall and two behind runners up Luton, a position they consolidated the following season. If the RA had been doing Portsmouth proud in the Amateur Cup, Saints were continuing to forge their reputation as doughty Cup fighters in its bigger brother, the FA Cup. Their success would make them arguably the most potent club in southern England by the early twentieth century. In 1894-95 they reached the first round proper for the first time – as they have done ever since – losing 1-5 to Nottingham Forest. That match underlined the growing popularity of the club and its inadequate facilities. More than 7,000 crammed into the Antelope Ground and when some enthusiastic spectators climbed onto the roof, it gave way scattering – according to contemporary reports – bodies in all directions. Mercifully, no serious injuries were recorded.

In 1897 the team were undefeated champions of the Southern League and in the same year Southampton FC was created. The St Mary's club reformed itself as a limited company, issuing £5,000 of shares and establishing a board of directors. The final link with the church was severed, although the new club had to ride the loss of their ground. The lease on the Antelope enclosure expired and they moved to the Hampshire Cricket Club ground at Northlands Road. The new venue was far from ideal, lacking proper terracing, but the club continued to thrive on the pitch, with its famous red and white striped kit – albeit with navy shorts in those days – finally established.

In 1897-98 the club, referred to in some quarters as the 'Cherry Stripes', retained the Southern League title and embarked on a memorable Cup run, disposing of Football League sides Leicester Fosse, Bolton Wanderers and Newcastle United on the way. In doing so they became the first professional side in the south of England to reach the semi-finals. A 1-1 draw at Birmingham against Nottingham Forest meant a replay at the famous Crystal Palace. It went ahead in a blizzard, with Saints conceding two late goals to end their hopes. Accounts of the game reveal that their goalkeeper, George Clawley, never saw the two shots that went past him, 'so choked were his eyes with snow' (Gibson and Pickford 1906).

At the end of that season director George Thomas, faced with regular crowds of 12,000, took the decision to build an enclosure at The Dell, a picturesque corner of the town a short walk from the cricket ground. In 1889 a contemporary painting of the area depicted, according to Inglis (1987), 'a tranquil pond in sunshine, surrounded by trees, with two ducks gently gliding over the water.' Ten years later the site was transformed. Thomas invested £10,000 in erecting a stadium on the four and a half acre site, which on completion he leased to the club for £250 a year.

His first task was to transform the pond into a series of underground streams, before work began on building two stands to seat 4,000 spectators. The boggy state of The Dell's pitch until the 1930s was usually attributed to the origins of the site. On the east side, a two-tiered stand ran 70 yards along one touchline, while on the west side a smaller stand was necessary on account of a house in the Archers Road corner, which was used by the club secretary. Steep uncovered terracing – already formed into the characteristic wedge-shape dictated by the boundaries of Milton Road and Archers Road – provided accommodation for a further 20,000. When completed, The Dell was among the best provincial stadiums in the country. Inglis details its facilities: 'In the Main (or West) Stand were six-feet deep plunge baths for the players, two showers plus ordinary baths. Around the terracing were very solid iron railings and there was even a special enclosure for spectators to store their bicycles during games at a penny a time.' The only problem was how to accommodate the press. They bemoaned the lack of desks as they sought to record for posterity The Dell's inaugural match on 3rd September 1898. The opponents were Brighton United, and Saints won 4-1.

The public interest generated by Saints' Cup and league exploits – in 1899 they retained the Southern League title for a third season and were awarded a special silk pennant by the league – saw revenues increase. In 1893 – the year before turning professional – the club generated income of £800. By 1897 the crowds flocking to see the Saints had taken that figure to £3,300 and in the wake of the semi-final run it was estimated more than £6,000 would find its way into club coffers.

If the prowess of the Royal Artillery, coupled with local backing, had established Portsmouth's credentials as a football town, it was the burgeoning balance sheet at Southampton which spurred the creation of a professional club. The Saints' success had not gone unnoticed. As F J H Young and T L Dines put it, in their 1927 account of Portsmouth FC's formation: 'Southampton had already embraced professionalism and it was making rapid inroads up and down the country. So its advent in a town of the size and importance of Portsmouth, with its wonderful cosmopolitan population, was inevitable'.

Correspondence had been exchanged in the *Portsmouth News* in 1897 regarding the establishment of a professional club. A letter from Nat Whittaker, Honorary Secretary of the Southern League, in January 1898 noted 'the potential for an astute consortium'. Not that the advent of professionalism was universally approved. Young and Dines recount a school of thought which saw the rise of professionalism as a bad thing. 'Steeped, as Portsmouth is, in the service traditions, the paid player was still an anathema to many of those sports stalwarts who had for many years run amateur clubs'.

However, once the plunge had been taken, they happily recorded 'to their credit, as well as to their sound judgment, let it be added that many of the most uncompromising of the club's opponents eventually became its most loyal and enthusiastic supporters'. Less well known is the fact that a second prospectus for a professional club in Portsmouth had been published, with the Southsea Rovers club – which had recently been elected to the Hampshire Senior League – aiming to raise £4,000 capital. The move was quietly abandoned after delegates scoffed at the plan (Smith 1999).

Unlike the Saints, professional football in Portsmouth was no evolutionary process. First and foremost the club was seen as a business opportunity – perhaps a touch ironic, given Pompey's predilection in the coming years to be anything but. On 5th April 1898 the decision was taken to establish a professional club for the country's principal naval port. The deed was done at a public meeting at 12 High Street, Old Portsmouth, attended by more then 70 people. Six local businessmen and six sportsmen raised capital of £8,000 in £1 shares to set up a limited company. Of this, £4,950 bought five acres of agricultural land near Fratton Station, and a further £16,000 was borrowed to construct a suitable stadium. The new board of directors included John Brickwood (of Brickwoods Brewery), George Oliver (founder of a private school), John Wyatt Peters (wine importer), William Wigginton (Government contractor) and Alfred Bone (architect and surveyor). In his book, Neasom recounts: 'In a matter of weeks [after the formation of the company], the Football Association's representative Mr W Pickford joined Mr Oliver to gaze over a five-barred gate only to see cows grazing on the five acres of land the company had bought – an improbable prospect now for Fratton Park' (1984). Before long, however, the new ground was levelled and drained and a 100 feet long stand, with seven rows of seats, constructed on the south side and a 240 feet covered terrace built to the north.

As yet, the club had no players and no league to play in. The appointment of Frank Brettell, with twenty years' experience in developing professional clubs at Liverpool, Bolton and Tottenham, was regarded as a coup. Within months he had secured the players who would catapult the club into the limelight. Matt 'Ginger' Reilly – goalkeeping star of the RA – was signed, while Brettell's contacts in the North enabled him to put together a competitive squad.

The Southern League voted unanimously to admit Portsmouth into an expanded first division for the 1899-1900 season, without having to prove themselves in division two. The demise of RA had paved the way, but the fact that only Reilly and full-back Turner switched from RA to the new Fratton Park club helped ensure the smooth transition of football power in Portsmouth. With Saints already established as one of the top sides in this league, a south-coast rivalry had been born or, perhaps more accurately, manufactured. The forthcoming season would provide conflicting evidence in the eternal argument as to which club could truly claim to be 'pride of the south'.

Chapter 2

~ ADVANTAGE SAINTS ~

The formation of the Southern League in 1894 proved to be a runaway success and was the launchpad for professionalism to spread across the south of England. The creation of the league was as a direct result of the growth of the Football League, six years its senior, which had rapidly expanded into a second division in 1892. A year later, the decision to elect two more clubs to even up the divisions at sixteen clubs apiece saw Woolwich Arsenal and Liverpool enrolled. The days of the competition being a bastion of the North and Midlands would be eroded, but in the meantime ambitious southern clubs needed a stage of similar prestige on which to display their talents. Led by Millwall Athletic – London's only other professional club at the time – the solution was sought in the creation of the Southern League, of which Southampton St Mary's were founder members.

By the turn of the twentieth century, the Saints were undoubtedly the major power in the new competition. After finishing third in their first two campaigns – behind Millwall and Luton on both occasions – Saints would be champions for three consecutive seasons, 1896-97 to 1898-99. For good measure, they had also made their mark on a national level through their FA Cup exploits. By reaching the semi-finals in 1898, losing to Forest in a replay, they had also become the first southern team in the professional era to reach that stage. Southampton's squad boasted a sprinkling of seasoned pros from the length and breadth of England and Scotland.

As yet, only Luton had followed Arsenal's lead and joined up with the 'northern' league, so to speak. The Hatters would return with their tails between their legs when they finished bottom in 1900 and sought readmission to the Southern League. In consequence, the Saints could be regarded as among the best, if not *the* best team south of Birmingham. Woolwich Arsenal were merely holding their own in the First Division of the Football League, but the Cup never pitched the Gunners against the Saints, denying any opportunity for an unofficial Battle of the South.

However, the fact that Saints had seen off the likes of Newcastle – beaten 1-0 at the County Ground in the second round – *en route* to that 1898 semi-final meant that by any yardstick they were an outfit to be reckoned with. It was therefore with great anticipation, but possibly some trepidation, that the newly formed Portsmouth club faced up to their first season in the Southern League, without opportunity for a dummy run in the second division of the competition. In addition to Saints, the league contained Millwall, Tottenham and Bristol City, all of whom had established a pedigree that Pompey must have thought difficult to match. As it turned out, they needn't have worried. Frank Brettell had done his job well.

The Portsmouth team that took the field for its first ever match, on 2nd September 1899 at Chatham – a fellow Royal Dockyard town – was not short of talent. In goal was former Royal Artillery goalie 'Ginger' Reilly, the 'broth of a Donnybrook bhoy' with a shock of red hair and a hangdog moustache. Reilly had been Brettell's first, and most popular signing, and his Gaelic football skills, honed back in Dublin, gave him a distinct advantage as he used hand, foot and eye coordination to propel his team forward. In those days goalkeepers were able to handle the ball outside their designated penalty area, although Reilly's prowess proved too much for the Football Association, who duly outlawed the practice. Robert Blyth was a Scottish half-back who had arrived from Preston and would give the club sterling service as player-manager, director and chairman. Bolton-born forward Dan Cunliffe would, in two spells for the club, play for England and score 159 League and Cup goals in 284 appearances.

In their salmon pink shirts, with maroon collars and cuffs – a combination which would make a controversial comeback in the ill-fated return to the First Division in 1987 – the team was dubbed the 'Shrimps', although the more common and contemporary moniker 'Pompey' was also used at the time. Harold 'Nobby' Clarke, the former Everton winger, had the honour of scoring the only goal of the game at Chatham and securing a winning start to the campaign.

The second league match the following Saturday saw Reading due at the newly-constructed Fratton Park. It was, however, the Saints who christened the new stadium in a friendly on the intervening Wednesday. The local paper heralded the new 'derby' and anticipated future confrontations: 'The first, of what is hoped will be a long series of historic battles between Portsmouth and Southampton took place on Wednesday at Fratton Park, as the new ground in Goldsmith Avenue has been named. There has always been a deal of rivalry between the two towns, but Southampton long-since took the initiative in securing the services of a good professional team. Last season, when the Royal Artillery met the Saints, there was a considerable amount of interest evinced and now that Portsmouth can also boast its own professional eleven that interest will be greatly increased'.

The bare match facts are that Pompey won 2-0, with goals from Cunliffe, after ten minutes – a 'clinking' shot, according to the *Evening News* – and midway through the second half from Clarke, who 'amid the greatest of enthusiasm … sent in a particularly fine shot which easily found the net'. The game kicked off at 5.15pm precisely, late enough to allow 5,000 spectators to assemble, and his Worship the Mayor – Alderman T Scott Foster JP – 'set the ball rolling' as Pompey defended the 'Milton End' of the ground with a slight breeze in their favour. Even the Saints admitted Pompey looked to have created a decent side: 'There is no doubt you have got together a very fine lot,' commented an anonymous opposition player to Brettell as the players came off for the interval. The local reporter gave short shrift to those who suggested the Saints weren't trying: 'Anyone who saw the match and understands the game cannot but admit that after Portsmouth had scored the Saints exerted every effort to get back on terms'.

Six weeks later the two teams locked horns again, when Saints made the same journey to meet Pompey in the Southern District Combination – a midweek league for first teams, not reserves – and once again local interest was immense. 'Long before the time fixed for the kick off spectators began to arrive in cabs, brakes and carts, as well as on foot in prodigious numbers,' commented the *Evening News*. By kick-off, more than 7,000, paying £125, were already in the enclosure with others still converging on the ground.

Again Pompey prevailed, this time by 5-1, but once again a question hung over the worth of the victory, as ten-man Saints had to make do without goalkeeper John Robinson for a considerable part of the match. He was carried off the field with 'severe contusions' and 'several doctors in attendance'. Brettell sportingly offered Southampton one of his players as a reserve – substitutes were not officially permitted until the 1960s – but the Saints declined and turned to forward Alf Milward, who went in goal, none too effectively as it turned out.

Fortunately, Robinson was none too worse for wear. The England international was a colourful character with impish good looks not unlike those of a young Paul Gascoigne. His misdemeanours were legion. In 1900 he received an FA reprimand for trying to poach legendary England forward Steve Bloomer from Derby for the Saints – in itself an indication of the high standing of the Southern League – and in 1902 he was suspended after punching a spectator in the face during a game at New Brompton. Pompey's keeper Reilly would suffer similar punishment a couple of years later when Swindon fans pelted him with clinker from behind the goal and he took matters into his own hands.

The return fixture – the first to be held at The Dell – was not scheduled until April. That was also the month in which the two fixtures which really counted, in the Southern League, would come – on Easter Saturday at Southampton, with the return on Easter Monday. A complicating factor was the emergence of another epic Saints Cup run, which began with a 3-0 thrashing of First Division Football League Everton in the first round at The Dell in January. In the next round Saints had been reduced to ten men by injury to forward John Farrell early on against another 'giant', Newcastle, but a blizzard forced the referee to abandon the tie in the 50th minute. In the re-match Saints won 4-1, setting up a home quarter-final tie with West Bromwich, which also went their way 2-1. The semi-final would be an all Southern League affair against Millwall, ensuring that a southern professional team would contest the English Cup final for the first time. The importance of 'the Cup' in this fading Victorian era cannot be underestimated. It was the trophy of trophies and would remain that way until long after the Second World War. Winning the Cup was the passport to national fame and fortune.

Lifting the FA Cup had been high on Saints' agenda from their first ill-fated entry in 1891. In those early forays, they would have a clear edge over their neighbours in the quest for football's oldest and most venerated trophy. In Portsmouth's first run at the Cup, Blackburn dumped them out at the first hurdle, albeit after a second replay. Their 0-5 defeat in the decisive match at neutral Villa Park was apparently blamed on goalkeeper Reilly, still in a state of shock after learning prior to the match via a telegram that he'd been selected to represent Ireland.

Southampton booked their place in the final by beating Millwall 3-0 in a replay at Reading after the sides had drawn 0-0 at Crystal Palace. Both ties were played before any of the matches against Portsmouth. To celebrate their accomplishment, Saints duly saw off Pompey 1-0 (Southern District Combination), but by the time Pompey arrived at The Dell twelve days later, on 14th April, Southampton's minds were focused on the impending final against Bury the following Saturday. Five defeats in eight games had already dented Saints' hopes of retaining the Southern League championship and there wasn't even a sizeable attendance to see Portsmouth win 2-0, thanks to goals from Cunliffe and 'Sandy' Brown. The homecoming to Southampton docks of General Sir George White – 'the Ladysmith hero' during the Boer War, who was soon to be awarded the Victoria Cross – claimed the attention of locals, if not the Pompey contingent. This was swelled by the one-day holiday for Portsmouth dockyard. According to the *Evening News*, large numbers made the journey from Portsmouth by train and charabanc to swell the gate to 4,000. The 'Pompey Chimes' – the famous chant in tune with Guildhall's on-the-hour reminder – were voiced loudly throughout the game.

Two days later Pompey completed the Southern League double over their rivals by the same scoreline. Brown was again on the scoresheet, as was William Smith. The crowd was 10,000. The two victories consolidated Pompey's final placing of second, behind Champions Tottenham, and was also decisive in ensuring they finished six points clear of third-placed Saints.

Of course Saints could claim, with some justification, that their Cup exploits had caused a fixture pile-up, ending their hopes of retaining the shield for a fourth season in a row. Southampton were also to know the bitter taste of a Cup final defeat. Bury cruised to a 4-0 victory in front of a Crystal Palace crowd of 69,000, swelled by an estimated 4,000 Saints fans aboard 'special' trains. Saints had attracted the backing of fans of other southern professional teams, keen to see the Cup come south. After the game, rumours abounded of a split in the Saints camp between Scottish and English players. Chalk and Holley (1988) say the alleged row was over the centre-forward position, with the English contingent wanting the temperamental but gifted Jack Farrell to play, despite the fact he had scored just once in nine matches, while the Scots preferred the hard-working Roddy McLeod, who had bagged three in four games before being dropped for the two Pompey fixtures over Easter. Farrell got the nod, as he had in the semi against Millwall, but the row so disenchanted him that he moved to New Brighton Tower – a club in what is now known as the Wirral – during the summer of 1900. The equally disgruntled, though for different reasons, McLeod, also departed, on the eve of the season to Brentford. Southampton's only consolation was that the Cup run put the club back in profit, if only to the tune of £31.

A south-coast rivalry was now up and running. There was, unsurprisingly, much satisfaction in Portsmouth that their club had performed so well in its first season, and to finish above Southampton was a significant bonus, beating them four times and losing only once into the bargain. However, for the first time, and certainly not for the last, the balance sheet had to be offset by Saints' undoubtedly higher profile and the fact that their Cup run had meant they had taken their eye off the league ball somewhat. The following season Saints put their upstart neighbour back in their place by storming to the Southern League Championship again – Pompey finished third. Having drawn 0-0 at Fratton Park in September, Saints went some way to sealing the title with a 2-0 win on 6th April at The Dell. Milward scored in each half but the gate was again disappointing, 4,000, and the overall decline in Saints' support led to a reported loss of £740. According to Chalk and Holley, the poor attendances were due to the imposition of the 'shilling [5p] gate' for certain matches, a high price which was popularly resented. Who says 'Gold' or 'Category A' matches are a new thing?

Pompey had the consolation of a Western League double – the Southern District Combination having given way to a new midweek competition. Both clubs made early exits from the FA Cup, although the death of Queen Victoria on 21st January 1901 at Osborne House, just across the Solent at East Cowes, disrupted football to the extent that Saints were forced to rearrange their home tie with Everton as the nation mourned. They then slumped to a 1-3 defeat, handicapped by the unavailability of star men Harry Wood and Arthur Chadwick. Pompey lost 0-3 at Newton Heath, who would shortly transform into Manchester United. Saints also made their first Continental excursion that summer, touring Belgium, Austria and Hungary, winning all six games they played.

The following, 1901-02, season saw Saints at it again in their pursuit of the FA Cup. Their thrilling run tested The Dell's capacity to the full. After victory in a replay over Spurs, a record gate of more than 20,000 turned out to see Liverpool beaten; then a full house of 25,000 witnessed the 1900 final defeat against Bury avenged in the last minute, as Edgar Chadwick rounded the goalkeeper to roll the ball in after Bert Brown's shot had rebounded from the crossbar. Brown, incidentally, was considered to be the 'fastest forward in the kingdom' (Chalk and Holley 1992). That goal gave Saints a 3-2 win and a semi-final tie with another former Cup adversary, Nottingham Forest, who would be given the runaround 5-1 at White Hart Lane.

Pompey at last embarked on a run of their own, seeing off Small Heath – that's Birmingham City today – Grimsby, after a replay, and Reading, before bowing out to Derby County 3-6 in a replay. The first game had ended 0-0 at Fratton in front of almost 23,000 on the same day that Saints beat Bury. Once again Saints proved to be the bridesmaid, although they made a better fist of the final, drawing 1-1 in the first game with Sheffield United, before losing 1-2 to an 84th-minute goal in the replay.

In the league it was Portsmouth's season: they remained undefeated against the Saints in four matches *en route* to a championship 'double' of Southern and Western Leagues. The most thrilling of the derbies – possibly the most thrilling ever – came on 2nd November 1901, when an estimated 3,000 Pompey fans journeyed by a variety of special excursions to see their side take the lead three times, only to be pegged back each time. With seven minutes remaining, however, Cunliffe scored a fourth and this time Saints had no reply. Scorer of two Pompey goals that day was Frank Bedingfield, a forward who was tipped for great things, perhaps even an England cap. With 50 goals in 58 league appearances Sunderland-born 'Beddy' was a Pompey hero, but three months after that game he caught a chill as Pompey prepared for their third round Cup-tie with Reading at Singleton. He recovered sufficiently to play, and even scored the winning goal, the 58th of his career in all competitions, but on the final whistle he collapsed in the dressing room. Tuberculosis was diagnosed and a public subscription raised £500 to send him to South Africa to recuperate. He died there in November 1904 aged just 27. Such was the esteem in which Bedingfield was held, his biography in the club's *Official Centenary History* (1998) recounts that after his death hundreds of mantelpieces in hundreds of homes bore his framed photograph.

Another legend playing in that match, for Southampton, was Charles Burgess 'CB' Fry. Clean-cut, with a neatly trimmed moustache, Fry was the archetypal 'all rounder', excelling at Association football, rugby, athletics –

he held the world long jump record until 1900 – and especially cricket. Such was Fry's sporting prowess that John Arlott, quoted in Iain Wilton's biography *CB Fry – An English Hero* (1999), was moved to describe him as 'a most incredible man … the most variously gifted Englishman of any age … the pre-eminent all-rounder, not merely of his own age, but, so far as is measurable, of all English history'.

Fry was much more than an elite sportsman, being a leading journalist and author, not to mention his cinema connections. His political influence even produced an offer of the throne of Albania. He is described in Chalk and Holley's *A-Z of the Saints* (1992) as 'possessing the physique of an Ancient Greek'. He enjoyed a prestigious career as an amateur footballer, picking up an Oxford Blue and also playing for the famed Corinthians. However, in 1900 he decided to turn professional, apparently to improve his chances of international recognition. At the time he was playing cricket for Hampshire and he opted for the Saints as they were closest to his West End home. His signing caused a sensation: 'a player who shines conspicuously among a constellation of football stars,' gushed the Southampton-based *Football Echo.*

On the field, Fry found the hurly-burly of league football less to his refined taste and his appearances for the Saints were rationed, usually to Cup-ties. He played in both Saints' losing finals and, despite misgivings about his tackling abilities, he remained popular with supporters. Holley and Chalk (1988) recount a stirring rendition of 'He's a jolly good fellow!' belted out by spectators at The Dell as he picked himself up on the touchline from a bout of cramp. His appearance at Fratton Park in October 1901 saw him earn 'loud applause' from the home crowd as he effected a clearance.

Fry even made the England international XI as they faced Ireland at The Dell in March 1901, bringing international football to the south coast for the first time. A large crowd saw Fry and two other Saints – goalie Jack Robinson and forward Archie Turner – represent their country that day. Farnborough-born Turner became the first Hampshireman to play for England. But Fry, now approaching 30, was on the wane. He was tried out at centre-forward in a couple of matches at the start of 1902-03, but his performances were inconclusive and in December 1902 he was transferred to Portsmouth, becoming the ninth international on their books. Fry's arrival set a trend which would be repeated much later in the century of fading stars departing The Dell for a swansong at Fratton Park. Not that Fry lasted long. Playing before 34,000 at Everton in the Cup on 7th February 1903, Fry was crocked by a bad tackle. Although he returned to the field after treatment, he was still in considerable pain and powerless to save his side from a 0-5 thrashing. Although he would continue to play top-class cricket with Hants until 1921, and appeared in 26 Tests for England (including a spell as captain without losing a Test), that injury brought his career in competitive football to a premature and painful end.

Player-exchanges between the south-coast rivals were common in those early years and the two clubs clearly had a cordial relationship. It has to be remembered that although the pair shared a common 'Hampshire' bond, the county was much larger then. Between the two football towns existed a huge rural swathe – Titchfield, Locks Heath, Burseldon and Botley were villages – unimaginable today in view of the urban M27 corridor that links them. The late, eminent sports writer and broadcaster John Arlott always referred to Portsmouth as the 'cockney' part of the county, on account of the London-esque accent to found down that way, as opposed to the more rural West Country twang that can be heard in Southampton. Either way, other than the special train and charabanc excursions to the respective venues on matchdays, it was unlikely rival supporters had much opportunity to meet, mingle and squabble as is taken for granted these days.

By way of illustrating the 'entente cordiale' of those early times it can be noted that a key element in Pompey's Championship winning side of 1902 was Arthur Chadwick. An England international centre-half, Chadwick had originally arrived at The Dell in 1897 from Burton Swifts, before signing for Pompey in May 1901. He had featured in Saints' 1900 Cup final defeat by Bury, and after a playing career that also took in Northampton, Accrington and Exeter, he became Southampton manager in 1925 after a spell in charge of Reading.

To prove this was no one-sided arrangement, making a move in the opposite direction in May 1903 was Albert 'Kelly' Houlker. An uncompromising half-back of stout build, Houlker stood just 5ft 6in. He had been capped by England while at Fratton, having joined Pompey from his native Blackburn. His move to The Dell was an undoubted success and he joined Chadwick in boasting a Southern League champions medal with each club after Saints won the title again in 1903 and 1904. Houlker's transfer, on account of his wife's health, upset Pompey fans. According to Gibson and Pickford, 'There was despondency in the naval town when he turned his back on them and joy in the ranks of the Saints when his accession was known, for a more popular and good-natured fellow and half back stands not in shoe leather.' That was high praise for one who was described as being 'as neat with his feet as a clog dancer in his native county'. He would win further England caps against Ireland and Wales. Houlker eventually left the south coast in 1906 to play a final season back with his hometown Blackburn before retiring. Or so he thought. So short were Rovers for a team during the Great War that Houlker received a summons in 1918 at the age of 45 to make up the numbers.

If Saints-Pompey relations were good during this period, they were probably strained somewhat in Portsmouth by a sequence of thirteen competitive matches – stretching more than three years from September 1902 – in which Saints remained undefeated against Pompey. In that time Saints also consolidated their position as the footballing power, certainly south and west of London, with their fifth and sixth Southern League titles in 1903 and 1904. The latter success gave Sammy Meston, Saints right-back, an unprecedented sixth medal.

Pompey were clinging valiantly to Saints' coat-tails, however, achieving top-four finishes in both seasons. In fact, the destination of the title might well have been different had Saints not taken three and four points off Portsmouth in those championship-winning seasons. Saints picked up another Southern League 'double' over Pompey in 1904-05, winning 1-0 at Fratton in November thanks to a goal from centre-half Bert Dainty, and 2-1 at The Dell in March. The sequence was finally broken in a Hampshire Charity Cup final at Fratton in November 1905. Organised by the local association as a fund-raiser for injured players in the county, the Hampshire Charity Cup would be contested periodically under different guises until shortly before the Second World War. In those days it was a midweek affair, and on the day in question it attracted around 4,000 spectators to see left-half E McDonald grab the only goal of the game. The match clearly carried some clout, as the medals were presented by the then secretary of the Football Association, Mr F J Wall. He was visiting a Fratton Park ground which had been substantially remodelled in the summer, with the building of a clock tower – a gift of director Sir John Brickwood – on the distinctive mock-Tudor pavilion at the Frogmore Road entrance to the ground.

Before Pompey could get too cock-a-hoop, Saints exacted revenge in another benevolent competition, the Southern Charities Cup, a fortnight later by winning 4-2 at The Dell. The sides were to meet one last time that month, on 30th November, when Pompey exorcised their saintly demons with a 1-0 win in the Southern League, courtesy of a late goal by centre-forward Willie Lee.

From a Pompey perspective it seemed like the curse had been lifted in the nick of time, for the FA Cup draw finally paired the Hampshire rivals in a clash the whole county had clamoured for. On 13th January 1906 twenty special excursions from as far away as Berkshire, plus special boats from the Isle of Wight, conveyed the masses to The Dell. Saints departed to a special training camp on the Tuesday and a tight contest was anticipated. Pompey, however, were struggling with injuries and when the talismanic Lee failed what we would these days call a fitness test, the visitors were always going to struggle for goals.

Saints, though, had problems of their own. Goalkeeper George Clawley was injured, as was his stand-in Tom Burrows. So it was eighteen-year-old local lad Bill Stead, with just the previous two league games to his name, who took the field to face Pompey. In *Match of the Millennium* (2000) Aldworth and Bull quote from a contemporary *Athletic News* report which described Pompey's early 'impetuous rushes calculated to unnerve a youngster'.

It didn't succeed. Instead, Saints' own tactical plan worked to perfection. Centre-forward Fred Harrison returned to the side at inside-right and George Hedley kept his place in the centre. The idea was to exert pressure on Pompey's veteran left-back, George Molyneux, well-known to the opposition, as he had moved across the county the previous summer. According to 'Above Bar', *Athletic News*' correspondent, Molyneux 'never played worse' in that match and Harrison's partnership with right-winger Isaac Tomlinson carried too much danger. Harrison scored the first goal after seven minutes, then Harry Brown headed a second from a 'perfect centre' by Tomlinson. Kirby pulled a goal back just after half-time, but once Hedley quickly made it 3-1 Pompey were run ragged. Brown added a fourth (his second), before Tomlinson rounded off a 5-1 rout. Ironically, Tomlinson would move to Fratton in the 1906 close season, but was not a success. Chalk and Holley (1988) reveal that he suffered acutely from nerves, especially before big games, and would often play poorly, especially away from home. Before kick-off he would take to walking around the stadium, rather than sitting in the dressing room.

Reaction in Portsmouth to the Cup debacle was scathing. 'Sentinel' didn't mince his words in Monday's edition of the *News*. 'Defeated – and disgraced! This, I think, was the general verdict of those who saw Portsmouth's pitiable exhibition … The score of five goals to one is in itself an all-sufficient commentary on Portsmouth's melancholy exhibition but does not in the slightest degree exaggerate Southampton's great superiority.' The forwards were singled out for particular censure: 'A more inept, ridiculous burlesque of an attack I have never seen'. The only Pompey players to shine amidst the carnage were goalkeeper Harris – 'time after time he came to the rescue of his side,' according to 'Sentinel' – and captain and half-back Albert Buick.

With a small, round-shouldered frame and lean legs, Gibson and Pickford (1906) had Buick in the 'fragile' category until he stepped onto the pitch. 'There is no whipcord tougher, no whalebone more pliant, no steel frame stronger. He is ferro-concrete.' So he proved that day against the Saints: 'The last time I saw him play was on that sad day at the Dell when Southampton, on top of their wonderful form, made common hacks of Pompey. On that day Buick was simply ubiquitous. With down hearted half backs to left and right, discouraged forwards in front and a scared back division behind, he strove to turn himself into a team.' The result would set in train another hoodoo, this time in Cup-ties between the clubs, which has yet to be broken.

Comparisons with the modern day are always hard, given that 100 years ago the Football League was in direct competition with the almost equally strong Southern League, but by any measure Southampton were a major footballing power at the beginning of the last century. They had been able to attract 'star' names, such as Fry, and their Cup exploits had put them on the map nationally.

Athletic News was a weekly journal with a predominantly northern readership. Its account of the 1906 Cup-tie, for instance, refers to Southampton as 'Saints' but Portsmouth as 'Portsmouth' reflecting what their readership would make of the two clubs. Although on the field of play there wasn't much to choose between Southampton and Portsmouth, it was Saints who enjoyed the 'cachet' of a club who could punch its weight. That aura would remain long after Southampton's star had begun to wane in the decade before the First World War. Gibson and Pickford (1906) underline the stature of the Southampton club in this period: 'Today, though their fame has somewhat dimmed, there is no southern club whose progress is more closely followed among northern teams and that is high praise'.

Football was changing, however, and neither Saints nor Pompey – given their remoteness from football's centre of gravity, the North, were well placed to influence the Football League's increasingly seniority over the Southern League. The maximum wage, already imposed by the Football League, would soon be adopted by its southern counterpart, ending its financial attraction to many northern-based players. The last occasion the hegemony of the Football League was challenged was in 1910, when Southern League champions Brighton beat their Football League counterparts, Aston Villa, to claim the FA Charity Shield and the unofficial tag of 'champions' of England.

Saints had built their club on the revenue generated by their Cup runs, and despite beating Pompey so comprehensively in that 1906 Cup-tie, they would bow out in the fourth round to Liverpool, ending hopes of another lucrative final appearance. One last tilt at glory lay just around the corner, however. Southampton were also facing problems with their landlord. George Thomas was no longer content to rent out The Dell for just £250 *per annum* and at the 1905 AGM demanded that figure be doubled. The board were reluctant and decided to seek alternatives. None could be found, not surprisingly, for the present ground was the best in the region at that time.

Portsmouth had never established an FA Cup reputation, so consequently their finances were even tighter, even though a year previously they had knocked out Football League Small Heath – soon to be known as Birmingham City – before succumbing 1-2 to Sheffield Wednesday in round three. The high hopes that had attended the club's formation were fast giving way to the realisation that running a professional football club was – as it still is – a ruinously costly affair. That the same could be said of their nearest neighbours, whose stock in the game was still considerably higher, was scant consolation.

Chapter 3

~ The Golden Era ~

(1906-20)

They wouldn't have realised it at the time, but Saints' high-water mark, certainly in the first half of the twentieth century, had passed. Their drubbing of Pompey in the Cup in 1906 had at least settled the argument about who was top dog on the south coast, even though Pompey exacted their revenge in March 1906, completing a Southern League double over their rivals by winning 2-1 at The Dell. As ever, sorting out the pecking order between the two is never that clear cut! Former Saint George Molyneux, who had moved to Fratton Park from The Dell the previous summer, scored one of the goals. Molyneux had earned three of his four England caps while at Southampton and he even played in the fated international at Ibrox in April 1902 which saw 25 people die as a terrace collapsed.

Saints would reach the semi-finals of the FA Cup again in 1908, losing 0-2 to Wolves at Stamford Bridge. It would prove the last time a 'non league', that is to say non-Football League, side would go so far. Pompey and Saints would suffer financially as other leading lights in the Southern League – Tottenham, Bristol City and Clapton Orient among others – 'defected' to the Second Division of the Football League, emasculating the Southern League in consequence. From time to time talks were aired to set up a unified national league, but these always ended without agreement.

According to East, in 1907 Southampton's AGM announced a deficit of £1,107, despite the widely criticised decision to raise admission prices to one shilling (5p) for some parts of The Dell for Cup-ties with Watford and Sheffield Wednesday. The 1908 semi-final Cup run put Saints back in the black, but by 1912 the club's liabilities had soared to almost £3,000, as the team slumped to the lower reaches of the table. A public appeal for funds in April of that year had to be postponed when public sympathy was distracted by the fate of the *Titanic*.

A fresh appeal was made in June, which enabled Saints to reduce its deficit, but the club remained strapped for cash and the glory years around the turn of the century must have seemed very distant. Down the coast, matters were even worse at Portsmouth. Indeed, Pompey almost folded in 1912. A catastrophic relegation to the second division of the Southern League in 1911 necessitated financially crippling journeys to the Welsh Valleys – Merthyr, Mardy, Pontypridd, Treharris and Aberdare, for instance – where the 'gate' money was negligible. Mercifully, Pompey staved off the crisis by sealing promotion at the first attempt, winning their last eight games to finish second on goal-average behind Merthyr. Attendances had returned to five figures in the closing stages of the season, but finances remained precarious. A year earlier, in the wake of relegation, a public subscription had raised £247 to keep the club afloat. But not even the relief of swift promotion could paper over liabilities of £10,000. For a few dark months the cessation of professional football in Portsmouth was contemplated. Happily, in July 1912 the company was restructured. One consequence was a break from the white jerseys adopted in 1910 and the adoption of the blue shirts and white shorts still worn today.

On the field, matches between Southampton and Portsmouth continued to be closely fought, even as their respective declines set in. In October 1906 Pompey became the first Southern League opponents to fail to score against Saints that season as they slumped to a 0-2 defeat at The Dell. This time it was Southampton's turn to celebrate a league 'double', winning 2-1 at Fratton in February, in a bad-tempered game that saw Pompey's E McDonald and Saints' Bill Clarke almost come to blows. A ticking off by the referee calmed the situation. For their part, Pompey had already taken four points off the Saints in the albeit less prestigious Western League, and, in the interests of fairness, each club had a charity cup win to their name.

It was a similar story in 1907-08, when the clubs had one Southern League and one Western League victory apiece to brag about. On a sultry afternoon in late September, Pompey recorded their first Southern League win of the season, with three second-half goals from McDonald, Kirby and Stephen Smith. More than 1,500 Saints fans swelled the gate to 18,000. The return, in late January, was watched by far fewer, just 6,000, which included a 'good number of Portsmouth excursionists'. This game was played in thick fog and Pompey's hopes of climbing above their mid-table neighbours were dashed when Bert Hodgkinson – a top-class baseball player too, believe it or not – scored the only goal with a deflected shot in the 32nd minute. Both clubs had an eye on forthcoming FA Cup-ties, and once again it was to be Southampton who grabbed the glory, beating West Bromwich *en route* to their latest semi-final appearance. Pompey achieved a 1-0 home win over Leicester Fosse, but their Cup dreams would be ended a fortnight later by Stoke City, who won 1-0 at Fratton Park.

Overall there was little to choose between the clubs, football-wise, although by now it was clear that a Western League victory carried nothing like the kudos of the Southern League. Attendances at these mid-week league matches rarely touched 5,000 at either ground, even for local derbies, and they increasingly became a stage for reserve-team players to show their mettle. So Pompey's 4-2 win over Saints in the Western League on 30th September 1908 – thanks to a hat-trick by William Reid, a prolific forward signed from Motherwell the previous summer – could not compensate for the pain of a 0-2 defeat at The Dell the previous Saturday in the

Southern League. The *Evening News* recognised the fact: 'As the points were at stake in the Western League it [the game] didn't create the same interest as Saturday's'. Then, first-half goals by John 'Jack' Bainbridge (who had signed from Pompey in 1907 after one season at Fratton Park) and Arthur Hughes (who had shone on Saints' first foray into Europe), did the trick.

Football was no longer the preserve of Perfidious Albion. In short, the Continentals were catching us up, although it would take until well into the 1950s for us to realise they'd long since overtaken us. Portsmouth and Southampton had toured Germany in the summer of 1907. Although the British had exported the joys of soccer – several French and Italian clubs had British roots – the 'Continent' and beyond were developing the game themselves. Hughes scored a hat-trick against The Hague of Holland during another Saints tour in May 1908, although he would not break into the Southern League first team until inside-forward George Smith collapsed and died in July 1909.

The Western League may no longer have had the same allure as the Southern League, but Saints decided the best way to avenge their 2-4 Western League reverse was to field their 'strongest eleven', according to the *News*, for the return on 28th October 1908. Pompey's scratch team, with six reserves, were no match and lost 1-4. Frank Jordan, an inside-forward in his second spell at The Dell, following his return from South Africa, scored twice, as did George McGhee, a teacher and local amateur. McGhee was being groomed for the first team, although injury would restrict his chances. Reid nabbed Pompey's goal, one of 40 in 45 appearances that season. Glasgow Rangers were alerted to Reid's prowess and he would move back to his native Scotland in the summer.

In many respects this can be regarded as the golden age for derby matches between Saints and Pompey. Meetings between the two were frequent, competitive, and cordial. Players moved between the teams without rancour and, above all, neither side looked like pulling significantly away from the other. The lure of the Football League was resisted by both clubs, fearful perhaps of the financial implications of a fixture list which would take them the length and breadth of England, so the pair were comfortably ensconced in a rivalry where there was always a 'next time' to avenge bruised local pride.

The prevailing mood was summed up on the eve of the return Southern League fixture at Fratton Park in January 1909 by the *Evening News*: 'No matter whether the teams are playing well or badly they "come out of their shells", so to speak, when they are pitted against each other. … Although the local rivalry is great, the matches have been played in a thoroughly sportsmanlike style – hard and vigorous, but perfectly fair'.

This time it would be Saints who would be looking forward to 'the next time' as Pompey took advantage of a side whose league fortunes were on the wane, after a bright start to the season. The previous week Saints had suffered their record defeat at The Dell, going down 0-6 to Swindon, and Pompey piled on the agony with a brace from Reid and another from William McCafferty. Saints could in part attribute defeat to injury to their goalkeeper Bert Lock, a brave but reckless custodian prone to his fair share of knocks. He received a kick to the back of the neck in the first period and was strongly advised not to continue. With typical courage he re-took his place between the sticks.

The most disappointing feature of the game was the crowd of 12,000, well short of the usual Fratton Park average for a Saints game, but this was put down to the public 'saving themselves for Sheffield'. The following week Wednesday were in town for an FA Cup-tie and Fratton's capacity would be tested as a record 27,853 poured through the turnstiles to see a 2-2 draw. Given Pompey's Cup track record, it will come as no surprise to hear they lost the replay 0-3.

As ever, 'the next time' wasn't that far away. In this 1908-09 season the two clubs would meet no fewer than *eight* times. Within a month the two were at it again at The Dell, as some unfinished business from the previous season was finally resolved. In the spring of 1908 Pompey had drawn twice with Millwall in the Southern Charities Cup semi-final, with the Saints awaiting the winners. The Lions had refused to play extra-time in the second game at Fratton and ultimately the competition committee awarded Pompey the match. It took until February 1909 for a suitable date for the final to be found. Pompey, regarding it as an 'end of season' fixture – that is to say the previous season – tried to field a side which most closely approximated to that of ten months beforehand. This was perhaps unwise, as Saints won 1-0 with a goal by Alf Ward, a rare personal highlight in a Saints career dogged by knee problems which forced his retirement at the end of the season.

Pompey's Millwall shenanigans the previous season were echoed in March, when Saints came to Fratton for the annual Hampshire Benevolent Cup. On a cold and stormy afternoon the sides played out a 1-1 draw in front of 3,000 wretched souls, with Reid giving Pompey a first-half lead before John Foster levelled. In view of the conditions, the two captains refused extra-time and the two sides re-convened the following month at The Dell, where Saints prevailed 4-3. For the record, Pompey won the other, the final encounter, in that current season's Southern Charities Cup, 2-1 at Southampton.

For the 1909-10 season, Saints and Pompey both withdrew from the Western League, enabling the pattern of matches to look more familiar to modern supporters. The days of eight derby days a season would be a thing of the past – in peacetime at least, but more of that shortly – and fewer matches meant greater weight would attend the outcome of those that remained. The first Southern League clash under the new regime was on 6th November 1909 (although the teams had already met in the Southern Charities Cup, Saints winning 3-2). The game was greeted, said the *Evening News*, with 'almost as much enthusiasm as for an English Cup match,' which, as we know, was no faint praise.

Pompey fielded their latest forward hope, Adam Bowman, registered in the nick of time after his move from Brentford in exchange for McCafferty. However, Bowman had not played for a couple of weeks and was 'not used' to his team-mates, and the paper concluded he was 'not happily circumstanced' by his debut. In modern journalese we can file him under 'struggled to adapt', especially in the intensity of a local derby, although Bowman would score nine goals in nineteen games before the season's end.

Instead, Pompey had an old hand, 'Sunny Jim' Kirby, to thank for a goal inside a minute, although Saints made their point with an equaliser by Joe Blake. 'Sentinel', the *Evening News*' football correspondent, was especially taken with the size of the crowd, 'considerably in excess of 12,000', including an estimated 700-800 from Southampton. On the Monday he was quite boastful about its significance: 'One thing about the match I was exceedingly pleased to see was the gate. It was the first time it had been fine for a home game this season and it proves what I have often said, that Portsmouth only wants a first class team to ensure them support second to none in the south of England'. By the genteel standards of the day that was throwing down the gauntlet, although there was little to choose between the two clubs in terms of gates in this period.

'Sentinel' had toned down his opinions by the following September, in what was to prove Portsmouth's nemesis season. Ahead of Pompey's first away game, at The Dell, he had reverted to a more conciliatory tone. 'The progress of Pompey is followed with almost as much interest in the neighbouring town of Southampton as it is in Portsmouth, while locally we watch the doings of the Saints with as much keenness as they do in Southampton. It is not to be wondered at therefore that when the two Hampshire rivals meet there should be a kind of local derby and unbounded enthusiasm'. An estimated 2,000 Pompey fans swelled the attendance to 10,000, and they 'gave vent to their lung-power early'. In view of the result they had to, perhaps. Percy 'PeeWee' Prince, Liverpool-born but Southampton-raised, completed the rout after Martine Dunne and Frank Jefferis – signed for £5 from Fordingbridge Turks – had scored in the first half.

How 'keen' 'Sentinel' was on Saints' 3-0 demolition of their rivals is not recorded, but he conceded: 'Southampton look like settling down to be a good side'. In fact, 'Sentinel' was mistaken. Saints were a poor side which would finish seventeenth. It's just that Pompey were worse. By the time the return in January came around, they were in desperate danger of relegation, finding themselves just four points above the bottom two, having played a game more than those around them. Beforehand, Pompey had restored a modicum of pride, winning the Hampshire Benevolent Cup, now named after William Pickford, 2-1 at The Dell, a match played on a pitch so treacherous that Pompey had wanted it postponed. In the end, the teams compromised and played 30 minutes each way. Pompey's poor form, and the waning appeal of Southern League football perhaps, meant just 9,000 turned out – the lowest-ever recorded derby attendance at Fratton Park – for what would be dubbed these days as a 'must-win' game for the home side. Instead they succumbed to a single second-half goal scored by Dunne, leaving the writing on the wall. A last-day victory over Brentford – their first since the end of January – couldn't save them and Portsmouth were down. Southampton were not far above them, but at least seventeenth place meant safety.

Pompey's relegation meant that for the 1911-12 season football supporters on the south coast would be denied a true derby day for the first time in thirteen years, although Saints did batter their neighbours 5-1 in the Pickford Benevolent Cup in October at The Dell. Not that Saints were prospering at their neighbour's expense. Despite spending £820 on six new players, they could only finish sixteenth that season. The club's losses were spiralling towards £1,700 for the financial year and a 'public appeal' for funds in January was wrecked by a coal miners' strike which caused considerable hardship in the Southampton area.

Portsmouth's priority was instant promotion, which, to their credit they achieved. Architect of Pompey's accession was new manager Robert Brown, who replaced the ultimately catastrophic management by committee of the previous three seasons, which had existed since the departure of Richard Bonney. Brown somehow 'fixed' the fixture list so that Pompey avoided too many railway trips to darkest Wales in mid-winter. He also assembled a squad of solid professionals, marshalled on the field by a veteran of the relegation campaign, John 'Jack' Warner, a Preston-born bricklayer. Warner had arrived at The Dell in 1902, having made a handful of appearances for his home-town club. A speedy full-back, who was a 'match for any forward,' according to Chalk and Holley (1992), from Saints' point of view Warner would prove to be one who got away. Apparently, the Saints board, believing his knee was suspect, authorised his transfer to Portsmouth in May 1906. Pompey had approached the player following his excellent performance in the January Cup-tie. Saints' error soon became apparent, as 227 Southern League appearances in salmon pink (then white, then blue) in ten seasons testified. Warner was forced to retire in 1915, ironically through a knee injury, but after the First World War he would become Pompey's trainer, a position he held until 1937.

The new season, 1912-13, saw the battle for Hampshire pride recommence. Poor old Saints would be on the receiving end as Pompey completed a clean sweep of all five matches contested. A new midweek competition had been instituted – the Southern Alliance – in a bid to attract spectators unable to attend on Saturdays, due to new shop laws which required them to work. The new competition would only endure for two seasons, reduced to an arena for reserves and watched by sub-1,000 attendances. It was still the Southern League which had any lure, and on 28th September 1912, 1,750 'dockyard excursionists' helped swell the largest Pompey contingent ever to descend on The Dell, according to contemporary accounts. It was a cracking match, too. Saints went into it off the back of a 0-5 drubbing at Swindon, and their morale would not have been helped by a Frank Stringfellow's last-gasp goal which gave Pompey the win by the odd goal in five.

'Ding Dong Dell' was the headline in the *Evening News*, illustrating that the art of alliteration, coupled with pertinent punning, were becoming the staple of sports sub-editors everywhere. The days of describing the game in terms of 'inflated spheres' and 'custodians' were all but behind us. On 25th January, Saints came to Fratton anxious to make amends, having lost the Pickford Cup and a couple of Southern Alliance games to Pompey in October and November, but to no avail. Despite their improved showing, and the backing of 1,000 Saints fans in the crowd of 14,000, second-half goals from Warner – whose knee was holding up – – and Stringfellow did the damage. Citing a 'palpably ineffective' attack, 'Sentinel' feared for Saints' prospects of avoiding the drop, but they survived, finishing seventeenth out of twenty, to Pompey's eleventh.

For the following season, 1913-14, the Southern League fixture committee pitted Saints against Pompey on consecutive days. Until the late 1950s it was traditional in the English game to play on Christmas Day and Boxing Day, so on 25th December 1913 a crowd of 14,000 saw Pompey continue their good run against the Saints with a brace of goals from Arthur Mountney. The following day Pompey's hero was unable to play, and Saints took advantage to win a thriller 4-3, with the crowd permitted onto the perimeter cinder track to ease the crush. Two goals from Sid Kimpton, who would find fame on the coaching staff of the Czech national team which reached the final of the 1938 World Cup, were the key to Saints' success. Their other goals came from Art Dominy – later to manage the Saints during the Second World War – and Len Andrews, who, by all accounts, packed a left-foot shot harder than any in the game. Pompey might have nicked a point, but Stringfellow saw a late, equalising 'goal' disallowed.

Despite war clouds gathering over Europe, professional football in Britain elected to press on with the 1914-1915 season as planned. The assassination of Archduke Ferdinand in June 1914 had set in train events which provoked Britain into declaring war on Germany. With the 'British Expeditionary Force ready to join the fray,' as Inglis (1988) put it, 'the league had every intention of carrying on, Huns or no Huns'.

The 1913 Christmas double-header was deemed so successful that it was repeated in 1914. This time Saints had the better of the two encounters, winning 1-0 at Fratton on Christmas Day then repeating their 4-3 win of twelve months previously in the return at The Dell, after Pompey had led 3-1 at one stage. There were 9,000 in attendance at Portsmouth and 7,000 for the return.

The financially crippling effects of the Great War were already starting to bite. Southampton had put out a flyer promoting the match to all and sundry, such as soldiers from around the country temporarily barracked in the town: 'At this juncture the Directors of the Club wish to return their thanks for the support which has been accorded to them this season. It is not, of course, up to average proportions – but then we did not expect it to be in view of the war; for thousands of our regular supporters are now away serving their King and Country ... Our players too are doing their little bit to protecting our hearths and homes. Over 20 are in military service and those entertaining you this afternoon ... are devoting several hours daily to drill ... Owning to the war, everything is abnormal and there has been a tremendous slump in our gates. Notwithstanding the most rigid economy on the part of the directorate and a monetary sacrifice cheerfully borne by the Players, the financial position is getting worse. The only immediate prospect of arresting this decline is for a bumper gate to be secured on Boxing Day when we play Portsmouth.'

In the circumstances, the public were not unduly bothered by the plight of a financially stricken professional football club. By now, the horrors of war were unfolding. Boxing Day newspaper headlines were dominated by the conflict and the fate of Allied forces, reporting 'sensible progress' in the Alsace, an air raid over the Thames, and the sinking of a French submarine. In another sign of the times, Mrs Emiline Pankhurst of suffragette fame, and leader of the Women's Social and Political Union, was reported as 'too unwell' to be arrested for her latest hunger-strike.

Football was about to take a back seat for four years and both Pompey and Southampton would be taken to the brink financially, both by the conflict and by the fact that the Southern League, in effect, left its clubs to fend for themselves. At the end of that 1914-15 season, Saints finished sixth and Pompey seventh, but more pressing was Southampton's financial deficit, which had ballooned to almost £4,000, while even the relatively new Portsmouth company had liabilities of £1,474.

The decision to suspend league football was taken at a meeting on 3rd July 1915 at the Winter Gardens, Blackpool, at a conference attended by the Football, Southern, Scottish and Irish Leagues, who agreed that settling issues of promotion and relegation in such circumstances would be grossly unfair. Clubs were finding it increasingly difficult to field eleven players, as their fit young men were called up or volunteered for active service. However, in reality the leagues had been virtually forced to shut down by the weight of public opinion, which voiced its distaste for footballers turning out in fancy colours while their countrymen in khaki were dying in the trenches.

The 1915-16 'season' was little more than a series of friendly matches to provide respite for troops returning on leave, although a South Western Combination league was formed in the second half of the season, embracing Swindon, Cardiff, Newport, and the two Bristol clubs. Portsmouth won it, clinching the title despite home and away defeats to Saints in their final two matches – the eighth and ninth time the two clubs had met that season. Better still was the organisation of a London Combination the following season, 1916-17, which saw the London-based Football League clubs agree to compete with their Southern League counterparts.

The soon-to-be-famous Woolwich Arsenal were scheduled to make their first (semi) competitive visits to The Dell and Fratton Park, along with the likes of Chelsea and West Ham. Again Saints took the honours in the local derbies, winning three of the four scheduled encounters. Saints even posted a profit of £228 that season, but in August 1917 the Hampshire clubs were stunned when the London clubs vetoed travelling south of the capital. Luton and Watford were also excluded on the basis that railway travel outside the capital was becoming increasingly impractical in wartime. Chalk and Holley (1988) state that Saints director Mr Bulpitt 'made an impassioned speech [at the crucial meeting] and even offered to pay the train fares of the 12 players from each club'. It was to no avail and the vote was lost nine to four, with Brentford abstaining.

In January 1918 the situation worsened when the use of petrol-driven vehicles for sporting activities was forbidden, 'except where life or limb was threatened', according to Inglis (1988). As a consequence, both Saints and Pompey were forced to arrange friendlies against local works teams – such as Harland & Woolfe and Thornycrofts Woolston – or local military establishments. For the record, Southampton and Portsmouth – notwithstanding the difficulties of fielding settled sides – ran up cricket scores against the likes of the Special School of Flying and the RN Torpedo School, in front of a handful of spectators. Visits from Bristol City, Reading and Swindon, coupled with a series of derbies, served to inject the fixture list with a degree of spice.

Also in January 1918, a South Hants War League was created to try to add a competitive element to matches. Some of the works teams, often fielding players with professional experience, were no mean outfits. For example, in January 1920 Thornycrofts Woolston even held First Division Burnley to a 0-0 draw in the first round of the FA Cup in a match played at Fratton Park as Saints were hosting their own tie against West Ham. The replay in Lancashire was lost 0-5. And Thornycrofts posted a better result at Fratton Park on 23rd March 1918 – winning 2-0 – than Saints, who the following week lost 2-4. Pompey won the SHW league that season, with Saints finishing a poor fourth.

Even though the War was nearing its end, it was decided regular football could not restart in time for August 1918, and with the London clubs still unwilling to travel south, it was the same routine in 1918-19. At least the Christmas 'double-header' between the Hampshire rivals was still on the menu, and Pompey would have enjoyed theirs, beating Saints 5-1 at Fratton Park on Christmas Day, then 6-3 at The Dell the following day. Stringfellow was the scourge of the Saints, scoring twice in the first fixture and a hat-trick in the second. To show that these were unusual times, the return matches at Easter – teams played each other four times – saw Saints draw 1-1 at Fratton on Good Friday then win by an unlikely 9-1 on Easter Monday. That defeat cost Pompey the chance of regaining the title, which went to the Harland and Woolfe side. In March 1919 there had also been an outbreak of crowd trouble at The Dell, although the cause was a fixture between Harland & Woolfe and Pompey in the Hants 'Victory Cup' to commemorate the end of 'the war to end all wars' on 11th November 1918. The shipyard side won 4-1, but reports told of battling supporters from both sides and the referee being forced to flee for the safety of the dressing room at the final whistle.

The Southern League resumed on 30th August 1919 with Pompey winning 2-0 at Southend, while Saints drew 1-1 at home to Exeter. But the days of the Southern League as a first-class competition were coming to an end. Indeed, in January of that year it had offered its first division lock, stock and barrel to the Football League, for the purpose of forming a third division, but the offer was declined, for the time being at least.

The Southern League's weakness stemmed from the fact that its leading advocate, Millwall chairman J B Skeggs, had been preoccupied with the war effort – for his trouble he received an OBE, records Inglis (1988) – and by the time of the Armistice the administrative infrastructure of the competition was in disarray. Another of its leading clubs, West Ham, had jumped across to the Second Division of the Football League, leaving the competition a pale shadow of that which had delivered FA Cup finalists – Southampton in 1900 and 1903 – and winners, Tottenham, in 1901.

During the 1916-17 season, the new 'London Combination' had seen Football League and Southern League clubs face each other on a regular basis. After the War was over, the Football League, under the stewardship of secretary Charles Sutcliffe, was keen to strengthen and broaden its power-base. The fact that the Football League's London representatives had operated pretty autonomously during the War was a concern. Shady horse-trading saw Chelsea, relegated in 1915, and – more controversially – Arsenal (who had finished seventh in Division Two, rather than the other relegated club, Tottenham) elected in 1919-20 to a First Division expanded from twenty to 22 teams.

The expansion was designed to head off the threat of a breakaway London league. Portsmouth were destined to be the last champions of a 'professional' Southern League and they made their intentions clear with a 5-1 hammering of Saints at Fratton Park on 18th October 1919. A 'fight or two' was also reported that afternoon, although the trouble was 'quickly quelled'. Public interest in football was on the rise again, and more than 20,000 crammed into the ground, although 'Linesman' – 'Sentinel's' replacement – indicated there was still plenty of room, with a 'great clamour for reserved seats, although admission charges have been increased'. He also reported that shares in the company were doing brisk business, especially when a £20 parcel included a reserved seat for all matches 'except English Cup ties'.

Not that that was really an issue. Pompey maintained their unhappy record in the FA Cup, losing 0-2 at Bradford in a replayed match, after the first had been abandoned at 2-2 in the 63rd minute. Saints, too, were lacking Cup comfort, falling 0-2 to West Ham in a first round replay after the sides had drawn 0-0 at The Dell. By the time Pompey earned a point at The Dell in March – with many travelling fans locked out – they were on their way to the title.

Saints at least had the consolation of lifting the Pickford Benevolent Cup at the end of the season, winning 2-0. Saints even allowed Pompey to bring on a substitute, after William Probert was forced from the field with an injury. However, the formation of a new Third Division of the Football League was far from a *fait accompli*, and it was not until the 1920 AGM of the Football League that it was agreed to offer 'associate membership' to the 22 clubs of the Southern League first division. In fact, it was only 21, as Cardiff City had already successfully applied to join Division Two of the Football League. They did so at the expense of bottom-placed Grimsby Town who, somewhat reluctantly, had to take their place in the new Third Division.

Despite Portsmouth's recent ascendancy, it is fair to say Southampton would metamorphose into a Football League club in August 1920 as the 'biggest' club on the south coast. Six Southern League titles, four FA Cup semi-finals and two FA Cup final appearances brooked no argument. Pompey's championship was only their second, and with an FA Cup record second to, well just about everyone, it is hard to make a case for their making any impact on the wider footballing world.

It is worth pitching this question of comparative status into the mix of the wider one of love-hate, because the conventional wisdom in Portsmouth is that Saints have never really amounted to much in terms of a club. In terms of trophies gleaned, there is perhaps some mileage in this point of view, but ultimately stature is only relative. By the standards of 1920, Saints still retained a cachet that Pompey had yet to emulate.

Chapter 4

~ The Race to the Top ~

(1920-27)

Aside from the additional long trip to Grimsby – Saints would have that pleasure in December, Pompey in April – the new Third Division fixture list was pretty familiar. Southampton kicked off with a win and a draw against Gillingham, plus a win and a defeat against Swindon, ahead of the first Football League derby, at The Dell on 11th September 1920. As Southern League champions, Pompey were expected to be among the front runners. Their own start had been marginally better and, with two wins and two draws, was enough to have them sitting on top of the table after four games.

Long-serving inside-right Frank Stringfellow had joined Portsmouth in 1911 and had the distinction of captaining them in their first Football League match, in the absence of Arthur Knight. He was the main threat, having scored four goals already. Pompey fans had been exhorted to 'get there early' and a special train leaving the town station at 1pm had been laid on. Any thoughts that the Hampshire balance of football power was shifting decisively to the east had to be put on hold. Southampton stormed to a 2-0 win, allowing them to leapfrog their neighbours in the table, although Exeter were now top.

Pompey complained of ill-fortune with both goals. The first, scored by Tom Parker, came from a corner which they claimed had been preceded by a handball, while the second was a penalty awarded when the ball 'kicked up' in a goalmouth scramble and hit Bill Probert's left hand. James Moore, who later that season became the first ever Saints player to be sent off, converted the kick. 'Linesman' in Monday's *Evening News* was not happy. 'Had the leather [1920s vernacular for the ball] passed him [Probert] Robson [the goalkeeper] could have cleared, so the right back was not preventing a certain goal even if he did intentionally knock the ball down. But he had no such intention and this was the verdict of the Southampton supporters who sat close to me in the stand … I did not think Mr Grinstead, the official, was the class of referee up to the standard required for a keen game such as this'.

The referee is, of course, always an easy excuse. More telling perhaps was the fact that Portsmouth were reduced to nine men for much of the game, with Willie Beedie sustaining a serious hip injury, while Jack Harwood 'crocked' his knee and 'might as well have been off the field for he could do no more than head the ball when it came in his direction at a convenient height'.

Seven days later – with Beedie and Harwood having missed Pompey's midweek draw at Gillingham and still sidelined – Saints' visit attracted more than 20,000 to Fratton Park, but again Pompey failed to deliver, losing to Bill Rawlings' first-half goal. Acknowledged as the better side, even by 'Linesman', Saints were suddenly on a roll. A 3-0 win at Swansea took them to the top of the pile, a position they held until they suffered back-to-back defeats against Grimsby.

With the Easter period approaching, Southampton were second behind Crystal Palace, whom they would play twice over the holiday period. Only the champions would go up, so these were critical games. Around 20,000 turned out at The Dell on 28th March, some of whom were hurt when a barrier collapsed at the Milton Road end. Moore gave Saints the lead, but a last-gasp equaliser took the wind out of their sails. Not even an honourable draw at The Nest, Palace's home in those days, could repair the damage, and Southampton ultimately fell five points short of the champions. Saints even progressed in the FA Cup, beating Northampton in a Dell replay and avenging the defeat at Blundell Park, before losing 0-1 to Cardiff at The Dell in round three – the equivalent of the fifth round these days.

By contrast, Portsmouth's season petered out. A 0-3 defeat at Second Division South Shields in the FA Cup in the first round was all too predictable, and the season ended with a pair of 0-0 draws against Queen's Park Rangers. At least, Pompey had the Pickford Cup to console them at the end of a disappointing campaign. Harry Buddery's second-half header settled the contest with Saints at Fratton on 11th May in front of a record attendance for the competition of almost 7,000.

Pompey could also be content with the returns at the gate. More than 25,000 had turned up for the Boxing Day win over Watford and never did attendances drop below 10,000. It is always risky to read too much into comparisons, as quoted attendances were often simply a reporter's estimate, but Southampton's good season did not prevent gates at The Dell frequently dipping below 10,000. By coincidence, Saints also ended their first Football League campaign with a brace of goalless draws, but only 7,000 saw the final home game, against Newport, less than half the number at Fratton Park for the equivalent end-of-season fixture.

The following, 1921-22 season saw a 're-branding' of the Third Division, with the addition of a 'northern' section. This spared the two south-coast clubs long journeys up north. In view of their location, no doubt Plymouth Argyle were even more pleased by developments.

It would prove to be an eventful Third Division (South) campaign for both Hampshire sides. The previous season, Saints had based their good form on a consistent defence, with full-backs Parker and Fred Titmuss proving ample cover, while centre-half and skipper Alistair Campbell was a rock. That form continued, but Saints also found a cutting edge, with Rawlings finally coming into his own. Thirty goals in 28 League appearances told its own story. Saints thrashed Charlton 6-0 and Northampton 8-0 at The Dell, Rawlings claiming three and four goals respectively, as Southampton vied with Plymouth for the top spot.

However, Portsmouth, were neatly tucked in behind the chasing pack as winter turned to spring. With FA Cup interest having again ended prematurely, Pompey were due to welcome Saints at Fratton on 18th March for a game which would prove vital. It was arguably the biggest clash yet between the Hampshire rivals, but Portsmouth needed the win more. Although only a point behind, they had played two games more than Southampton and defeat would end hopes of promotion. The permanent berthing of *HMS Victory* in No 2 Dry Dock, where she remains to this day, earlier in the week might have proved portentous, had the home side won.

In the event, a record crowd of 26,382, swelled by a sizeable travelling contingent, crammed into Fratton Park, but that man Rawlings broke Pompey hearts again. Rawlings had been decorated in the Great War, earning the 1914 Star with the 2nd/3rd Wessex Field Ambulance, and the Andover-born centre-forward had been snapped up by Southampton as an amateur in 1918 (Holley and Chalk 1992). He was now at the height of his powers. His goals, even in the Third Division, had persuaded the England selectors to award him a full cap earlier that month, when he led the line against Wales. Against Pompey, serviced by winger Charlie Brown, Rawlings scored a goal in each half and Pompey could do no better than strike the crossbar twice. In effect, the title race was now a two-horse affair. Saints trailed Argyle by a couple of points, but crucially had two games in hand. The pair were also scheduled to meet twice in April.

Portsmouth were in no mood to roll over in the return at The Dell. Conceding another penalty – although Henry Johnson handled before being felled in the box – Rawlings converted after just seven minutes. Pompey quickly equalised through Percy Cherrett, but three minutes later goalkeeper Ned Robson was carried off unconscious following a brave save to prevent Johnson from restoring Saints' advantage. With Robson's index finger dislocated and blood pouring from a head wound, left-back Shirley Abbott went in goal and, down to ten men, Pompey had to reshuffle the back line. Centre-half John Brown held the side together to earn a 1-1 draw. According to contemporary reports, the 'auburn-haired Scot performed feats of tackling and generalship which left the Saints fans gasping and resulted in Rawlings … being kept entirely out of the picture'. Robson was allowed out of the Royal South Hants Infirmary on the Sunday and was driven by motor car to his home in Talbot Road, 500 yards from Fratton Park. It was to prove Robson's last game for the club, as in the summer he joined Sunderland for £150.

Southampton continued their pursuit of Plymouth, and even though Saints only managed one point in four against Argyle, four wins and two draws in the next six games left the situation tantalisingly poised. On 6th May, Plymouth were in the box seat, two points clear and needing only a draw at QPR to secure the title and promotion. Saints were at home to Newport County and had a better goal-average, so if they won and Argyle lost, Saints would pip them. According to Chalk and Holley's *Saints: A Complete Record* (1988) two Southampton directors, George Muir and Mr Hammock, were sent to Loftus Road to keep everyone abreast of developments by telephone. The days of portable radios were still many years off. Saints did their bit, thrashing Newport 5-0, leaving most of the 9,000 crowd who had remained in the ground waiting anxiously for news. When the telephone rang in the secretary's office it brought news that Plymouth had obligingly lost 0-2. Southampton were champions. Early that evening a telegram was delivered to the Southampton club's offices. It read: 'To the Chairman of Southampton Football Club and directors. Hearty congratulations on promotion. Your gain is our loss. Portsmouth Board of Directors.'

Next season there would be no more lucrative League derbies, but there was still the Pickford Cup to be decided on the Monday at The Dell. Saints fielded the side which had clinched promotion, and secured the cup with two goals in as many second-half minutes from 'Art' Dominy and Rawlings, the former having seen his first-half goal cancelled out by Jerry Mackie. It was noted that the gate was somewhat disappointing for the charity match.

Now, in 1922-23, Southampton would play in a national as opposed to a regional league, the first occasion a south-coast club would do so. The financial, not to mention physical, strains were underlined by the fact the only other 'southern' sides in Division Two of the Football League were West Ham, Fulham, Crystal Palace, and Clapton Orient. Saints' opening fixture was in the north east, at South Shields, a journey that Chalk and Holley (1988) reveal took twenty hours, but the team would have been satisfied with a point from a 0-0 draw. Saints would travel 8,000 miles this season, getting to know the intricacies of the railway timetables. Saints initially struggled, losing four and drawing two of their opening six fixtures. Their first goal didn't come until that sixth game – a 2-2 home draw with Barnsley, Bert Shelley having the honour.

Meanwhile, Pompey set off on their Division Three (South) campaign at a gallop. Following a 0-0 draw in the opening game with Bristol Rovers, Pompey won their next six, still without conceding a goal, to top the table at the end of September. A 0-0 draw at Newport stretched their defensive blockade to a club-record eight matches, but their momentum was broken by back-to-back defeats against Plymouth, who were still a force, despite the previous season's disappointment. After that, Pompey never quite picked up the threads – their uncertain form included a 1-7 thrashing at Brighton on Boxing Day – and they limped in sixth, thirteen points behind champions Bristol City. As for the FA Cup, need you ask? A replay defeat in the first round against Leeds ended dreams of a trip to Wembley, the new stadium nearing completion as part of the preparations for the British Empire Exhibition a year later, in 1924.

Southampton finally found their feet in the Second Division after earning their first win, in their seventh game, at Blackpool. By Christmas they were safely in mid-table and would finish the season with a perfect palindromic record: played 42, won 14, drawn 14, lost 14, points 42. Saints also scored and conceded the same number of goals – 40.

With the threat of relegation behind them, Southampton focused on the Cup, producing a thrilling run which saw First Division Newcastle defeated 3-1 at The Dell in a first-round replay. Another top-flight side, Chelsea, suffered a similar fate in the next round, this time by a single Dominy goal, a feat he repeated in the third-round replay against Second Division counterparts Bury. In the quarter-finals, Southampton were given a home tie against promotion-chasing West Ham and again the game was tight. Vic Watson gave the Hammers the lead, but Jack Elkes levelled with a header. The replay at the Boleyn Ground finished 1-1 too, but Saints were beaten 0-1 in the second replay at Villa Park. West Ham went on to reach the famous 'White Horse' final, losing 0-2 to Bolton, as an estimated 160,000 spectators flocked to the new stadium and had to be shepherded patiently off the pitch by PC Scorey on his white horse before play could begin. From then on, the FA Cup final would become an all-ticket affair.

Saints and Pompey were left to compete for two local cup competitions. Partly to compensate for the loss of league derbies, a Portsmouth businessman, Jack Rowland, put up a trophy, at a cost of 100 guineas (a guinea being 21 shillings, or £1.05 in decimal currency), to be contested annually for hospital charities. The proceeds would be shared between the Royal Portsmouth and the Royal South Hants and Southampton hospitals, and 'as well as doing good would provide opportunities for old rivals to meet in serious football'. Adverse weather affected the attendance at the inaugural match at Fratton Park on 16th April, the 7,500 attendance providing receipts of £412. Pompey had already beaten Saints in a friendly at The Dell earlier in the season, 3-1, but Saints' superior class told this time. Johnson and Rawlings scored twice in a minute in the first half, before Parker pulled one back late on. The Mayor of Portsmouth, Alderman FG Foster, presented the winning team with their medals, provided by the *Evening News* and *Hampshire Telegraph*. In his speech he said he understood the *Daily Echo* would do likewise the following season.

Seven days later came the annual Pickford Cup at The Dell. The proceeds of £253 were deemed by comparison with the Hospital Cup effort at Portsmouth to be 'not so satisfactory'. In fact, throughout the 1920s Pompey had the edge in terms of attracting the public, with league attendances invariably higher at Fratton Park even when Saints were in a higher division. Pompey looked set for revenge as goals from Billy Haines and Mackie saw them into a 2-0 half-time lead, but Johnson and Dominy secured a draw. A toss of a coin, won by Dominy, meant Saints would hold the shared trophy for the first six months and Pompey the next.

The arrival of Billy Haines galvanised Portsmouth and 1923-24 would prove to be a momentous season for the club. Legend has it that 'Farmer's Boy', as he came to be known, only signed after a supporter – Fred Prescott, Traffic Superintendent of City Tramways – was delayed by a motor car accident while on holiday in the West Country. According to Roger Holmes in his *Pompey Players 1920-2001* (2001) Prescott decided instead to take in a Somerset League game involving Haines' club Frome Town. Haines scored six goals in an 8-0 win. Portsmouth manager John McCartney was duly alerted and attended the next match himself, offering Haines terms there and then in December 1922. After two months' training he scored a hat-trick on his reserve-team debut and three goals in his first two League matches.

As Pompey scorched to promotion, Haines bagged 28 League goals in 31 matches and might have had many more but for an ankle injury which kept him out for seven matches in the spring. Pompey clinched the title with a game to spare, beating Swindon 4-1 at Fratton Park, although the restored Haines failed to score. The Rowland Cup, as the hospital charity trophy was renamed, and the Pickford Cup matches, scheduled for an end of season double-header on 5th May at The Dell and 7th May at Fratton respectively, took on added significance. The games would prove a useful barometer of the Second Division clashes to come. And Saints had no mean side. Another slow start in 1923-24 had been offset by six wins and three draws in eleven games from November. With Rawlings still banging in the goals, by the end of February Saints were in contention for promotion. They were also living up to their Cup fighting tradition, with First Division Chelsea losing a replay at The Dell for the second year running. Promotion rivals Blackpool were beaten in the second round 3-1, then Saints forced a 0-0 draw with Liverpool, who fielded six internationals, in a third-round tie at The Dell. A 0-2 replay defeat was no disgrace, but the effort told. With regulars Parker, Campbell, Titmuss and Jimmy Carr injured, back-to-back League defeats were recorded against eventual champions Leeds in early March. Not even a storming finish, taking 24 points out of 33 available, could compensate and Saints finished fifth, three points adrift of second-placed, and promoted, Bury.

Once again the weather kept the gate down for the Rowland Cup at The Dell, but nevertheless more than £200 was raised. Those who turned up were treated to a thriller which Pompey took by the odd goal in five. A brace from Haines had given them a 3-1 lead, after Rawlings had cancelled out Stephen Dearn's opener. George Harkus's effort came too late, and in any case the margin would have been wider but for Jimmy Martin missing a penalty.

It was also a sad evening for 22-year-old home winger Sam Meston, son of former Saint Sammy Meston, who played for the club at the turn of the century. Signed from Hampshire League Sholing Athletic in 1921, he had established himself in the first team earlier in the season, but broke his leg against Bristol City on 6th October. The Rowland Cup marked his come-back, but a collision with a Pompey defender saw him carried off with a fracture of the same leg. He would never be quite the same, and drifted away from The Dell to Gillingham, although improbably he was later signed by First Division Everton and played alongside the legendary 'Dixie' Dean.

At the presentation of The Rowland Cup, the *Echo* kept its promise and presented each player of the winning team with a cigarette case. With one cup in the bag, Pompey crowned a marvellous season two evenings later by capturing the Pickford Cup, the Portsmouth public again turning out in numbers. The 7,496 attendance was a record for the fixture and provided receipts of £404 to helping injured players in the county. Beedie scored after three minutes, then Haines made the match safe on the hour. Pompey had struck a psychological blow for the battles to come.

Portsmouth clearly found the Second Division to their taste. By the time they visited Saints on 27th September 1924 they were already in the leading pack, having picked up eight points out of ten, winning three times and drawing twice. Southampton were already three points in arrears, having played two games more, although they had yet to concede a goal at home. At the end of 90 frenetic minutes both sides could take comfort that their respective records were intact. Saints had the better of the first half, Pompey the second, and even claimed a penalty, but the referee, Captain A J Prince-Cox, said Parker's handball was unintentional. Rawlings should have settled the game in Saints' favour late on, but he fired wide from close in.

By the time of the return two months later, Saints were still trailing Pompey, who had consolidated their position, although an excess of draws kept them from looking promotion contenders. As ever, this latest derby proved the form-book could be torn up. Dominy gave Saints the lead midway though the second half with a 'splendid shot' from the edge of the area. Shortly afterwards Bill Henderson hit a Pompey post, but with time running out Mackie juggled past three defenders and slipped the ball to

Haines, running in from the left, who equalised. Once again Prince-Cox, the referee, was praised by all sides, despite suffering from a sprained leg muscle.

Although games between Southampton and Portsmouth stretched back less than a quarter of a century, they already totalled 94, with a perfectly balanced record of 41 wins apiece, and twelve draws. For most of this season though, Pompey were in the ascendant, an eight-match unbeaten run guiding them to fourth place, nine points behind second-placed Manchester United and eleven behind champions Leicester.

Saints finished in similar style, but their record included six draws out of eight games and they ended the season three points behind their rivals in seventh place. Saints manager Jimmy McIntyre had resigned in December, whereupon the board chose not to appoint a successor, taking on the task themselves. The decision didn't prevent Saints once again showing their Cup pedigree, although the elements almost robbed them at the first hurdle. Leading Third Division Exeter 5-0 in the first round, the fog blanketed The Dell with ten minutes left. The referee abandoned the game, despite some Saints fans running on the pitch in an effort to let it continue – according to Chalk and Holley (1988). The teams had to start all over again four days later. Justice was done as Saints won 3-1 and another Third Division side, Brighton, were dispatched by a Parker penalty.

Saints' luck of the draw held in the third round, when Second Division Bradford City succumbed 0-2, but the visit of Liverpool in the quarter-final promised to provide a much tougher test. The First Division team were confident of repeating their previous year's win, but Rawlings' opportunism put Southampton in the semi-finals for the first time since 1908. Had left-back Titmuss not reported sick just before kick-off against Sheffield United at Stamford Bridge – he was replaced by Ted Hough – things might have been different. However, Titmuss's absence disrupted Saints' defensive balance. Right-back Tom Parker sliced into his own net, Parker had the chance to equalise from the spot after Rawlings was tripped, but missed, then got into a tizzy with his goalkeeper, Allen, to present United with their second and clinching goal.

The now-traditional end of season charity double-header saw Pompey take the Rowland Cup at Fratton Park, through first-half goals by Haines and Mackie, although the Pickford Cup ended all square, Dominy cancelling out Martin's early opener before half-time. Saints had their reserve goalkeeper Harry Yeomans to thank for saving Harry Foxall's second-half penalty. Southampton won the toss again to determine who retained the trophy. Afterwards, Councillor A E Hooper, vice chairman of Portsmouth, stressed the importance of municipal support for the two clubs and floated the idea of a joint Portsmouth-Southampton team to face a 'City of London' or 'Sheffield' representative side on an annual basis. That interesting idea proved to be stillborn. The post-match dinner was deemed a 'ladies night' and Saints director George Muir proposed a toast to the 'fairer sex', emphasising the 'pleasure of football officials and players that ladies were taking such an interest in the game'. To ensure women knew their limits though, the *Evening News* reported that his daughter, 'Miss Muir', replied in 'charmingly appropriate terms'.

The start of 1925-26 saw a fundamental change in the laws of football and, like everyone else, Saints and Pompey took time to adjust to the new offside ruling. Previously, three players had to be between the attacking player and the goal when a forward pass was made, but that had now been reduced to two. With chaos reigning, goals flooded in all over the country. Saints scored just two and conceded eleven in the opening four games, while Pompey fared even worse, conceding thirteen. Five of these came in a 1-5 pasting by Middlesbrough, which took the edge off the ceremonial opening of the new South Stand, built at a cost of £20,000. However, of the seven goals Pompey had scored, three were at The Dell on 5th September, earning a first win of the season. Three of Pompey's all-Scots forward quintet scored, Mackie, Beedie and Alex Merrie – in for the injured Haines – grabbing the honours, with Saints' goal coming from Fred Price.

'Linesman' had some salutary advice for Southampton: 'They are attempting the impossible this season in trying to run a successful side without a manager. This policy landed Pompey in the second division of the Southern League and may land the Saints back in the Third Division.' Perhaps the warnings of 'Linesman' were heeded, for former Saints and Pompey centre-half Arthur Chadwick, the Reading manager, was appointed manager of Southampton in October. His arrival helped stabilise the club and a relegation battle was avoided, but Saints could finish no higher than fourteenth.

In March, the Saints board sold Parker to Arsenal, the £3,250 transfer fee being necessary to acquire the freehold of The Dell, but the sale left supporters far from happy. Unusually, Saints were also knocked out of the FA Cup at the first attempt. A reorganisation of the Cup meant that First and Second Division clubs now postponed their entry until the third-round stage. For the third season running Saints were paired with Liverpool, losing 0-1 at Anfield in a replay. Pompey's interest lasted only marginally longer, a third-round second replay against Derby at Leicester settling the matter.

About this time, Saints and Pompey squared up for the return derby, at Fratton. With goalkeeper Allen having fractured his ribs the previous week against Liverpool, and Campbell suffering from 'gastric trouble', Southampton's problems were multiplying. An Arctic blast swept the country, the south coast wasn't spared, and 100 men were out shovelling to clear the pitch of snow. They must have wondered why they bothered. Frank Matthews gave Saints an early lead, then Haines levelled. Foxall hit the crossbar before the break, but Rawlings scored the clincher and stand-in goalie Len Hill stood tall as Pompey vainly chased an equaliser.

Despite their defeat, Pompey held their own in the League, notwithstanding a wretched three days in the North East in October, when they lost 1-7 to Darlington and 1-5 at South Shields. Eleventh place, with 44 points from 42 games hardly suggested the fireworks to come. The balance of power in south-coast football was shifting, however, and was emphasised by the outcomes of the Rowland and Pickford Cups. The two games, on 3rd and 5th May, were played against the backdrop of the General Strike, called by the Trades Union Congress in support of the striking miners. The headline and sub-head in the *Evening News* on the Monday said: 'General Strike Due To Start – There Is Hardly A Glimmer Of Hope In The Situation.' Prime Minister Stanley Baldwin's speech to a packed House of Commons made the Stop Press: 'The course adopted by the TUC, if successful, would substitute tyranny for freedom,' said Baldwin. The newspaper also lamented that for the first time in 50 years it couldn't provide a 'full supply of news from the day' on account of striking print workers. With the strike still biting 24 hours later, the paper found a few column inches to report on Pompey's 4-2 win at The Dell. The gate of £105, suggesting around 2,000 turned up, was affected by the 'industrial situation'. By the time of the Pickford Cup game, things were improving, although not for Saints, who this time succumbed 1-5, Haines helping himself to a hat-trick.

Under Arthur Chadwick, Saints were rebuilding. By the start of the 1926-27 season Art Dominy had gone to First Division Everton, leaving Harkus appointed club captain in his place. The prolific Rawlings – 105 goals in six seasons – was still around, however. With him, Saints could pose a threat to anyone and by a quirk of the fixture list it was Pompey at Fratton who would be the first to try to stop him. Pompey gave a debut to summer recruit Murdoch McKenzie, 'the Darlington goal getter' who had scored twice against Pompey the previous season. With the temperature soaring to 82 degrees, a record crowd of 28,200 packed Fratton Park, despite the counter attraction of Essex batting first against Hampshire at the United Services Ground. With many Saints favours evident in the ground, Rawlings hit an upright, Haines gave Pompey an early lead, only for Saints debutant Sam Taylor to cancel it out. After the turnaround Pompey won the game when Henry Goodwin lobbed Allen and McKenzie added a debut goal. Despite their loss, it was Southampton who actually made the early running in the League. Going into the New Year they were two points behind leaders Middlesbrough, a point clear of Pompey. However, four straight defeats in January saw Saints drop off the pace.

In a twist to conventional wisdom, it almost seemed as though Saints had faded in the League in order to focus on the Cup. Squeezed among those four defeats were a 3-0 home win over Norwich in the third round and a 4-1 Dell win over First Division Birmingham in the fourth. Saints looked up against it in the fifth round, however, despite their tenth consecutive home draw in the competition, yet First Division champions-elect Newcastle were beaten 2-1, thanks to a brace from Rowley. The luck of the draw at last deserted Southampton in the quarter-finals, but a 0-0 draw at Millwall ensured another Dell Cup-tie, settled by Rawlings' two goals, which took them into the semi-finals for the sixth time in their history.

By contrast, Pompey were mounting a serious promotion bid, which was sparked by a 2-0 victory at The Dell in January. A near-20,000 crowd, paying record receipts of £1,269, were entertained before the kick-off by an 'open air music festival', including the Royal Artillery Band and the Grenadiers Band, who led community singing conducted by a 'jolly fellow in white jersey and flannels'. Cook gave Pompey a first-half lead after Allen failed to hold a Mackie 'hot shot'. Then, ten minutes from the end, Haines scored from the spot after Hough had tripped him. The win took Pompey into second place for the first time in their history. The question was: could they stay there and could Saints finally win the Cup?

Saturday 26th March, 1927 looked likely to prove a pivotal day. Saints would meet Arsenal at Stamford Bridge for the right to play at Wembley, while Pompey entertained League leaders Middlesbrough at Fratton Park. Having been toppled 3-7 at Boro earlier in the season, Pompey were always going to be up against it, and the second-half goal that sank them looked to have shattered hopes of First Division football for another season. For Saints, it was Cup heartbreak again. Chalk and Holley (1988) neatly summed up the contest: 'In the traditions of Southampton semi finals, Hough obligingly put Arsenal into the lead … with an own goal. Charlie Buchan increased that lead but five minutes from time Rawlings pulled a goal back. In the meantime, according to Saints – particularly director Mr A A Wood – they should have been awarded three penalties at least. All the complaining in the world did not alter the fact that Southampton would have to wait a good deal longer for their first Wembley appearance'. In fact, it would be 36 years before Saints got to another semi-final.

While Saints reacted to their defeat with a run which saw them win just once more that season, to finish thirteenth, Pompey bounced back with a vengeance. Haines netted seven goals in the next three matches as Pompey ran in nineteen goals. The run included a club record 9-1 win over Notts County at Fratton, and despite losing twice to Barnsley over Easter, Portsmouth remained in contention for promotion. A 0-0 draw at rivals Chelsea in the penultimate game kept them second, leaving a straight fight with Manchester City for the final spot on the last day of the season.

Pompey's home fixture with Preston kicked off fifteen minutes after City's with already-relegated Bradford City at Maine Road. With Pompey leading 4-1, news filtered through that Manchester had won 8-0. Frantic calculations with pencil and paper dictated that Pompey needed another goal to pip them on goal-average. Who should oblige but the Farmer's Boy Haines himself, carving a niche in Pompey folklore with his 40th goal of the season, to clinch promotion by the narrowest of margins. After the game it was noted that 'no more hearty wishes could have been expressed than by those directors of the Southampton club'.

Two days later Saints and Pompey convened at The Dell for the Pickford Cup. The celebratory mood was helped by the fact it was the silver jubilee of the charity game, which had raised more than £4,000 in its time for needy footballers. Whether or not it was the hang-over from the promotion celebrations, Pompey were no match for their hosts, who won 4-1, Rowley and Rawlings helping themselves to two goals apiece.

The trophy's sponsor, William Pickford himself, was present, and after the match he made a speech to players, officials and spectators as he presented the trophy. To cheers he congratulated Pompey on their promotion and hoped Saints would follow them and, in time, his home town team Bournemouth and Boscombe too. The Mayor of Southampton added his own best wishes and added how he 'regretted the way in which Saints were put out of the Cup at Stamford Bridge'.

Pickford concluded proceedings by making a prediction: 'Never mind about them [Pompey] being beaten this evening. You wait until Wednesday!' He was right too, as Pompey exacted revenge, 5-1, in the Rowland Cup. Before the game, 'Linesman' reminded readers of the part that Saints, even in modest form, had played in ensuring Pompey's promotion – taking points off Manchester City, Chelsea and Nottingham Forest. At the time Southampton met those clubs, Saints had nothing to play for and, if Portsmouth went up, they were also facing the potential loss of their largest gate of the season. 'In the circumstances it is an outstanding instance of the purity of the game that their players should have been so keen to do Pompey a good turn … They deserve special cheer from the crowd when they come out tomorrow.'

Whether the Fratton faithful obliged isn't recorded, but it is more than likely they did. The sentiments summed up the evident civility of the rivalry in the late 1920s. For the first time, however, the two clubs were on significantly different trajectories. It would be more than 30 years before they would meet in competitive circumstances again. By then the world would be greatly changed.

Chapter 5

~ Parting of the Ways ~

(1927-39)

Portsmouth FC arrived in the Big Time on 27th August 1927, maintaining their proud record of never having been beaten in their first outing in a new competition. They also had a new manager, Jack W Tinn, from South Shields. He replaced John McCartney, who had resigned on health grounds, citing the strain of that tension-racked Preston game as a contributory factor. He died six years later.

A 3-3 draw at Sunderland, who had finished third the previous season, was no mean feat, but it could have been better. Pompey had led 3-0 in the first half – Jerry Mackie, Billy Haines and Freddy Cook grabbing the goals before the home team launched their fightback. Four days later Aston Villa – six League titles and six FA Cup wins to their illustrious name – were beaten 3-1 at Fratton Park before a new record attendance of 32,050. That was followed by a 2-2 home draw with Derby County on the second Saturday of the season, making for a highly encouraging start to life in these plush new surroundings.

The contrast with Southampton's (mis)fortunes couldn't have been starker. Any hopes entertained in the immediate post-promotion back-slapping of two south-coast clubs soon being in the top division were quashed by four straight defeats. These included a humiliating 3-6 reverse at home to Stoke, while Pompey were being pegged back at Roker Park. Money was short at The Dell, mainly because the transfer fee picked up for the sale of Tom Parker went into constructing the West Stand, which opened officially on 7th January 1928. At the time, it was regarded, say Chalk and Holley (1988), as being 'one of the best in the country'.

That the stand was christened with a 1-4 defeat to Leeds was an apposite counterpoint to the paucity of talent on the field. Gates tumbled as low as 4,619 for the visit of Fulham in November 1927, but with Bill Rawlings in the team, Saints looked like having enough goals to keep relegation fears at bay. That is, until March, when Saints' directors accepted a £3,860 offer from Manchester United for the player. Supporters were outraged, but the board moved swiftly to sign his replacement, Portsmouth's veteran forward Mackie, for a fee of £1,000. The Motherwell-born 34-year-old had been out of Pompey's first team since Christmas, as manager Jack Tinn sought to build for the future. Mackie made an immediate impact, scoring a hat-trick on his home debut, a 6-1 win over Barnsley. All told his six goals in seven games helped Southampton avert relegation by two points.

For Portsmouth, the First Division proved tougher than their initial flush suggested. Goals were leaked alarmingly on their travels. Villa avenged their defeat by inflicting Pompey's first, 7-2, in early September, and Liverpool thrashed Pompey 8-2 in October. Five goals were shipped at Middlesbrough and six at Blackburn as the season reached its climax in April, but Pompey's home form was good enough to keep their heads above water. They concluded the season with four consecutive defeats to finish one place above the trap-door, but this had been an unprecedentedly evenly-matched campaign. Had Pompey drawn those four games they would have finished in the top half, and had they won them they would have finished fourth! As it was, their dreadful goal-average meant they finished twentieth out of 22 teams with a respectable 39 points, the same as The Wednesday – as they were still called – from Sheffield, who finished six places above them. It was one of the tightest ever finishes to a First Division season, as Tottenham, 21st and relegated, amassed 38 points and bottom-of-the-table Middlesbrough 37.

The important thing was that Pompey could look forward to another season in the top flight, and the new Hants pecking order was re-affirmed as Saints and Pompey met at Fratton in the Pickford Cup, raising another £188. Four goals by John Weddle, a 23-year-old from the North East, who had impressed in a trial and had by now replaced the legendary Haines, added to one apiece from Bobby Irvine and David Watson, secured a 6-1 win. Saints' goal came from Charles Petrie. The Rowland 'Hospital' Cup game was cancelled because the Saints board were apparently 'finding it inconvenient to field a team'. Instead, *HMS Excellent*, the Portsmouth-based Navy Cup winners, met RAOC (Hilsea), the Army Cup winners, at Fratton. Following a 1-1 draw, RAOC prevailed 3-0, watched by 2,000 spectators.

In the summer of 1928 Billy Haines, still only 28, was allowed to leave Portsmouth, despite his record of eleven goals in 26 Division One games and a career tally of 128 in all competitions. He duly signed for the Saints, dropping down one division. His impact at The Dell was immediate. Although troubled by injuries, his sixteen goals in 27 League appearances made him Saints' top scorer in 1928-29. Coupled with former Pompey colleague Mackie, who weighed in with ten, and Gosport-born Stan Cribb, twelve, Saints stayed on the fringes of the promotion race all season. In the end they fell five points short of second-placed Grimsby and they had to settle for fourth place – their best season yet in Division Two.

Portsmouth were finding it even harder to come to grips with the First Division and opposition goals continued to fly past goalkeeper Dan McPhail, among them a record-breaking five in each half at Leicester in October. Legend has it ten swans flew over Filbert Street that afternoon. Shortly afterwards, McPhail broke his arm at West Ham. His replacement arrived in December from Hearts. Jock Gilfillan signed, along with John McNeil, and Gilfillan would establish himself over time as one of the club's greatest-ever custodians. With relegation rarely a serious worry, if only because Cardiff and Bury were so far adrift, Pompey were able to concentrate on the FA Cup. McNeil was on target in the third round home win over Charlton and again in the 2-0 fourth round beating of Bradford at Fratton. In a fifth-round replay, Chelsea were despatched by a solitary Weddle goal, setting up a home quarter-final with West Ham. Interest in the game was such that it attracted a record crowd of more than 39,000. Fratton's capacity had been increased to 40,000 since the concreting of the Milton End terrace the previous summer. This was the first occasion that the vast wealth of untapped support for a successful south-coast club became apparent.

In a see-saw game, Weddle netted the decisive fifth goal of the game to propel Pompey into the semi-finals, where they would face Aston Villa at Stamford Bridge. In the build up, Pompey retreated to the Isle of Wight, as they had before previous rounds. The air was clearly invigorating and Pompey clinched their first ever final appearance through a first-half penalty, converted by Jack Smith, a £2,000 signing in December 1927 from Tinn's former club South Shields.

According to Neasom (1984), Cup final fever swept Portsmouth: 'The club's allocation of Wembley tickets was just 3,750 – applications totalled 15,000. Forged tickets now appeared in the city and the police investigated, but no one was charged'. The BBC tried to secure rights to broadcast the final on radio, but were rebuffed by the FA. Instead, as detailed in the club's *Official Centenary History*, Pompey installed a Marconiphone Super Loudspeaker at Fratton Park to relay events minute by minute to supporters who went along to watch a Portsmouth XI take on a Portsmouth FA representative side (Farmery, Jeffs and Owen, 1998).

Portsmouth's hopes were high, especially as their opponents were fellow strugglers Bolton, but a first-half injury to half-back Tommy Bell, reduced to a passenger with a muscle injury, proved too much of a handicap and Pompey lost 0-2. While their record still hardly bore comparison with those doughty Cup fighters from Southampton, Pompey had at last started chipping away at a pillar of Saints' overall perceived higher standing in the game.

There were still a couple of lesser Cups up for grabs. The first one went to Southampton, who beat the Wembley team, minus the crocked Bell, 2-1 at Fratton Park in the Rowland Cup on 6th May. The result was perhaps no surprise, as Saints were in form, having won six of their last nine matches, while Pompey had failed to win any of their last five. Two days later the outcome was the same, Saints recovering from 0-1 behind to win the Pickford Cup 3-2. An Arthur Bradford penalty on the stroke of half-time put Saints level and goals from Dick Rowley and Bert Coates made the game safe, before Jimmy Easson – another recent Tinn signing – halved the deficit with his second goal of the evening.

The 22 players, managers and trainers received cufflinks, while Pompey skipper McIlwaine was also presented with a gramophone player and records. It had been a somewhat forlorn Dell that evening. A few hours after the season's final League game, against Swansea, the East Stand had gone up in flames. Chalk and Holley (1988) record the *Echo* reported the blaze with the witty headline 'East Stand goes West', and that the likely cause was a smouldering cigarette end discarded during the match by a supporter. The club had to borrow £10,000 to rebuild the stand. A heavy shower during the Pompey game sent spectators scurrying for cover under the only other shelter to be found; the recently built West Stand.

There would be no repeat of Pompey's Cup heroics the following season – 1929-30. Third Division neighbours Brighton caused a sensation in the fourth round by knocking out their rivals at Fratton Park – 0-1. At least First Division survival was assured with a best-yet 40 points, although that was only four more than relegated Burnley mustered. Still, a final placing of thirteenth suggested a club becoming more accustomed to its surroundings.

With Haines and Mackie – despite his dismissal at Barnsley (the first Southampton player to be expelled in eight seasons) still around and scoring, Saints were again playing the role of promotion outsiders. The driving force, though, was Dick Rowley, in prolific form with 25 goals in 25 League games to January. An FA Cup exit at Bradford City prompted the board to cash in and accept a £3,750 bid for the player from Tottenham. The rebuilding of the West Stand, and now the forced reconstruction from the embers of the East, necessitated belt-tightening at The Dell. The sale of Rowley ruled out any chance of promotion, and Southampton subsided to seventh.

On 5th May Saints and Pompey played out a rare 0-0 draw at Fratton Park to share the Pickford Cup, although the *Evening News* reported disappointment in the crowd that neither Haines nor Mackie took the field for the visitors. Two days later an experimental Pompey team travelled west and beat Saints 2-0 in the Pickford Cup. Harold Methven, a recently signed inside-forward from Gresley Rovers, scored both goals.

Accusations that Saints' directors lacked ambition were answered in the summer of 1930, when the club paid a record £2,650 fee to buy 26-year-old Pompey centre-half John McIlwaine, who had captained his side at Wembley. It was an ill-starred move. The player was struck down by injury in the first month of the new season and didn't play again until the end of November – as centre-forward, strange for a player standing just 5ft 9in in his socks.

While Saints' season lumbered towards upper mid-table respectability, followed by the shock departure of manager Arthur Chadwick in April, Pompey were by now establishing a solid First Division track record. A fourth-place finish and 84 goals scored meant the club were now punching with the heavyweights. The events of May 1931, however, would suggest that Southampton were looking increasingly lightweight. 'The Dell Bombshell', as it was dubbed, was about to explode. The Pickford Cup was an established fixture, but when Pompey arrived at The Dell on Monday, 4th May 1931 they found no Saints team to play. The crisis arose when fifteen dissident Saints players, including McIlwaine, each of whom had refused terms for the next season, went on strike.

Their collective view – voiced by skipper Mike Keeping – was that if they played, the club's insurance wouldn't cover them. Saints' officials pleaded that the current season's cover did not expire until 9th May. Irony of ironies, it was the benevolent fund in question that provided the reason for the match, and which would have assisted in the event of injury. The pleas fell on deaf ears. It seems the match was being used as a bargaining chip in the players' wider dispute with their employers. An unnamed Saints player denied that was the case, but told the *Evening News*: 'We asked if the match could be postponed either for a few days or until early next season. There has been a cut in wages all round and we are sticking together to get better terms.'

Saints had re-engaged just five players, all of whom were prepared to play, so the Hampshire Football Association decided to use these five as a core and raise a 'County XI' to fulfil the fixture, calling upon four former Saints professionals – Art Dominy, Bill Rawlings, George Harkus and Len Butt – to make up the numbers. A goalkeeper called W J Soffe from the New Forest played in possibly the biggest match of his life, but given that Pompey sent out their first team it was little surprise he was overworked – Easson, Weddle, and Sepp Rutherford (two) completing a 4-0 rout. At the post-match presentation, the embarrassed Southampton directors pledged that the club would fulfil the Rowland Cup game scheduled for Fratton Park two days later.

The row rumbled on, however, and the following day the aggrieved Saints players made it clear they would not budge. 'Practically all 15 of us have been offered reduced wages. In some cases the cut means as much as £90 and £100 a year to a player. Football is our living and if we got hurt in the charity match and were unable to play again for a long time, where should we be? The club insurance would give us 30s [£1.50] a week and the Hampshire Benevolent Fund could not do very much,' commented another anonymous rebel. He was at pains to point out that Mike Keeping was not the ringleader of the revolt. 'He is, as captain of the side, simply voicing the views of the players concerned'.

Saints director Major R C Sloan Stanley countered: 'We have never treated a player badly while I have been with the club and we would not do so now had it happened that one or other had received an injury while playing in this charity match.'

Southampton were true to their word and, despite fielding a scratch side at Fratton, they did well, holding out for a 2-2 draw. Pompey were in experimental mode, giving trials to three players and according to 'Spectator' in the *Evening News*, 'inclined to take things rather easily'. Goals by Easson and Weddle had seemingly put Pompey on course, cancelling out an early goal by Allen, who seems not to have been a professional at The Dell, as no trace of him can be found. After 66 minutes Saints levelled through Arthur Haddleton. In the boardroom afterwards the destination of the trophy was decided by a toss of a coin and Pompey skipper Dave Thackery guessed right. The brouhaha had affected the gate, however, with just over 2,000 turning out, raising £127. This sum included ten guineas donated by Rowland himself.

That same day, Pompey signed a Saints player. Full-back Ted Hough, a Dell stalwart since 1921, was allowed to move for a 'moderate fee'. At almost 32, he seemed an unlikely Tinn purchase, given that the manager was supposedly building for the future, and so it proved. Hough made just one League appearance, in October 1931, as Pompey crashed 0-3 at home to Aston Villa. Hough moved shortly afterwards to Bristol Rovers.

Pompey had started the 1931-32 season poorly, with just two wins in twelve games, while Saints, under new manager George Kay, by September were top of the Second Division for the first time in their history. Haddleton set a club record by scoring in Saints' first eight League matches, but the good start soon fizzled out. In December, Plymouth inflicted Southampton's record home League defeat, 0-6, just seven days after Saints had succumbed 0-5 at Notts County. Only a spurt of good form around Easter, harvesting nine points out of ten, kept relegation at bay. But attendances were haemorrhaging. The final match of the season at The Dell, drawn 1-1 with Manchester United, attracted a mere 6,128.

Pompey's season improved dramatically and an eight-match unbeaten run from 14th November to 16th January pulled them clear of danger. The FA Cup briefly promised some joy, after replay victories against Middlesbrough and Aston Villa, but a fifth-round pairing with Herbert Chapman's reigning champions Arsenal ended any Wembley hopes. The Gunners won 2-0 at Fratton Park.

The conclusion to that 1931-32 season was spiced by a new competition, the Hants Combination Cup, involving all four professional sides in the county. While Aldershot met Bournemouth, Saints entertained Pompey at The Dell on Monday, 18th April. Saints were forced to make four changes, due to injuries incurred in their 2-1 win at Plymouth, which had all but secured Second Division safety. Pompey were the favourites, fielding the side – aside from new signing Jimmy Nichol from Leith, in place of Weddle – which had thrashed FA Cup finalists Newcastle 6-0 on the Saturday.

However, it was soon clear this was going to be a tempestuous game. The Saints crowd took exception to an early disallowed John Arnold goal, and as the protests ensued, stones were thrown at Pompey full-back Alex Mackie, considered to be at the heart of the problem. The referee tried to intervene, but was forced to call upon police assistance to calm things down. Mackie was then subjected to jeers and ironic cheering every time he touched the ball and it was clear his feud with Arnold was still bubbling away. On the hour the pair were at 'loggerheads' again and the referee sent the Pompey man off. Shortly afterwards Arnold fired home the winning goal.

Oddly, Mackie never served a suspension for the dismissal, surprising given that to be sent from the field of play in the 1930s was virtually unheard of. Instead he was rested, for no apparent reason, when the Rowland Cup at The Dell came around three weeks later. His place went to a young Bill Rochford, who would have a significant say in both clubs' histories in due course. Heavy rain on the afternoon meant the gate was so small it didn't even cover expenses, so the hospital charities didn't receive a penny and the fixture was now on its last legs. On the field, Saints led twice, through Dick Neal and Arthur Holt, who incidentally often opened the Hampshire batting with his Saints colleague, Arnold. Easson and Fred Worrall evened things up each time. The toss of the coin went Saints' way after the final whistle. Two days later a Saints side fielding several reserves were beaten 1-5 at Fratton Park in the Pickford Cup.

There was no denying that, taking the long view, Southampton were a club in decline. One of the most significant departures from The Dell in the summer of 1932 was McIlwaine. The centre-half could not agree terms, but as was the practice in those days, his registration was retained by the club after his contract had terminated. According to Chalk and Holley (1988), the club sought a £2,500 fee, but unsurprisingly there were no takers and the player drifted out of the Football League to 'guest' for Welsh League side Llanelli.

Good home results in 1932-33, with fifteen wins out of 21 games, was promotion form, and centre-forward Ted Drake – a Southampton-born gas meter inspector who was playing for Winchester when Kay persuaded him to turn pro – was banging in the goals, twenty in 33 games. However, the financial position was still precarious at The Dell and yet again key players were sold at a crucial time of the season. In February 1933 Keeping and Arnold were sold to Fulham for a combined fee of £5,000. The frustration felt by the club's supporters was underlined when just 2,949 turned up for the next home League game, against Bradford City – the club's lowest pre-Second World War attendance so far. Away from The Dell, Saints were frequently travel sick, and even the seventeen-mile trip to Fratton in October for the semi-final of the Hants Combination Cup made them queasy. Saints lost 0-6.

Portsmouth were now very much an established First Division club, and they retained their status comfortably, finishing ninth. The growing gulf in the respective clubs' standing was underlined in a joint Rowland/Pickford Cup final in May, which saw Pompey run out 5-0 winners. Match reports suggest there was still a hint of needle, as there was 'one unpleasant scene where players nearly came to blows'.

Saints' miserable away form continued in 1933-34, when they failed to earn a single victory, leaving them reliant once more on good home results to stay up. Their away form was not helped by an Easter fixture list which decreed that Saints play at Blackpool on Good Friday, then at Plymouth the next day. In the circumstances, following a 2-4 defeat at the seaside, a 0-0 Home Park draw after a gruelling coach journey through the night implied they were more resilient than their results suggested.

Southampton also lost another jewel in Ted Drake, whose 22 goals by March had the big boys sniffing around. In the end it was Arsenal – *en route* to the second of three consecutive League titles – who stumped up the £6,000 needed to secure his transfer. Even the shock return to The Dell of McIlwaine could not avert another lower mid-table finish.

Saints' Cup lustre was also beginning to tarnish. Since reaching the semi-finals in 1927, the club had failed to progress past the third round and this season was no different. Third Division (South) Northampton beat them 1-0 in a replay at the County Ground. By that time, Saints were also out of the Hants Combination Cup, losing 0-1 to a goal from Wallbanks, a reserve who never again played in Portsmouth's first team, in the semi-final on 22nd November. Visibility that afternoon was so poor that the two teams agreed to play without a half-time interval.

Portsmouth were clearly acquiring what used to be Saints' FA Cup taste. In 1934 they would even up the final appearances record at two apiece with a storming run in the competition. Manchester United, Grimsby, Swansea and Bolton were all accounted for, then in the semi-final First Division rivals Leicester were brushed aside 4-1 to set up a final with Manchester City at Wembley.

Again fortune did not smile on Pompey. After Rutherford had given them the lead after 27 minutes, skipper Jimmy Allen was reduced to a passenger and eventually carried off with concussion with twenty minutes to go. While he was off, Fred Tilson shot home the equaliser and, although a dazed Allen returned for the final few minutes, the disoriented Pompey defence allowed Tilson to sneak in and grab a winning goal at the death.

Rumours spread that Allen had died after the match as a result of his injuries but these were scotched when he appeared, fit and well, at the post-match banquet.

Portsmouth might have lost a Cup final for the second time, but Southampton's Cup pedigree was but a fading memory now. Pompey could claim to be well on the way to being not just the League, but also the Cup kings of the south coast. To rub in the fact, four days after losing at Wembley, Pompey swatted Third Division (South) Bournemouth 8-2 in the final of the Combination Cup. The Pickford/Rowland Cup at The Dell was almost as one-sided, ending 4-1 to Pompey. Beforehand, Hampshire Schoolboys took on their counterparts from Le Havre, but in a classic foot-shooting exercise, a dispute about something or other meant no Southampton boys were in the squad, cutting the gate dramatically. Following the senior game it was reported that 'the French lads, who obtained the Pompey players' autographs ... were amazed by the way the first division players passed the ball speedily and accurately'. Whether they were as keen on the Saints' players' signatures and style is, perhaps diplomatically, not recorded.

During the summer of 1934 the financial woes at The Dell were underlined by the fact that players were asked to defer their close season wages until the start of the new campaign. Perhaps surprisingly, in view of their earlier militancy, they agreed A bumper August pay packet didn't lead to improved results in 1934-35, and with just one win in the first eleven matches the club faced an uphill battle against the drop. A win in the FA Cup third round, 2-1 at Walsall – who the previous season had stunned Arsenal 2-0 – failed to lift morale and Saints failed to win any of the next ten matches. That should read eleven, if we include the 0-3 fourth-round defeat by Birmingham, although a record gate of 28,291, paying welcome receipts of £2,676, reinforced the notion that 'there was plenty of potential support in Southampton for a successful team' (Chalk and Holley 1988).

If that sounds a bit like, well, the bleating of Portsmouth fans in the late 1960s and early 70s, at a time when Southampton were establishing themselves in the First Division, the reader could be forgiven. The comparison arguably sums up the relationship between the two clubs during the 1930s. Pompey were still the upstart club, manufactured at the turn of the century when Saints were, if you'll excuse the phrase, in their pomp. Now Pompey had gone and stolen their Cup-fighting clothes, while finding themselves a highly fashionable tailor called 'First Division'. It must have been galling to be a Saints supporter at this time. At least their team averted relegation, with the last four home games won, or else this tale might have taken a different course altogether. Had the chill financial wind of associate membership of the Football League – that is to say, Third

Division football – ever blown around the corridors of The Dell, Saints might never have recovered.

Not that Portsmouth covered themselves in Cup glory in 1935. After beating Huddersfield in a third-round replay at Leeds Road, they could only draw 0-0 with Third Division Bristol City at Fratton Park, before being dumped out in an Ashton Gate replay by two second-half goals. Pompey's League form slipped, too, fourteenth place being the lowest position in five seasons, but their Hampshire superiority was maintained with a 1-0 win over Bournemouth in the Combination Cup, now renamed the Professional Cup. The game was played at Dean Park on Monday, 6th May in front of a bumper 6,500 attendance – the country enjoying a public holiday to celebrate the Silver Jubilee of King George V.

Two days later, Rutherford scored the only goal at The Dell, so that both Pickford and Rowland Cups would reside for twelve more months in the Fratton Park trophy cabinet. The Saints team that day included five local-born players, the fruits of their junior side, established in 1932, which played in the Hampshire League. In an article headlined 'Success of Southampton FC Nursery', 'Ranger' in the *News* reported his surprise at learning after the match the enterprise cost not £1,000 per annum, but just £500, meaning it had to produce just one player per season to justify its cost.

The 1935-36 season would see Southampton commemorate their Golden Jubilee, but optimism was not high as the campaign approached. Supporters had to raise £200 to keep the club going over the summer (Chalk and Holley 1988). However, galvanised by the signing of Vic Watson, the experienced West Ham forward, and the dependability of McIlwaine at centre-half, Saints won five and drew two of their first eight games to go top by late September. It was illusory. By February Saints had won just three more matches and were out of the FA Cup at the first hurdle yet again, beaten 0-1 at First Division Middlesbrough. A stunning 7-2 win over Nottingham Forest, with Holt and Watson both getting hat-tricks – 38-year-old Watson being the oldest Saint ever to achieve this feat – snapped them out of their nosedive. Although relegation was again avoided, matters would get worse before they got better. On 28th March Saints suffered their record League defeat, 0-8 at Tottenham, two weeks after promising young goalkeeper Bill Light had left to join the White Hart Lane club.

On the following Monday afternoon, admittedly it was wet and not a Bank Holiday, just 1,875 spectators clicked through the Dell turnstiles for a match with Port Vale. To put such a gate into perspective, it needs to be remembered that in the 1930s football was not the boom sport it would become in the immediate post-1945 period. The Great Depression may have been on the wane, but Southampton, relying on the docks and the notorious 'tally' system for allocating employment on a casual basis, was not an affluent place. Fratton Park only attracted 10,000 for the penultimate home League match, against Grimsby, and attendances across football were extremely erratic. Saints' biggest home gate had exceeded 21,000, against Spurs.

It was clear that Southampton's hopes of joining Portsmouth in the First Division looked remote in the immediate future. At least they kept the Pickford Cup (the Rowland Cup being defunct) competitive, taking an early lead at The Dell on 27th April through Watson. Pompey hit back before half-time through Bill Bagley, then a Bill Adams own-goal after the break ensured that the regional pecking order was maintained. However, the fixture was descending into farce. The *Evening News* correspondent, 'Ranger', was unhappy at the way the players of both sides approached the game: '[The players] thought nothing of stopping the ball with their hands when unable to reach it with any other part of their body', he moaned, noting that the crowd found it highly amusing when the referee did not spot a blatant handball by McIlwaine. 'Rules are there to be observed even in semi competitive matches,' he added. The fixture quietly lapsed into oblivion.

With Saints manager Kay moving to Liverpool, the summer of 1936 was one of upheaval at The Dell. Nine directors resigned and George Goss succeeded Kay as secretary-manager, assisted by McIlwaine. But by the end of the season, both had gone. Chalk and Holley (1988) identified the worsening financial plight as underpinning the club's woes, although £1,000 was found that summer to recruit Arsenal's Irish forward Jimmy Dunne. Fourteen goals were a reasonable return from Dunne, but fourth from the bottom and four points clear of the relegation zone was a bitter disappointment. Home form was reasonable and Saints' attendances improved. A new Dell record crowd was enticed for the third round FA Cup-tie against champions Sunderland, 30,380 seeing Saints claw back two goals after trailing 0-3. There were also five goals that afternoon at Fratton Park, but they were all in the Pompey net as Second Division Tottenham stunned the 32,000 crowd. That result was a blip in an otherwise healthy League campaign, which might have seen a best-ever final placing, save for the fact that Pompey lost their last five games. They finished ninth.

That poor run in should have acted as a wake-up call. It didn't, and the following, 1937-38, season saw Portsmouth floundering. The first win did not arrive until 20th November and the team was marooned at the foot of the First Division. It looked odds on that Saints and Pompey would be renewing their competitive acquaintance from August 1938 – in Division Two.

Despite an almost equally dismal start — Southampton's first win didn't come until 25th September – things were looking up at The Dell. With former Saints full-back Tom Parker, previously manager at Norwich, now in charge, the club was beginning to turn the corner. Certainly the fans liked what they saw and only once did attendances dip below 10,000, despite the fact that the team finished fifteenth and suffered their now-customary third round Cup exit. Saints even diced with relegation, but they were saved by a splendid run in February and March, which brought five wins and three draws. The upturn coincided with the introduction of young inside-forward Edward Bates, who had been signed from Parker's old club, Norwich, in the summer. Another Parker success was Harry Osman, who arrived in the close season from Plymouth and weighed in with 22 goals.

If Saints' recovery was impressive, Pompey's was extraordinary. Having lost ten of their first fifteen fixtures, they lost just seven more all season, although survival wasn't assured until a last-day 4-0 demolition of Leeds.

Although the status quo was maintained, the Hampshire giants did, in fact, renew their rivalry as the 1938-39 season got under way. As part of the Golden Jubilee of the Football League, it had levied clubs with a target of £100,000 to help injured old professionals. First Division clubs were expected to come up with £1,000 each, and Second Division clubs half that amount. To assist their own efforts, Saints and Pompey arranged a series of derby matches. Saints travelled to Fratton Park on 20th August 1938. Saints looked to build on the previous season's success and fielded new signings Charles Wilkinson from Sheffield United and Reg Tomlinson from Grimsby. Fred Williams, a full-back from their nursery system also debuted. Saints went ahead within a minute and although Pompey ran out 4-1 winners it had been a fast and furious affair which drew nostalgic praise in the *Evening News*. 'The game was reminiscent of the days when we used to crowd ourselves into Fratton Park to see the Hampshire rivals do battle in the Southern League,' a misty-eyed 'Ranger' recounted on the Monday. The 14,577 attendance was the 'tenth best of the day' and raised more than £800 towards the two clubs' joint target.

Once the League started, new season optimism quickly faded. Saints had it all to do after losing their first four games, although they would rally to finish eighteenth, four points clear of 21st-placed Norwich. Pompey, too, failed to fulfil the hopes of supporters, ending up needing three wins in a row during April to keep the relegation wolf from the door.

By then, Portsmouth had booked another Wembley Cup final date. The run had started routinely, with a 4-0 home win over Lincoln in the third round and then a 2-0 win over Second Division West Brom, also at Fratton Park. The luck of the draw was with Pompey and the fifth round presented a winnable home tie with another Second Division side, West Ham. On 11th February 1939 a new Fratton gate record was established – 47,614. The Jimmy Allen Stand – known as the North Stand these days – was packed. It had been named after the record £11,000 transfer of Pompey's centre-half to Aston Villa in 1934, which paid for its construction. The crowd saw wingers Fred Worrall and Cliff Parker score the second-half goals that put Pompey in the quarter-finals.

Another home tie? You bet. Coupled with manager Tinn's 'lucky' white spats, which he wore in every round, the bookmakers were beginning to wonder if Pompey had their own magic touch – their name on the Cup. More than 44,000 saw Jock Anderson score the only goal of that game. Anderson was on the scoresheet again as Pompey came from behind to beat Huddersfield 2-1 at Highbury in the semi-final, Bert Barlow netting the decisive goal.

In the Wembley final Pompey were the underdogs. Wolves, under Major Frank Buckley, were a crack outfit, finishing second the previous season and looking likely to finish second this time. On the day, for whatever reason – their controversial use of 'monkey gland' treatment is often cited – they didn't perform and Pompey scorched to one of the biggest final upsets of all time, by winning 4-1. For the record, Barlow, Anderson and a brace from Parker did the damage. The Cup was coming south of London for the first time and Pompey's relationship with their neighbours was fundamentally realigned.

Southampton were magnanimous in acknowledging the achievement. The 'Celt', who covered Saints for the *Evening News* and *Football Mail,* reported on their final home match, which was played concurrently with the Cup final: 'Whilst Portsmouth were making football history at Wembley last Saturday, the Saints were winning their last home match of the season against Burnley at The Dell by the odd goal in three. Only about 4,000 people watched the play and those were more interested in the growing Portsmouth score displayed at frequent intervals, than anything that was happening on the field before them. No doubt thousands of Saints' usual followers were in their homes listening to the broadcast of the final and that accounted for the small numbers at The Dell. There is real pleasure here at the triumph of Portsmouth … and the Mayor of Southampton (Cllr A H Powdrill) immediately the final score was known telegraphed the town's congratulations. It was indeed a great victory'.

With war clouds gathering over Europe, Portsmouth could rightly claim to have eclipsed anything achieved by the great Southampton teams of the late nineteenth and early twentieth centuries. In a little under twenty years they had usurped Saints' justifiable claim to be the major footballing power on the south coast. The question now was how the looming war would affect the respective clubs' futures.

Chapter 6

~ THE WILDERNESS YEARS ~

(1939-55)

The imminent threat of war claimed one of its first football casualties before Prime Minister Neville Chamberlain declared it on 3rd September 1939. Jimmy Guthrie, Portsmouth's Cup-winning captain, was on an FA coaching course at Leeds University when, during a black-out practice, he was involved in a motor car accident. The incident prompted the club to ban its players from travelling in cars.

Guthrie's injuries ruled him out of the start of the 1939-40 season, making him the only one of Pompey's Wembley heroes to miss the season's opening fixture against Saints at The Dell on 19th August. The match was to raise money for the League's Jubilee fund. Not that Guthrie's absence hindered Pompey's performance. They won 3-0 with a Jock Anderson hat-trick. A crowd of 8,747, paying £518 was respectable enough, considering it was, according to the *Evening News*, 'almost too hot to be watching or playing football.' Saints fielded Portsmouth-born George Smith, a twenty-year-old half-back raised in Guernsey. Oddly, he remains the only Saints player called 'Smith' to play League football.

Portsmouth had been asked the bring the FA Cup with them to The Dell, and Dave Bull's biography of Ted Bates, *Dell Diamond* (1998) recalls the irony of the occasion: 'The side with only one FA Cup win in 12 seasons entertained the FA Cup holders … Portsmouth rubbed it in by parading the trophy and let the home fans experience what it felt like – literally if you were standing down the front – as the Cup was taken round the ground. The Saints players also had a feel. Tom Emanuel [a full-back], for one was "really thrilled" to have the Cup in his hands.'

Bull also reminds us that 'Commentator', the *Echo* football writer, remarked that even the visitors' shirt numbers seemed more prominent. That seems an unusual metaphor for Pompey's superiority during this period, but apt, given that shirt numbering had only been made compulsory the previous season.

The League programme got under way the following Saturday. While Pompey were beating Blackburn 2-1 at Fratton, in front of 23,000, Saints lost 1-3 at newly promoted Newport County, but it was clear these were far from normal times. Plans were being made to evacuate schoolchildren from high-risk areas, including Southampton and Portsmouth, and black out 'practice' was now for real.

Saints slumped again in midweek, losing 1-3 at home to Swansea, and by the time they secured their first win, 3-0 at home to Bury, on 2nd

September, it was clear that football was about to be shut down. Just over 5,000 attended that match, well below 'normal' expectations. Pompey, too, played before substantially reduced gates as they lost their first two away games, at Derby and Bolton. Once Chamberlain declared that Britain was at war with Germany, the Football League – recalling, no doubt, the debacle in 1914 – announced an immediate suspension.

With Southampton designated an 'unsafe area', due to the production of armaments in the town (Chalk and Holley 1988), The Dell was a no-go for football matches. However, Saints quickly arranged a friendly at Bournemouth for the following Saturday and drew 2-2. Seven days later they travelled to Fratton Park for Pompey's first wartime friendly. Portsmouth, despite its Royal Dockyard, was apparently considered safe to stage football. On safety grounds, the capacity had been slashed, with a maximum of 8,000 allowed. The local Chief Constable had powers to fix a lower limit or even forbid the use of a ground. Tickets had to be bought in advance and the crowds 'evenly distributed'.

What the 50,000-capacity Fratton Park looked like with 3,000 souls dotted around for Saints' match on 23rd September can only be imagined. However, the *News*' football correspondent 'Ranger' didn't like the prospect one bit, fearing for football of this sort. 'Had one been seeking an answer to the question of whether friendly football amongst professional teams has any bite in it he need have gone no further than Fratton Park on Saturday … the answer was there for all to see. The first thing, which prepared one for a negative answer, was the "crowd", which was hardly large enough to merit the description … The ground wore a deserted appearance and the football was for the most part of a "friendly" character with scarcely a thrill in the whole 90 minutes.'

'Ranger's' mood was hardly helped by the fact that Saints raced into a 3-0 lead after just eighteen minutes, Reg Tomlinson showing Anderson that anything he could do, he could do better, as he bagged a hat-trick. Pompey pulled a couple back before half-time, through a Bert Barlow penalty and a goal from winger Ron Candy, but that's the way it stayed.

Discussions between the FA, the Football League, and the municipal authorities sought to pave the way for the reintroduction of competitive regional football. However, initial talk was of restricting travel to a radius of 50 miles, a scandalous proposal, according to 'Ranger', who spluttered: 'If this becomes the law and is rigidly applied it will prevent the Cup holders from taking part in first class football as long as the war lasts.' It would not have done much for Saints' prospects, either. However, common sense eventually prevailed. 'Ranger' for one, was sure 'the service authorities in Portsmouth are most anxious there should be the best possible standard of competition football provided for the troops in the neighbourhood'. On 21st October 1939 Saints and Pompey kicked off in the Football

League South 'B' against a core of London teams, supplemented by the other two Hampshire clubs, plus Reading and Brighton. Saints were even allowed to play football at The Dell again, but they couldn't have felt less welcome as Bournemouth snatched a 2-1 win on the 'opening day'.

The Football League decreed that players should be paid 30 shillings a match, and initially Saints and Pompey were able to conserve the core of their professional staffs, only calling on guest players stationed in the area when required. For the 'derby' meeting at Fratton Park on 7th December, Pompey were able to recall Guthrie for his first appearance of the season, and he was given a warm welcome by the crowd of around 4,500. Servicemen could obtain entry into the ground for a reduced sum of sixpence (2½p), instead of the usual shilling (5p). Pompey also fielded the Chelsea goalkeeper John Jackson, deputising for Harry Walker, who was performing 'best man' duties at former teammate Donaghue's wedding. Portsmouth won the game 4-1, Barlow netting a hat-trick, and Bill Bagley getting the other. John Bradley scored Saints' late consolation from the penalty spot.

Six weeks later, on 20th January 1940, Saints took their revenge, winning 2-0, taking an early lead when Guthrie's back-pass was too strong for Walker. According to contemporary reports, Saints' players were properly appreciative, several of them running up to shake the scowling Pompey skipper's hand. Another mix up between Rochford and the goalkeeper presented Fred Briggs with the second goal. Pompey also announced the return of former centre-half Jimmy Allen, unable to play competitive football because it had been banned in Birmingham. This had left his club, Aston Villa, temporarily mothballed. Allen would make just seven appearances for Pompey. The day after he played in Pompey's Good Friday defeat at Brentford, he was left out of the side to play Saints in a Football League 'C' fixture at Fratton Park as he had just signed for the opposition! Allen was in the twilight of his career and in four years at The Dell he only played eight times.

Portsmouth put aside their feelings about Allen's departure by winning 3-1. Southampton made amends in the return a month later on 24th April, winning a 'rousing game' 1-0 at The Dell. Allen impressed for the Saints, but a Pompey youngster called Reg Flewin also took the eye. Flewin had already made his First Division debut, aged eighteen, twelve months beforehand. He had made the centre-half position his own, since regular centre-half Tommy Rowe joined the police force on the outbreak of war. Flewin was a championship star in the making.

Portsmouth contrived to finish bottom of that 'C' League, which did not finish until 8th June, matching the inglorious record of Saints in the 'B' League. The following, 1940-41 season would prove to be grim for both clubs, not least because of the fearful pounding at the hands of the

Luftwaffe in the Battle of Britain. With aircraft factories such as Follands and Supermarine, home of the Spitfire, shipbuilders Vosper Thornycroft, the commercial port and the oil facility at Hythe, the Southampton area was as much a target as the more obvious Portsmouth, bristling with military wherewithal. Matches at The Dell were frequently interrupted by air raids during that autumn, but in November a bomb actually hit. It blew, say Chalk and Holley (1988), 'an 18 feet wide crater in the Milton End penalty area, smashing a culvert carrying a stream under the pitch and flooding the ground to a depth of more than three feet for a month.' All Saints' remaining fixtures in the Southern Regional League had to be played on opposing grounds.

Relying on emerging young players from their nursery, Saints won just four out of 31 matches, although one of those was a gratifying 2-1 affair at Fratton Park on Christmas Day 1940. Boxing Day fixtures were cancelled that season. Pompey fared better, winning sixteen matches, and they also had the bonus of a more attractive fixture list – the big London clubs considered Southampton a step too far. Saints returned to Fratton four more times in 1941, losing league games 2-5 on 8th February and 0-6 in March. The week after that February visit, Saints also played a 'home' match at Fratton, Brentford graciously deigning to travel no further than Portsmouth to meet Saints in the War Cup. But Southampton lost that fixture too.

War football was a peculiar brand. Players would be whisked away without notice to play their part in the war effort, leaving clubs having to beg, steal or borrow replacements, sometimes from the crowd. Results, too, were completely unpredictable, with double-digit scores not uncommon. Perhaps the strangest Fratton Park score saw Pompey overcome Aldershot 10-5 after extra-time, having been losing 1-3 at half-time, in the semi-final of the Hants Combination Cup in May 1941. Pompey's 8-1 mauling of Saints on 2nd June in the final, bringing down the curtain on the season, was almost as fanciful. Two days beforehand, Pompey had lost 2-9 themselves ... at Aldershot.

For the 1941-42 season, Southampton found themselves even more isolated from top class football. Aldershot had the pick of the Army players at their disposal, which made them one of the country's foremost teams. Aldershot and Portsmouth had joined the London War League, leaving Southampton to feed on the scraps of matches against Bournemouth, Luton, Cardiff and Bristol City, supplemented by friendlies with the service sides.

Fratton Park, on the other hand, attracted a five-figure gate for the first time in more than two years, once restrictions were relaxed. Almost 16,000 saw Arsenal demolish the hosts 5-1 on 27th September 1941. Pompey were prolific, scoring 105 goals. Their results included an all-time record

16-1 thrashing of Clapton Orient in February 1942. Pompey also reached Wembley again, reaching the semi-finals of the London War Cup, eliminating Crystal Palace and Chelsea in a round robin. In the semi, Charlton were beaten 1-0 at Stamford Bridge, with a goal by Scotland international forward Andy Black, guesting for Pompey from Hearts.

In the final Pompey met Brentford, but in a scene echoing the 'Dell Bombshell' nine years before, the game nearly didn't take place. Pompey skipper and union representative Jimmy Guthrie exploited the occasion to try to persuade the board to stump up wages docked from players after the outbreak of war, even though they had been registered with the club. Eight minutes before kick-off, with an expectant all-ticket crowd of 72,000 in the stadium, a deal was done and the match went ahead. Portsmouth's *Official Centenary History* notes: 'It was small wonder that Guthrie, after all the vitriolic negotiating which had gone on in the dressing room, had what he admitted was a "stinker" and missed a penalty' (Farmery, Jeffs & Owen 1998).

Southampton were back in the London fold for the following, 1942-43, season and even had the 'Preston Plumber', winger Tom Finney, playing for them at The Dell against Arsenal. Despite striking up 'quite an understanding' with inside-forward Bates, Saints lost 1-3, although the attendance was a healthy 11,000. With the war situation buoyed by news of victory at El Alamein, the traditional Christmas/Boxing Day double-header went ahead. Saints beat Pompey 3-2 at Fratton, with guest Bradford City forward Alf Whittingham scoring twice and Bates once. Pompey got their revenge 24 hours later, winning 2-0 at The Dell.

In April the rivals met again in a friendly at Fratton, achieving that rarity in the goal-laden war years, namely a 0-0 draw. Saints' best win that season was 11-0, at home to Luton in January. Whittingham's eight goals in one game matched Black's feat the previous season for Pompey against Clapton Orient. The season ended with Pompey fourth and Saints fifth, just two points separating them in the new League South competition they had both entered.

The goals continued to flow in 1943-44, Saints being on the receiving end of a 1-10 mauling at Aldershot, their worst ever defeat. Although the Shots team was packed with internationals that day, and they were justly regarded as a top team in wartime football, their league record that season was modest – they finished in lower mid-table. Saints and Pompey also served up a couple of treats over Christmas. At The Dell on 25th December an injury to Guthrie derailed a side leading 2-0 and Saints ran out 6-3 winners, two own-goals not helping Pompey's cause. The match was described as 'full-blooded with a Cup tie atmosphere'. Two days later (26th December falling on a Sunday, so Boxing Day was the Monday), Pompey won 4-2 at Fratton Park. Taking some tentative steps in both games was a young left-half from Alton serving in the Navy, Jimmy Dickinson, who had impressed the previous season in a trial. Two more friendlies in April – won by Pompey 2-1 at Fratton and Saints 3-0 at The Dell – kept the record parallel for the season, although Pompey again finished higher.

Even with the invasion of, and advance in, Europe during the late summer and autumn of 1944, football war-style remained as gloriously erratic as ever. On 26th August Saints thrashed Watford 9-0 at The Dell, on the same day that Pompey beat Clapton Orient 5-1 at Fratton Park. By the time the sides met at Fratton on 30th September, Pompey had scored fourteen goals in five matches, while Saints had nineteen in the credit column. This time it was Pompey who prevailed, after Saints' early pressure 'petered out'. Charlie Wayman, a 23-year-old Newcastle United forward, scored one of the Pompey goals. He was guesting for the south-coast side and would find fame – if not fortune in these days of the maximum wage – just seventeen miles away, after signing for Saints in October 1947.

By the time the return came around in January 1945, Wayman's fleeting contribution to the Pompey cause – seven games, six goals – was done, but a new, local discovery was making waves. Peter Harris, who had represented Portsmouth Schools but shown no inclination to become a professional, had joined Pompey from Gosport Borough. At eighteen he scored twice on his home debut against Aldershot, in a 3-0 win in October, and was soon an established figure on the wing. At The Dell, having turned nineteen, Harris gave the perfect demonstration of the goalscoring winger's art, bagging a hat-trick in a 4-2 win. The league 'double' and even a 7-4 friendly win over Southampton at Fratton in April 1945, couldn't prevent Saints from finishing in fifth place, while Pompey languished in twelfth.

The end of war in Europe in May 1945 paved the way for the normalisation of football, but with the conflict still raging in the Far East it was deemed imprudent to resume 'normal' league fixtures. For the 1945-46 season the League South was reinforced by a number of Midlands clubs, such as Derby, Birmingham and Aston Villa, and a 42-game programme was reintroduced. The FA Cup made a popular return to the sporting calendar, with matches scheduled over two legs to sate the public desire for live football.

The use of guest players was still permitted, as players continued to be at the whim of military call-ups. Dickinson was drafted to sea and missed most of the season, although he did play in the 3-2 league victory over Saints at Fratton Park on 8th September. The Portsmouth directors also took the opportunity to remind their Southampton counterparts that they still 'held' the FA Cup, placing the trophy on the boardroom table for the occasion (Bull 1998). Pompey had kept the Cup under lock and key during the war years and, at six years, could now claim to have kept hold of it for longer than anyone else, thereby giving rise to a popular trick quiz question. Pompey's 3-2 win was settled by first-half goals from Harris, Petersfield-born Fred Evans, and Ray Haddington, a guest from Bradford Park Avenue. After half-time Bradley hit back with a couple, but Pompey held on. The attendance was 23,000.

That match also underlined the fact that far from being a golden age of good manners, young rowdies were quite capable of getting up to mischief. The *News* reported that youngsters had thrown stones at players on the pitch and lectured its readers: 'It is a practice which should be stopped at once and adults around the ground can do much to stop it by checking any youngsters they see acting in this stupid way'. No arguments there then. Pompey were also upset by the news that one of their pre-War stars, Jimmy McAlinden, had apparently signed for Shamrock Rovers after being 'tapped up', it seemed, by the Dublin side.

A week later the return was played. With Dickinson at sea, Pompey's defence were metaphorically all at sea too. Their side, packed with six local players, went down 1-3, Bates, Bradley and Don Roper getting the Saints' goals. Pompey's reply was scored by 22-year-old Sheffield-born Jack Froggatt. Tinn had signed Froggatt on amateur forms, as the player had been called up by the Royal Air Force and was unable to attend a trial. But once stationed back on the south coast Froggatt became a regular.

Southampton fared better that season than Pompey, finishing sixteenth and reaching the fourth round of the FA Cup, although Saints' 3-5 aggregate defeat by Queen's Park Rangers, who were playing in the league below, was a huge disappointment. Pompey's grip on the Cup was also loosened at last, as they lost 0-1 over the two legs in the third round to Birmingham, who were *en route* to becoming the champions of League South. Pompey finished fourth from bottom. Part of their problem was that many players had service commitments. Only goalkeeper Harry Walker, with 40 appearances, could be counted as a fixture in the team. By contrast, Saints had Roper as an ever present, while Bates and Albie Roles played 40 times apiece. Three other Saints made 30 or more appearances.

It was fortunate for Pompey, if not Saints, that the composition of the leagues in August 1946 bore no relation to their performance in that first post-War season. If it had, both clubs would have ended up in the Second Division. However, given the difficulties of fielding teams, to use the 1945-46 season as some sort of benchmark would have been an injustice. Instead, the divisional breakdown of 1939-40 was restored, with Pompey back in the First Division and Saints in the Second. Fixtures from 1939-40, interrupted after just three matches, were played seven years later.

So, in August 1946 almost 31,000 were at Fratton to see Blackburn beaten 3-1. McAlinden was back in favour, Pompey having tempted him back, but the affair was clouded by the whiff of illegal payments, never proved nor disproved. The result was one goal better than the aborted August 1939 effort against Rovers, when Pompey had won 2-1. For their part, Saints visited Newport County, in effect the reigning Division Three (South) champions from 1938-39. A freak rainstorm forced a postponement, however. The intervening war years had affected the South Wales club perhaps more than any other. Their 'championship' side dismantled, they would end up relegated in their first season in Division Two, cast adrift at the bottom and with a 0-13 reverse at Newcastle on their record. Saints finally got their campaign up and running a week later against Swansea at The Dell, winning 4-0. Although both Hants clubs would end the season in mid-table, the seeds for future glory, or at least, in Saints' case a darn good stab at it, had been sown.

During the War, Saints had been assembling an exciting blend of youth and experience. This was initially under Tom Parker, then, on his resignation in 1944, secretary-manager J R Sarjantson, finally by the combination of Art Dominy and Bill Dodgin. One such experienced character to join the club was left-back Bill Rochford. Surplus to requirements at Fratton Park, the only Pompey captain to lift a trophy at Wembley still commanded a £550 transfer fee, even at the age of 33. His no-nonsense approach and fatherly influence was considered useful for developing the talents of future England right-back Alf Ramsey. Ramsey had spent time at Pompey as an amateur during the War while based in Hampshire with the Army. Bill Ellerington, son of a former Saint, vied with Ramsey for the position and also benefited from Rochford's guidance. He would be another to play for England, as well as securing the right-back spot at The Dell, once Ramsey moved to Spurs in 1949. The foundations were being laid of a side which would come within an ace of bringing First Division football to The Dell.

Meanwhile, Portsmouth's greatest-ever team was also taking shape. Tinn's re-building was radical, although he would have controversially left the club by 1948, allowing Bob Jackson to take the helm. By the end of the 1946-47 season, only inside-forward Bert Barlow and winger Cliff Parker of the 1939 FA Cup-winners were still regulars. Pompey's scouting network had scoured near and far to construct a side which would be the best in the land for two seasons running.

A myth frequently peddled about Pompey's championship side, not only by Saints fans, is that the club benefited from its military connections in wartime by having the pick of service players. Leaving aside the fact that, despite this available talent, Pompey's war record was average, the core of the championship team had been scouted playing elsewhere, not in service teams. Goalkeeper Ernie Butler signed in 1938, having been spotted playing in the West Country pre-War. Right-back Phil Rookes had signed from Bradford City in 1939. Left-back Harry Ferrier was bought from Barnsley in 1946 for £1,000, while centre-forward Duggie Reid was a pricey £7,000 from Stockport in the same year. Harris, Froggatt, Flewin were all local bred, if not born, while Dickinson had come from local football. Even tough Scottish half-back Jimmy Scoular, who impressed while playing for the RAF in a representative match at Privett Park Gosport, was initially signed by Gosport Borough, before coming under the scrutiny of Pompey's talent scouts. Of the core championship-winning side, only one player – Shoreditch-born inside-forward Len Phillips, a Royal Marine and veteran of the D-Day landings, and recommended by a marine corporal – joined directly from the armed forces.

In 1948-49 Pompey were imperious throughout. Backed by a superb home record – eighteen wins and three draws in 21 matches – they cruised to the First Division title. They were the best in the land and by some distance. What is also often forgotten is that Pompey could, and in the eyes of diehard supporters should, have become the first team in the 'modern' era to achieve the League and FA Cup double. In March 1949 all that stood between Pompey and a fourth Wembley Cup final was lowly Second Division Leicester, but inspired by centre-forward Don Revie the Foxes caused a sensation, winning 3-1 at Highbury. In the final Pompey would have met Wolves, a side they had thrashed 5-0 at Fratton in April.

While Portsmouth were homing in on the ultimate domestic prize, Southampton looked set to join them in the First Division. The previous season Saints had finished third, four points adrift of second-placed Newcastle, and had reached the last eight of the FA Cup before going down 0-1 at home to Spurs in front of 28,000. The signing of Charlie Wayman in October, supplementing Ted Bates and Eric Day, had made Saints a potent attacking force. Nine points from the final ten available had supporters eagerly anticipating the new campaign, and with good cause. In a manner that Pompey fans would appreciate more than 40 years later, when Guy Whittingham tore up the goalscoring record books, Wayman did likewise. His 32 goals included five in a 6-0 home win over Leicester in October. His 32nd goal came in a crucial 1-0 win at White Hart Lane on 2nd April against promotion rivals Spurs, watched by 69,000. Although a virtual passenger with a torn thigh muscle, Wayman defied his immobility to fire home the winning goal with eight minutes to go. With seven games remaining, Saints found themselves eight points clear at the top. The Hampshire derby to end all derbies looked set to finally arrive.

With Wayman out of action, however, and no adequate replacement available, the goals dried up. Saints managed just two goals in those seven games, picked up just four points, and were agonisingly overtaken by West Brom and champions Fulham. In the penultimate game, a Dell full house of 30,500 saw the Throstles bag a vital draw, when a win would have all but ensured promotion. On the final day, a patched-up Wayman was pitched into the game at Chesterfield, but Saints lost 0-1 and that was that.

Southampton boss Dodgin left the club that summer to join Fulham, and it was widely expected that the players' choice, Bill Rochford, would get the nod. Instead the job was given to Sid Cann, who was faced with lifting a demoralised set of players. A dreadful start to the 1949-50 season – three straight defeats – provoked worries about relegation, never mind promotion. However, the restored Wayman was soon back in the groove and another 24 goals, added to sixteen from Bates, saw Saints up among the front-runners again. On the last day, a 3-0 win over West Ham at The Dell would have seen Saints promoted, but the lowly Hammers stunned the 25,000 crowd by taking a two-goal lead. What had started as a 3-0 target was now 7-2 – due to the vagaries of goal-average. Although Saints commendably recovered to win 3-2, it left them fourth, level on points with the two Sheffield clubs, but with a marginally inferior average of 1.333 to United's 1.387 and promoted Wednesday's 1.398.

On the same day, seventeen miles to the east, the climax to an even more incredible tale was being played out at Fratton Park. When table-topping Manchester United knocked Portsmouth out of the FA Cup, 3-1, in a fifth round February replay at Fratton, it seemed Pompey's season was over. Although still in the top six, retaining the title looked a long shot. Seven teams remained in the hunt and Pompey were four points off the pace. However, a storming run of six wins and a draw in eight games – the last at Manchester United won 2-0, left Pompey in pole position again.

Fratton Park was bulging at the seams for the visit of losing Cup finalists Liverpool on 30th April. The official attendance was counted as a shade over 47,500, well short of an estimated 60,000 capacity, although this was never likely to be threatened as the gates at Fratton were customarily closed once around 47-50,000 people were inside. The figure was smaller, too, than the record 51,385 which had turned up in March 1949 for an FA Cup quarter-final with Derby, or even the 50,248 which had witnessed the 1-1 draw with Wolves back in October. Without computerised turnstiles, in those days the gates were shut whenever it was believed 'capacity' had been reached. Thousands were often left stranded outside. That afternoon, those locked out had to make do with a running commentary relayed from the ground, which told of Pompey's vital 2-1 win, leaving them within touching distance of the title.

A 0-2 midweek defeat by Cup winners Arsenal at Highbury left the champagne on ice, but with a colossal goal-average advantage over second-placed Wolves, two points from the final match, at home to Aston Villa, would suffice. *Portsmouth: Champions of England* sums up how events unfolded: 'Shortly after 4.20pm Portsmouth and England left-half Jimmy Dickinson threaded a pass through the middle of the field ... allowing makeshift centre-forward Bill Thompson to run on and crash an unstoppable shot past the Villa keeper Rutherford. The goal put Pompey 4-0 up and, although there were still eighteen minutes to play, it ensured the south-coast club would become the first team since Arsenal to retain the League Championship trophy.' The trophy was actually positioned in front of the South Stand, even before the final whistle (Farmery 2000).

It turned out that there were actually around 5,000 fewer spectators inside Fratton than for the previous match a fortnight earlier. This fact attracted the attention of the official Saints magazine in a June 2004 article on the clubs' rivalry, in which it was claimed that Pompey are the only champions to post a smaller gate for their last home match than for the one before. In fact, this is untrue, but it highlights a desire among some of the Saints persuasion to downplay the impressiveness of Portsmouth's attendances in the late 1940s. In this instance, the most likely explanation for the drop – given that Southampton were playing their own do-or-die match at The Dell simultaneously, was that those living closer to Southampton, who normally followed both clubs, opted to watch Saints that afternoon. Similarly, Saints' gate was also probably affected by the fact that those to the west of Fareham might have chosen Fratton as their ground of choice. For Southampton's crunch clash with promotion rivals Sheffield Wednesday in April 1950, when Pompey were playing away, 28,000 had packed The Dell. Certainly until the 1970s, there remained a significant core of fans along the Solent who were happy to watch and support both sides on alternate weekends.

It has been argued, on the basis of anecdotal evidence, that the principal reason Pompey averaged around 37,000 in their two championship seasons was that servicemen were let into the ground for free and therefore were counted. Neither contemporary pre-match previews in the local press nor the club's official programme made reference to any such concession, and it is difficult to see how such a gesture would have benefited the club. Entertainment tax was levied on declared match receipts – a Football League minimum admission charge of 1s 3d (6p) also applied – and the visiting club was entitled to a share of the gate money. If these alleged freeloading servicemen 'counted' in Pompey attendances, in effect the club would have had to stump up for them, despite having received no revenue. Like the 'Scum' docks' strike story, this sounds like yet another apocryphal tale, weaving its erroneous way into the fabric of the derby debate. As the previous chapter detailed, servicemen were allowed into Fratton Park for 6d as opposed to the normal shilling during the early War years, but there is no evidence to suggest even this policy was continued once the conflict was over. Some servicemen probably did receive 'complimentary' tickets from time to time. However, the ritual doling out of 'comps' on match days has been usual practice at all clubs for time immemorial.

However, that said, Pompey fans' current claims for the club being a 'sleeping giant' on the evidence of attendances in the late 1940s and early 50s are more tenuous. Pompey's gates in their hey-day, despite their unprecedented success, were distinctly 'mid-table'. An average of 37,000 compared unfavourably to the 'big' clubs of the day. Arsenal's average was more than 50,000, while gates at Manchester United, Everton, Newcastle and Aston Villa all topped Pompey's, which had more in common with the likes of West Brom, Middlesbrough and Birmingham – that is to say solid, rather than spectacular, provincial clubs. Viewed with hindsight, even the former 'greatness' of the Portsmouth club, a genuine claim in the dark days of the 1960s and 1970s perhaps, is now less potent. More accurately, Portsmouth – like Derby and Nottingham Forest in the 1970s or Blackburn in the 1990s – were a respectable club suddenly blessed by unique circumstances which allowed them to touch greatness. Pompey's was a significant contribution to the fabric of football for sure, but more than 50 years on, it hardly constitutes a claim to be a fallen giant.

Southampton's decline following their double promotion near-miss was rapid. After a couple of mid-table finishes, by 1953 the club found itself relegated back to the Third Division (South) from which it had escaped 30 years previously. Stars like Wayman had to be sold and were not adequately replaced, although the club was still forward thinking in many respects. Floodlights had been installed at The Dell for training purposes, at a cost of £600. Once the FA had sanctioned their use for friendly matches, Pompey were one of the first visitors to play under them, in October 1951. Three weeks before that, Saints had staged what is believed to be the first competitive match under lights in Britain, when Spurs were entertained in a reserve-team fixture in front of more than 13,000 (Chalk and Holley 1988).

The Fratton Park club were considering erecting their own floodlights and the outcome of the game at The Dell convinced everyone of their viability. More than 22,600 attended and 'Ranger's' report was enthusiastic: 'There is something different about this floodlit football. The play looked faster and the passing seemed more accurate, but whether this is due to the lighting I am not able to say ... the white ball is much easier to follow in the air or on the ground and it is never lost to sight as the normal ball is when it passes before part of a crowd'. From today's vantage point, it is hard to comprehend the novelty value of football under lights. For the record, that match ended 2-2, with John Beale's 30-yarder and Duggie Reid cancelling out John Edwards' opener. Frank Dudley headed a late equaliser for Saints from Henry Horton's cross.

In fact it took Portsmouth almost eighteen months to stage their own floodlit match and, fittingly, it was doomed Saints who did the honours on 2nd March 1953. With just six wins all season to their name, this was one of the poorest Saints sides in memory, but they gave their all against a Pompey side who had finished fourth in 1951-52. Ferrier gave Pompey the lead from the spot before half-time, after Ellerington had fouled winger Gordon Dale. Roy Williams, a 5ft 4in pocket dynamo scrambled Saints' equaliser three minutes into the second half., whereupon the game took on 'the tempo of a cup tie'. Chances came and went, but the score remained the same. The only downside for the 22,000 crowd was the mist which obscured much of the action.

Southampton's bid to bounce back to Division Two in 1953-54 faltered: they won only two of their last fourteen matches to finish sixth. Portsmouth's great side was gradually disintegrating. Scoular would soon be off to Newcastle, while the likes of Flewin, Butler and Reid were getting no younger. Pompey were on the slide, finishing fifteenth in 1953 and fourteenth a year later. With hindsight, the 1954-55 season would prove a pivotal one. With Phillips having now adapted to become an accomplished right-half, Dickinson still England's left-half, and Harris's goals still flowing – ably assisted by two youth products, Portsmouth-born Johnny Gordon and Scot Jackie Henderson in attack – the club were back in the running for a third championship in six years. Eventually they had to be content with third, their hopes fading after they failed to beat eventual champions Chelsea at Fratton at Easter.

On Monday, 7th March 1955, Pompey returned to The Dell for another floodlit friendly. It was a snowy evening which saw Saints keeper Fred Kiernan clad in tracksuit bottoms – a rarity in those days – and the Saints players warming up beforehand with tracksuits tops. By contrast Pompey followed conventional wisdom at that time by delaying their appearance until a couple of minutes before kick-off. As a result, for an hour or so Pompey were given the runaround, but Saints could only score once, Eric Day converting a penalty in the 53rd minute. Finally, Pompey roused themselves with three goals in six minutes – Ron Newman, Ron Rafferty and Derek Rees scoring. By the conclusion of the season, Saints lay third, but with only runaway champions Bristol City going up, promotion was never really a realistic hope. Pompey remained two divisions above their rivals and it was approaching 30 years since they had been in the same division. Of course, nothing is permanent, but the Fratton Park club's hegemony seemed as dominant as ever.

Chapter 7

~ The Pendulum Swings ~

(1955-66)

Portsmouth's undisputed mastery of the south coast – Bournemouth and Brighton accompanied Southampton in the Third Division (South) – was not going to be undone in 1955-56, which would see Saints occupy the lowest League position in their history. Following an opening day win over Swindon, five defeats and a draw had dumped Saints close to the foot of the Football League, and gates had dipped below 8,000. Manager George Roughton resigned in early September, but his replacement would turn out to be a masterstroke. Ted Bates had been successfully coaching the reserve team since retiring in 1953 and his work had not gone unnoticed.

However, Bates had to work against a perilous financial situation. Bull (1998) relates a crunch board meeting in March 1955, attended by the club's bankers, at a time when making half the squad become part-time professionals was seriously considered. The worst was avoided, as was the fear of having to re-apply for League status. Bates galvanised the squad, and with goals from Eric Day (28), Derek Reeves (18) and Tommy Mulgrew (16), Saints scored heavily enough (they were the fourth highest scorers in the division, with 91) to reach safety. However, a final placing of fourteenth in the Third Division (South) broadly equates with seventh in the Fourth Division, had it existed then, which was pretty much the same as Pompey's League nadir in the 1970s. The aforementioned Brighton and Bournemouth both finished above Saints, to rub in their fall from grace.

For their part, Portsmouth's championship-winning side was now all-but gone, but manager Eddie Lever – who had taken over from Jackson in 1952 – continued the club's knack of unearthing fresh talent. Phil Gunter, cricketing-footballer Mike Barnard, Johnny Phillips and England amateur international Pat Neil were all local lads in first-team contention. But, as at Southampton, gates were on the wane. The 1955-56 season's best at Fratton was a respectable 38,000 against Sunderland in October, but by the spring, as the season fizzled out, sub-20,000 gates were frequent. One such was the visit of Newcastle in late February, when a mere 15,800 witnessed a little bit of football history as the two clubs played the first Football League match under floodlights. For the record, the Magpies won 2-0. At the end of that season another link in the title-winning chain was broken as Duggie Reid retired, but few supporters could have predicted the horror of the 1956-57 season to come.

At Christmas 1956 the unthinkable (in Portsmouth terms) or blissful (in Southampton's) looked a distinct possibility – the rivals seemed to be converging on Division Two. Saints topped the table, as Bates' summer addition Jimmy Shields from Sunderland racked up the goals. A 2-1 win at Crystal Palace on 29th December kept them at the summit, while Portsmouth lost 1-3 at Fratton Park to Manchester United, a result which left them languishing in 21st place.

A run of five straight defeats, shortly after they had re-signed forward Don Roper from Arsenal, took the wind out of Saints' sails, but the introduction of seventeen-year-old Winchester-born winger Terry Paine, who had signed pro forms earlier in the season, helped reinvigorate their season. The dramatic shift in the clubs' fortunes was underlined in a February friendly at The Dell, hastily arranged to cover their inactivity on FA Cup fifth round day. Saints outplayed their so-called 'betters', opening a 3-0 lead shortly after half-time, thanks to goals from Reeves either side of one from Day. Syd McClellan then netted for Pompey. As it happened, a more significant feature of the afternoon was Bournemouth's sensational 3-1 Cup win over First Division Spurs at Dean Court. The shoestring exploits of Bournemouth manager Freddie Cox were being sized up by the Pompey board. However, we are getting slightly ahead of ourselves.

For Southampton, promotion was still theirs for the taking as they prepared for the three-game Easter period – two of them against title rivals Torquay. The holiday weekend would also be crucial for Pompey, four points adrift of safety. But with two games against fellow strugglers Cardiff City, salvation was just about in their own hands. Three victories did the trick for Pompey and the drop was avoided. Alas for Saints, their own schedule yielded just one win rather than the two required and the promotion dream died.

Nevertheless, for Portsmouth the clock was ticking loudly. Defensive inadequacies – 92 goals conceded in 1956-57 and 88 the following season – were barely concealed by a reasonably proficient attack, although a run of five defeats and a draw in April 1958 left Pompey clinging precariously to First Division status on goal-average ahead of Sunderland. Nor could silverware, in the shape of the newly instituted Southern Floodlit Challenge Cup – in effect a forerunner of the Football League Cup – paper over Pompey's cracks. Manager Lever was relieved of his duties and Cox installed in his place. It was to prove a catastrophic decision.

Pompey's scouting network unearthed another Pompey lad, Ray Crawford, and a young self-confident Irishman called Derek Dougan. These two forwards hinted that there might be enough goals in the tank to ward off relegation. Alas, Cox didn't see it that way and sold them off for a song, replacing them with lower division journeymen. Crawford would subsequently earn England honours and a League championship medal at Ipswich. Dougan would enjoy a highly successful career in the top flight and regularly represent Northern Ireland. At the end of a traumatic 1958-

59 season Pompey found themselves doomed by the end of March and accumulated just 21 points. The last of their six League wins was back on 22nd November, and gates had slumped to under 13,000 for the penultimate home match against Everton.

Southampton had established themselves as one of the most prolific teams in the country in the late 1950s. In 1957-58 they amassed an incredible 112 goals – 78 of them at The Dell – but could finish no higher than sixth on account of the 72 they let in. That position was enough to secure them a place in the new national Third Division instigated for the 1958-59 season. Its fixture list offered exotic trips to Rochdale, Accrington, Halifax and Tranmere, among others, for the first time, but again a suspect defence ruined the good work done by the forwards. Eighty-eight goals should have got them into the top six, but the 80 they conceded left them below halfway.

Ted Bates responded by putting fourteen players on the transfer list and reshuffling his squad. Of the nine arrivals, Cliff Huxford, a wing-half from Chelsea, was in the eyes of Chalk and Holley (1988), the most significant: 'He soon became Saints' skipper and a tower of strength on the field.' Saints were also reaping the fruits of their youth policy, dubbed 'Ted's Teenies' by Bull (1998). This involved an innovative partnership with a local engineering company, CPC. In effect, the company 'sponsored' – long before the term was coined – the Saints youth team, employing its own football coach-cum-engineer Ernie Jones, who had left The Dell in 1951. Given Saints' parlous finances, this was another brilliant stroke by Bates and eighteen months after its inception they became the first side to beat the famous 'Busby Babes' in the FA Youth Cup. Their 3-2 success at Old Trafford in April 1957 wasn't enough to overturn a 2-5 defeat in the first leg, but it was the first time United had lost a game in the competition since its inauguration in 1953.

One advantage for Saints of being in the new national Third Division was that two promotion places were up for grabs, rather than one. Not that they needed a second place in 1959-60. Veterans of that youth side, wingers Paine and John Sydenham, were a cut above Third Division football and Saints blitzed their way to the title, scoring 106 goals. Derek Reeves – who ironically had been on Pompey's books early in his career, but had been allowed to leave — bagged a Saints record 39 of them. Although a hiccough in March and early April raised the spectre of 1949's collapse, promotion was clinched four games from the end of the season with a 1-0 home win over Reading, watched by 25,000. Saints had also caused a sensation in the FA Cup, winning 5-1 at First Division Manchester City, Reeves helping himself to four goals. The fifth came from another of Bates' summer signings, George O'Brien from Leeds United. The inside-forward ably assisted Reeves, banging in 23 League goals himself, but O'Brien could so easily have ended up a Pompey player. While he was still at Dunfermline he had been deemed too pricey by the then Saints boss George Roughton. Lever, too, turned his nose up at the chance to sign him, and it was left to Bates several years later to show them how it was done (Bull 1998).

How Portsmouth could have done with O'Brien's talents. While Saints were soaring to the title, at Fratton Park things were going from bad to worse. Nine consecutive defeats in September and October left them bottom of the Second Division. It took an upturn in form to avoid a second successive relegation, but Pompey were indebted to the ineptitude of Hull and Bristol City as much as to their own improvement. For the first time in almost 30 years, Fratton hosted a sub-10,000 gate for a League game, although the stayaways missed a treat as Middlesbrough suffered a 6-3 pre-Christmas pasting. Southampton's average home gate of more than 18,000 was almost 2,000 higher than Pompey's, the first time they had bettered their rivals since the advent of the Football League's Third Division in 1920.

When the 1960-61 fixture list was published, the dates of the first competitive derbies since 1927 were the first to be sought. Fans would not have long to wait, Pompey making the trip to The Dell on 27th August. It was difficult to decide who to install as favourites, both teams having started the new campaign with a win and a defeat. As a club, Portsmouth were undeniably the bigger. Two League titles, an FA Cup win and twice losing finalists, coupled with more than 30 consecutive years of top-flight football, had put Pompey on the football map. Saints' illustrious best was now a matter of 60 years past. In gaining promotion back to the Second Division, they had, in the eyes of Pompey fans, merely rediscovered their 'natural' level. Any thoughts that Saints were back on a par with their neighbours would have been treated with disdain.

Football is no respecter of reputation, however, and on the day Saints slaughtered Pompey. After 23 minutes Huxford fired a 25-yarder past Dick Beattie and by the interval the game was over. Three more goals in seven minutes had left Pompey reeling. First, O'Brien converted a penalty in the 36th minute, after the same player had tumbled under Sammy Chapman's challenge. Then Paine scored from an acute angle after Reeves had hit a post. Two minutes from the interval, Mulgrew's header made it 4-0. Ron Newman restored some lost pride, but the final goal of the game saw veteran Jimmy Dickinson, fast approaching 600 League appearances for the club, deflect Mulgrew's shot into his own net. Almost 29,000 had crammed into The Dell and the gates had been closed just before kick-off, even though the ground was 1,000 short of its declared capacity. Any Pompey fans who failed to gain access would have been the lucky ones. According to the chairman of the Portsmouth Supporters Club, Billy 'Farmer's Boy'

Haines – the Pompey legend and former Saint who had scored twice in the last League meeting in January 1927 – the best side won: 'Southampton have a fast young team, full of enthusiasm, and should do well in the second division.'

And do well Southampton certainly did. By the time the return came round on New Year's Eve, they were handily placed fourth, four points behind leaders Ipswich with a game in hand. Poor old Portsmouth were still struggling to adapt to Second Division football, with a dreadful 47 goals conceded in fourteen away matches to date. Fortunately, their home form was holding up. More than 31,000 turned up for the return, the biggest gate since 1958 and the fourth highest of the day in all divisions. It was estimated that 10,000 Saints fans made the short trip, but they would have left in buoyant mood. After twelve minutes Saints' keeper Ron Reynolds left the pitch with a burst blood vessel in his throat, but returned before half-time. During his absence, and with danger-man Terry Paine in goal, Pompey failed to muster a shot on target. They would be left to rue their profligacy. With fifteen minutes to go, Pompey scored against the run of play after Dick Connor had fouled Pompey's Jimmy White. Harry Harris dummied the free-kick, leaving it for Chapman to fire past a startled Reynolds. 'An old trick, but it worked,' noted 'Linesman' wryly. In the 81st minute Saints had a golden chance to level when Harris fouled Paine in the box, but Beattie dived to his left to grab John Page's spot-kick on the line and, after clearing the ball, proceeded to do a dance for joy. In the last minute, however, a final surge saw Paine and Reeves have shots blocked before Mulgrew forced the ball home.

Despite that late point earned, Saints' promotion hopes eventually ran out of steam, a run of six defeats and two draws in March and April ending their hopes. But for Pompey, their nightmare continued. Five straight League defeats – sandwiched by an FA Cup third round exit at home to League new-boys Peterborough and a loss at Rotherham in the quarter-finals of the new League Cup – saw them back in the relegation frame. Results perked up in April, but it was too late. A 0-3 defeat at Middlesbrough in their penultimate match sealed Pompey's fate. It would be Third Division football at Fratton Park, and for the first time since 1924 Saints would be lording it in a superior division.

Shortly before the drop was confirmed, Freddie Cox was relieved of his manager's position, to be replaced by straight-talking Yorkshireman George Smith. Smith's 'sergeant-major' approach was just what traumatised Portsmouth needed. Optimism slowly returned, helped by a pre-season victory over Saints at The Dell in August 1961. 'Spirit' and 'quality' were two terms not applied to a Pompey team in some time, however those words appeared in the *News*' sub-headline describing the performance that day. One of Smith's first decisions had been to restore Jimmy Dickinson as captain, and it proved well-judged. Johnny Gordon, back at the club after a spell at Birmingham, scored the opener just before half-time, before centre-forward Ron Saunders – one of the few successful Cox signings, in 1958 – sealed the victory.

Southampton looked short in defence, with centre-half Page playing apparently in the knowledge that Bates was keen to replace him. On the eve of the season Tony Knapp arrived in a club record £27,500 deal from First Division Leicester. Knapp shored up the back line and, with O'Brien shouldering the goalscoring responsibility – 28 in 38 appearances – Saints again looked a good bet for promotion, until another spring slump saw them end up sixth.

The returning 'feel-good' factor at Fratton was well-founded. Pompey looked a class above the rest when sauntering to the Third Division title, losing just eight games. As with Saints two years before, promotion had lent Pompey impetus, and for part of the following, 1962-63 season Saints were back in their neighbours' shadow. Food for thought on the old debate about relative attendances was provided by the fact that Pompey's average of 16,900 was about 1,100 short of Saints' equivalent two years earlier.

After eight games Saints were bottom, and although a couple of wins – secured by goals from new signing George Kirby from Plymouth – lifted them out of the bottom two, it was Pompey who had made much the better start, four wins and four draws in ten games putting them in upper mid-table. Saints returned to Fratton on 15th October, 1962 and Pompey's relative buoyancy enticed the biggest gate yet for a local derby – 32,407. 'Linesman' was the first to concede that the early table had perhaps been a shade economical with the truth: 'After the first two or three weeks of the season, Pompey were at the top of the table and Saints were at the bottom and envious eyes were being cast in Fratton Park's direction. Now there is absolutely nothing between them if Saturday's match is a true indication,' he suggested, following a 1-1 draw. Tony Barton, a winger signed twelve months previously from Nottingham Forest, had opened the scoring with a 'brilliant volley' after 33 minutes. O'Brien's neat flicked header from Paine's corner levelled things shortly after the break.

The return fixture was scheduled for March, but by then the 'big freeze' of 1963 had taken its icy grip, wrecking the fixture list. Between Boxing Day and 23rd February neither Saints nor Pompey played a League game. Clearly the lay-off did Saints less harm as they produced their best form of the season to thrash the Fratton Park side 4-2. Tommy Traynor's own-goal, after being pressured by Barton, had given Pompey the perfect start after fifteen minutes, but a flurry of goals before the break – with Saints down to ten men – changed the course of the game. David Burnside headed home, with full-back Stuart Williams off the field having treatment to a gashed leg. Then Paine's snap-shot caught out goalkeeper John

Armstrong. With a minute of the first half remaining, Williams returned to the fray. His first task was to score an easy goal after Paine's shot rebounded from the crossbar. In the second half Saints were in complete control, but only added a Burnside goal when Armstrong failed to hold his shot. Saunders pulled one back and winger Micky Lill, on his debut, hit the bar, but Saints were well worth the win.

Southampton were also enjoying a useful FA Cup run. Owing to the weather, the ties were all over the place, but the draw was kind. The home third round tie with Fourth Division York was postponed nine times before Saints eventually won 5-0 on 13th February. A fortnight later Third Division Watford went the same way, 3-1 at The Dell. Then, on 16th March, Kirby headed the first-half goal which secured a 1-0 win over First Division Sheffield United. Two titanic battles with Nottingham Forest, also from Division One, ended all-square. In the replay at The Dell, Saints had trailed 0-3 with twenty minutes to go, but Burnside's late goal crowned a marvellous comeback. The second replay was at White Hart Lane, where an estimated 25,000 Saints fans saw their side outclass their supposed superiors 5-0. The Cup was finally cheering again for Southampton as they made their first semi-final appearance since 1927. Dreams of Wembley were shattered at Villa Park, though, as Denis Law gave Manchester United the victory. Belated revenge, thirteen years later, would be particularly sweet.

In the League, Southampton's form picked up as Pompey's faltered, and they finished safely in mid-table. After Pompey's own second replay Cup exit against Third Division Coventry – the fourth round tie was not settled until three days after Saints fifth round win – Pompey lost six straight League games and had to content themselves with sixteenth place.

Since relegation from the First Division in 1959, Portsmouth had managed just two draws in four encounters with their neighbours, and few expected that trend to be reversed on 28th September 1963. Two draws and two defeats in their opening four home games contrasted with Saints running into form, beating Newcastle and Swansea in their two previous games. In the event, the fact that Saints goalkeeper Reynolds was in the wars again, having to leave the field with a dislocated shoulder after fifteen minutes, suggests Pompey's 2-0 win had a touch of fortune about it. Huxford stood in between the sticks, but Pompey were already two goals to the good. Saunders' 'superb' header from a Micky Lill cross had given Pompey the advantage after just 25 seconds, Saunders' momentum carrying him into the massed photographers behind the goal. After eleven minutes, Brian Lewis – a recent recruit from Luton – strolled through to score at the second attempt, despite Williams' efforts to clear off the line. In a bruising encounter, Pompey too had their problems, Phil Gunter being reduced to a passenger after a clash with Kirby.

The niggling nature of the contest was summed up by Pompey full-back Roy Lunniss's battle with Terry Paine, which would become a running feature of these 1960s derbies. The Saints winger exacted retribution for an earlier foul by launching a 'foot up' challenge on the former Crystal Palace defender. Lunniss was forced off for treatment and irate teammate Lewis chased Paine in a fury. Apocryphal stories tells of Lewis brandishing the corner flag at the winger. Referee Norman Burtenshaw confirmed afterwards that he booked the pair. Saints manager Ted Bates had no doubt who was the man of the match: 'If we could have scored a goal it would have put us back in the game with a chance. As it was I thought Dickinson won the match for Pompey'.

By the time of the return on 8th February 1964, Portsmouth were slithering downwards, without a win since early November and tossing away a 3-1 half-time lead at home to Scunthorpe in their last match to lose 3-4. Saints, by contrast, were once again scoring goals for fun. In their last home game, on 29th January, against that same Scunthorpe side, they had won 7-2. Two of the goals had been scored by eighteen-year-old striker Martin Chivers, a former Tauntons Grammar Schoolboy, who apparently 'didn't fancy going to Fratton Park' when Pompey's scouts came knocking at his door in the autumn of 1962 (Bull 1998).

Pompey's loss was Saints' gain. Early on, Chivers saw a shot hit the bar, but football being a funny old game it was Pompey who took control. Winger John McClelland spoiled Tommy Traynor's 499th League match for Saints, robbing him by the corner flag and setting up Saunders to cross for Albert McCann to head past Tony Godfrey. In the 23rd minute it was 2-0. Saunders hooked home after McClelland had set up the chance with a headed pass. Chivers pulled one back with a cross-shot before the interval, but McClelland restored the two-goal cushion when he followed up a Saunders shot eight minutes into the second half. Saints didn't score again until it was too late, Paine flashing home Burnside's pass with two minutes to go. Once again Dickinson was singled out for praise, with even Saints fans nominating him man of the match. 'What a wonderful player he is. He hardly gave Kirby a chance. How he stands up to the pace at his age beats me,' commented Mr W Wilson of Shirley afterwards. With Dickinson fast approaching his 39th birthday, it was not clear how Pompey would replace their veteran talisman.

Lunniss's mastery of Paine had again been the key to Portsmouth's success, the winger being forced inside to try to escape the Pompey full-back. The bad blood between the two probably explained an extraordinary incident at a reserve game at The Dell six weeks later. As the teams were trooping off at half-time a Saints 'fan' leant over the tunnel wall – situated in the corner of the ground – and abused the Pompey man. A tall, muscular, 'rough and ready' character, Lunniss confronted his tormentor and, according to eyewitnesses, threatened to jump the barrier and sort him out. He was hustled away by teammates and the lure of a half-time cuppa diffused what might have developed into a Cantona-style incident.

Following their League win at The Dell, Pompey kept their good form going. By the end of March they looked set to finish above their rivals. However, Saints' five wins in their last seven games, which brought twenty goals in the final four, took them to 100 for the season. Pompey's League double was left counting for naught in the final League standings. Saints finished fifth with 47 points, with Pompey four points adrift in ninth.

With the 1964-65 season approaching, Southampton keeper Reynolds retired through injury. This was unsurprising, as he is almost certainly the only visiting goalkeeper to have been twice carried off at Fratton Park. Reynolds was replaced by John Hollowbread from Spurs. Pompey kept faith with most of the previous season's squad, but there was consternation among supporters in late August when Smith sold star striker Saunders for £15,000 to Third Division Watford. It seemed an odd decision at the time, as Saunders had bagged 33 goals the previous season, and already had three in this, although the gathering financial storm-clouds enveloping Fratton might have played some part in the decision. To replace him, Smith turned to Gosport-born Ray Hiron, signed for a song from Hampshire League Fareham Town. The gangly twenty-year-old would now make his debut against Saints at Fratton Park. The date was 12th September, 1964.

On paper, both teams looked out of sorts, but on the field it was the Blues who were made to struggle. Saints had conceded ten goals in five games, but – gamely though Hiron tried – it was men against boys. 'His lack of professional experience was almost savagely exposed in a match which, by tradition, no quarter is asked and the tackling ruthless,' wrote 'Linesman'. With Paine, by now an England regular, mastering Lunniss, and O'Brien a constant thorn, Saints strolled in the autumn sun. Pompey keeper John Milkins might have saved Ken Wimshurst's shot in the eighteenth minute, but the ball squirmed free and Chivers tapped it in. Dodson hit a post as Pompey rallied, but with half-time approaching Harris's poor back-pass yielded a corner which Paine headed in. Ten minutes into the second half Sydenham fired in Saints' third, after being set up by O'Brien, which prompted a celebratory pitch invasion by banner-waving Saints fans. That was a red rag to a bull, and Pompey 'hotheads' were quickly among them. 'Pitched battles broke out,' forcing police to intervene to clear the pitch while the players stood by and watched. Hooliganism had arrived, and the nature of the rivalry had changed for good.

By the time the two teams met again, at The Dell on 16th January 1965, the respective paths suggested by the Saints' September win had become predictably well-trodden. Pompey were wretchedly bottom, while Saints were handily placed in the chasing pack, hoping to launch a blind-side bid for promotion. Pompey had received a couple of recent boosts, however. First, their youth side had triumphed in the FA Youth Cup against Saints on the Monday; and second, they had new forward Dennis Edwards – bought using the Saunders' proceeds – making his debut. Dickinson was making his 750th League appearance and the two teams formed a guard of honour to applaud him onto the field, while the crowd sang 'For he's a jolly good fellow!' Saints started brightly and should have scored more than the one goal credited to their own new signing, Jimmy Melia, who cost £30,000 from Wolves – twice what Pompey had paid for Edwards. Melia stabbed home a loose ball in the 35th minute after a corner wasn't properly cleared. But for Milkins' defiance, Saints would have been well ahead. But comparable slackness in the Saints defence five minutes later allowed Lewis to score with a shot off the far post, following an Albert McCann corner. In the second half, Pompey seized the initiative, to the delight of their fans in the 23,911 crowd, and deserved the lead given by the blossoming Hiron's fierce shot after 57 minutes. But seven minutes later it was back to 2-2. Sydenham skinned Ron Tindall and crossed for Melia to guide home the equaliser. Both sides had chances to win the game, but had to settle for a point apiece.

Southampton failed to win any of their next five games, leaving their promotion hopes on ice for another season, but although Portsmouth rallied, four straight defeats in March landed them back in deep trouble. With Pompey's debts coming under increasing scrutiny from their creditors, desperate economy measures were needed. Even before the relegation outcome was determined, it was reluctantly decided to do away with the youth and reserve sides at the end of the season, and make do with a first-team squad.

A young full-back from Godalming called Michael Mills, who will feature later in this story, would prove to be the highest-profile casualty of the club's short-sightedness. Pompey's fraught relations with their bankers gave rise to a conspiracy theory that was widely held, certainly among the financial community in Portsmouth. Although the local branch of the club's bank was in the city, the regional office was in Southampton, and it is said that pressure was brought to bear on the local manager to be hard on Portsmouth. The received wisdom was that there was a desire to keep the financial screws turned on the club: if not to actually force it into receivership, then at least ensure it could not effectively challenge Saints. Whether or not these accusations are groundless, Saints continued to mop up the floating support which clearly existed east of Southampton and west of Fareham, helping to establish itself as the leading club on the south coast.

Matt 'Ginger' Reilly, who had the distinction of playing for the Royal Artillery, Saints (on loan), and Pompey. *(Glory Gunners)*

The Southampton team which took part in the first ever FA Cup-tie between the clubs in January 1906. *(Association Football and the Men Who Made It)*

The Echo advertises newsreel footage of Saints' 2-0 win at Fratton Park in March 1922, the week after the game at the King's Theatre, Southampton.

Pompey's young striker Andy Stewart tussles with Saints defender Paul Bennett in the Boxing Day 1974 encounter at Fratton, won 2-1 by Saints. (*The News*)

Pompey's Goals Against the Saints

Worrall scoring the first goal for Portsmouth

The second goal was headed by McCarthy

Three of Pompey's goals in the 6-0 Hampshire Professional Cup win over Saints in October 1932, captured by the *Evening News*' photographer.

Below: Portsmouth-born Bobby Stokes scores Saints' winner in the 1976 FA Cup final against Manchester United. Fifteen months later he joined his home-town club. *(The News)*
Right: Stokes during his time with Pompey.

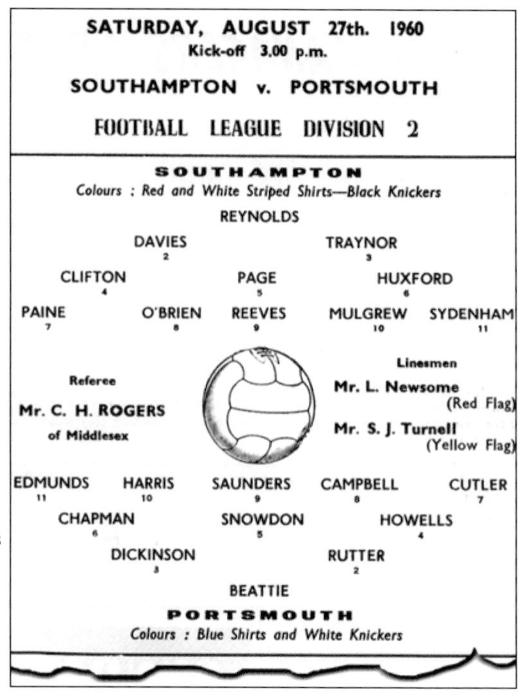
SATURDAY, AUGUST 27th. 1960
Kick-off 3.00 p.m.

SOUTHAMPTON v. PORTSMOUTH

FOOTBALL LEAGUE DIVISION 2

SOUTHAMPTON
Colours : Red and White Striped Shirts—Black Knickers

REYNOLDS

DAVIES 2 TRAYNOR 3

CLIFTON 4 PAGE 5 HUXFORD 6

PAINE 7 O'BRIEN 8 REEVES 9 MULGREW 10 SYDENHAM 11

Referee
Mr. C. H. ROGERS
of Middlesex

Linesmen
Mr. L. Newsome (Red Flag)
Mr. S. J. Turnell (Yellow Flag)

EDMUNDS 11 HARRIS 10 SAUNDERS 9 CAMPBELL 8 CUTLER 7

CHAPMAN 6 SNOWDON 5 HOWELLS 4

DICKINSON 3 RUTTER 2

BEATTIE

PORTSMOUTH
Colours : Blue Shirts and White Knickers

Programmes and teams for the first league meeting of the sides since 1927. Saints won 5-1.

Pompey's Arjan De Zeeuw brings down Saints' James Beattie for the penalty which ensured Saints won 2-0 in the Carling Cup, December 2003. *(The News)*

Take that and don't come back

SAINTS did not just win, they dished out a right good spanking to dispatch Pompey with an arrogance which seemed to say: "Don't come back until you are good enough!"

After all the hype and talk, this turned into something of a one-sided anti-climax — not that the supporters celebrating in red and white cared.

They loved every minute of a day they have waited for eight years to savour. And with the rare cushion of a three-goal lead, they were able to relax and make it party time for the last 10 minutes.

They danced to all their favourites songs: "There's only one team in Hampshire", "Bye bye Pompey" and "Easy, easy".

And they even spared a thought for those suffering the big screening ...

Graham Hiley reports from The Dell

There was only ever going to be one team coming out on top. Saints won because they are the better side and made absolutely sure they proved it on the day.

They won because they were more incisive, rock solid at the back and scored at vital times. And they won because they wanted it more.

Saints were up for this one from the off. The atmosphere around the ground was deafening as they ran out and the players responded.

They knew how much it meant and after letting the fans down at Reading, they emphatically stamped the words "Account paid in full" on their ticket to the fourth round of the FA Cup.

After the Nightmare on Elm Park, this was a dream start to 1996 as they gave fans everything they had demanded ...

► ONE-NIL: Jim Magilton gets the ball rolling as he hits Saints' opener.

SAINTS 3 POMPEY 0

Dave Beasant had only one serious save to make ... a fingertip stop from ...

The Echo sums up Pompey's wretched 0-3 defeat at The Dell in the third round of the FA Cup in January 1996.

Ron Davies, regarded as one of the best headers in football in the late 1960s, served both clubs in typical style. *(The News)*

Left: Saints full-back Mark Dennis is tended after being hit by a coin thrown from the crowd. *(The News)*

Below: How *The News* reported the incident.

WANTED

£200 reward on Pompey coin yobbos

The programme cover and teams for Saints' visit to Fratton in February 1966. Saints won 5-2.

PORTSMOUTH Royal Blue Shirts, White Shorts	v.	SOUTHAMPTON Red and White Striped Shirts, Black Shorts
John Armstrong	1	Campbell Forsyth S
Alex Wilson S	2	Tommy Hare
Ron Tindall	3	Stuart Williams W
Johnny Gordon	4	Ken Wimshurst
Frank Haydock	5	Tony Knapp (Capt).
Harry Harris (Capt.)	6	Cliff Huxford
Brian Lewis	7	Terry Paine E
Cliff Portwood	8	Martin Chivers
Dennis Edwards	9	Norman Dean
Albert McCann	10	Jimmy Melia E
John McClelland	11	John Sydenham
Ray Hiron	12	David Walker

OFFICIALS

eree: Mr. E. D. Wallace (*Swindon*)

Linesmen: Mr. G. Keeble (*Red Flag*)
MR. D. G. Mead (*Yellow Flag*)

Pompey winger Vince Hilaire tussles with Saints Glenn Cockerill during Pompey's 2-0 win at The Dell in January 1988. *(The News)*

Saint Michael Channon of Portsmouth. The former Southampton star spent a season at Fratton Park in the mid-1980s. *(author's collection)*

Nat Whittaker, Secretary of the Southern League, who was a powerful advocate for professional football in Portsmouth. *(Association Football and the Men Who Made It)*

Pompey take the field before their vital Third Division (South) clash with Saints in March 1922. Pompey's 0-2 defeat ended their hopes of promotion, while Saints went on the win the title. *(source unknown)*

MR. TED BATES'S TEAM MUCH THE STRONGER IN ATTACK

Triumphant Southampton Stun Pompey

NO NEED TO FEAR ANY SECOND DIVISION SIDE

(By LINESMAN)

IT will take Pompey a long time to win back the prestige they lost at Southampton on Saturday. For the Saints' players and officials there were triumphant smiles after their 5—1 win. For Pompey, there was just humiliation.

Pompey have had plenty of unkind things said and written about them in the past few seasons, many of them justified on the results obtained. But if they had won, or at least put up a show in this match, they could have done themselves immense good among their wavering followers in Hampshire.

They still have the chance, of course, to get their own back on the confident Saints in the return match at Fratton Park on the last day of the year. Unless there is a big improvement by then, however, Pompey will be left behind in the Second Division by a team so much stronger in attack.

It was 33 years ago that Pompey left Saints behind when they went up into the First Division. Ever since then, the Saints have been waiting for the chance to put things right. Now their own outstanding form and the decline of Pompey gave them the chance.

H[illegible]shire [illegible]

despite the early promise of new outside-right John Fraser.

Whether it proves possible to complete any exchange deals remains to be seen.

The names of Bill Curry and Adrian Thorne, of Brighton, and Wilf Carter, of Plymouth, are being linked with Pompey. What a difference a couple of them would make to the outlook.

It took the Saints 23 minutes to put themselves ahead. And what a great goal it was — a 25-yard shot from Huxford which went like a flash past goalkeeper Dick Beattie and into the corner of the net.

After 26 minutes, O'Brien went sprawling in a clash with Chapman and, although many thought the decision a little harsh on the left-half, a penalty was given. O'Brien took the kick and deceived Beattie to make it 2—0.

Paine made the opening for the third goal three minutes later and eventually scored it himself from a narrow angle, after a shot by [illegible] Derek Reeves [illegible]

SPECTATORS' VIEWPOINT

Wingers Sydenham And Paine Impress Mr. Billy Haines

(By JANUS)

WHILE Mr. Billy Haines, Chairman of the Portsmouth Supporters' Club, was disappointed at Pompey's display in Saturday's long-awaited local Derby, he sportingly paid tribute to the skill and speed of the Southampton side.

Mr. Haines, scorer of both Pompey's goals in the previous league match between the two clubs at The Dell, in 1927, met many old friends in the Boardroom after the Saints 5—1 victory.

"The best side won today," he said. "Southampton have a fast young team, full of enthusiasm, and they shoud do well in the Second Division.

"I liked outside-left John Sydenham. He has more than one trick up his sleeve. And with Terry Paine, Southampton have a fine pair of wingers."

Mr. Haines said it was good to see one team, at any rate, putting on a football display for the big crowd.

A Saints player after he left Fratton Park, Mr. Haines said he finished playing league football at The Dell back in season 1932-33. This was his first visit to the ground in post-war sea[illegible] who has been [illegible]

MR. BILLY HAINES

The Evening News sums up the outcome of this August 1960 clash between the sides.

Action from the 2-2 draw at The Dell in January 1965. *(The News)*

Saints' Matt Le Tissier up against Pompey's Mark Stimson during Saints' 3-0 FA Cup win of January 1996. *(The News)*

Alan Ball, with his trademark flat cap, enjoyed a successful spell as Pompey manager, as well as playing for and managing Saints. *(author's collection)*

James Beattie's late diving header seals Saints' superiority in their 3-0 win over Pompey in their first Premiership clash, December 2003. *(The News)*

Saints Graham Baker (right) goes shoulder to shoulder with Pompey's Barry Horne, who would later play for Saints, during Pompey's 2-0 win at The Dell in January 1988. *(The News)*

Pompey's expensive winger Peter Marinello tussles with Saints defender Paul Bennett in the Boxing Day 1974 encounter at Fratton, won 2-1 by Saints. *(The News)*

This War League game in 1939 featured Jimmy Guthrie, Pompey's skipper, back from injury after a summer car crash. Pompey won 4-1

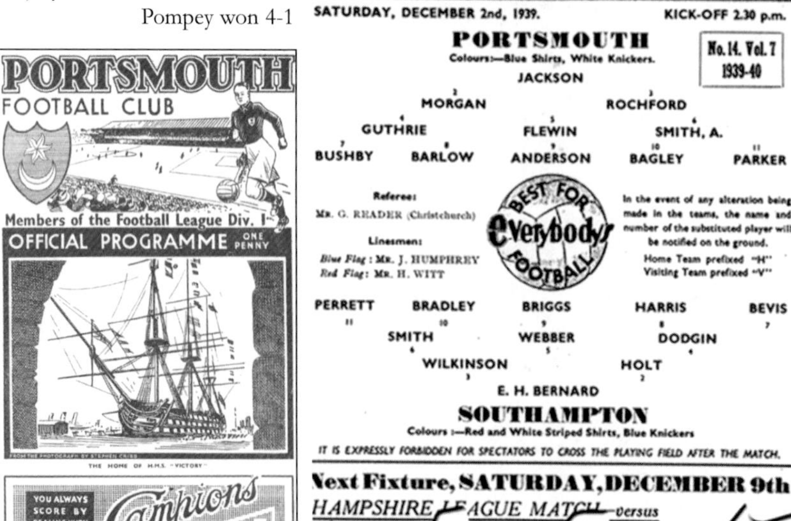

SUNSHINE ALE BREWED BY BRICKWOODS

come ... ROAD HOUSE
At the CITY ENTRANCE—PORTSBRIDGE
Open till the Early Hours of the Morning.
— Fully Licensed —

SATURDAY, DECEMBER 2nd, 1939. KICK-OFF 2.30 p.m.

No. 14. Vol. 7
1939-40

PORTSMOUTH
Colours:—Blue Shirts, White Knickers.

JACKSON

2 MORGAN — 3 ROCHFORD

4 GUTHRIE — 5 FLEWIN — 6 SMITH, A.

7 BUSHBY — 8 BARLOW — 9 ANDERSON — 10 BAGLEY — 11 PARKER

Referee:
MR. G. READER (Christchurch)

Linesmen:
Blue Flag: MR. J. HUMPHREY
Red Flag: MR. H. WITT

BEST FOR FOOTBALL Everybody's

In the event of any alteration being made in the teams, the name and number of the substituted player will be notified on the ground.
Home Team prefixed "H"
Visiting Team prefixed "V"

PERRETT 11 — BRADLEY 10 — BRIGGS 9 — HARRIS 8 — BEVIS 7

SMITH 6 — WEBBER 5 — DODGIN 4

WILKINSON 3 — HOLT 2

E. H. BERNARD

SOUTHAMPTON
Colours:—Red and White Striped Shirts, Blue Knickers

IT IS EXPRESSLY FORBIDDEN FOR SPECTATORS TO CROSS THE PLAYING FIELD AFTER THE MATCH.

Next Fixture, SATURDAY, DECEMBER 9th
HAMPSHIRE LEAGUE MATCH versus

William Pickford, Secretary of the Hants FA and later the Football Association. *(Association Football and the Men Who Made It)*

Pompey's Yakubu celebrates his winning goal against Saints in March 2004, in what was Pompey's first home derby win since 1963. *(The News)*

The Echo sums up Saints poor display when losing 2-4 to Pompey in April 1970 for John Sydenham's testimonial.

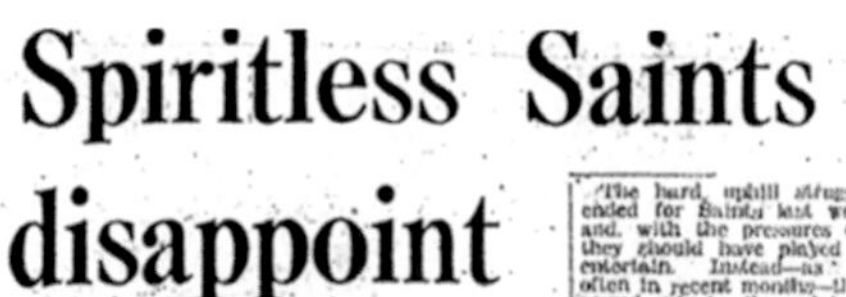

Spiritless Saints disappoint

By BOB LEVER

Southampton 2, Portsmouth 4

JOHN SYDENHAM'S former colleagues must have disappointed him last night for some of them never did justice to his final appearance for Saints at The Dell. Ten thousand fans turned up to pay their tribute to Sydenham's 13 years of full-time service to the club and show they cared. Pompey played in attractive, forceful style—but Saints did not respond as a team, nor did they catch the mood of the night.

Let me not detract from Pompey's showing. They deserved their win. Their effort saved this testimonial game from dying; they fought to preserve their pride. But Saints only partly re-acted. For the first half-hour they matched the Pompey challenge, but then they fell apart.

Briefly, the attack sparkled. Sydenham, himself, fed from midfield by Terry Paine, zipped merrily down the left flank. One of his crosses skidded right across an open goal and from one of his corners, Paine crossed for Mike Channon to bring a good save from John Milkins.

Rising shot

Brian Bromley cracked a rising shot into the nearside top corner in the 22nd minute to put Pompey ahead, but Saints came straight back for Jimmy Gabriel to head in the equaliser from Gerry O'Brien's cross a minute later.

Pompey's response was another goal when Nick Jennings turned in Eoin Hand's hard, low cross in the 27th minute. From Saints there was only despair.

They substituted Duncan MacLeod for a below-par Hugh Fisher at half-time, but Pompey—by now in complete control—took a 3—1 lead in the 53rd minute. Ray Pointer, who replaced David Munks, gave Ray Hiron the chance to beat Martin.

Initiative

Fred Kemp came on to replace David Walker, who had been working hard with Jimmy Gabriel to stem the Pompey tide—yet still Saints failed to recapture he initiative. Hiron made it 4—1 in the 73rd minute with a swerving shot that Martin touched, but could not save.

Sydenham, by his time, was left stranded by tiring colleagues who seemed only anxious to defend. O'Brien and Kemp tried to inject some fire, but with Channon and Frank Saul completely over-shadowed, they had little success. Channon's goal ten minutes from time took some sting from the defeat, but that was all.

The hard, uphill struggle ended for Saints last week and, with the pressures off, they should have played to entertain. Instead—as so often in recent months—they served only to disappoint.

Teams: Saints—Martin; Kirkup, Fry; Fisher (MacLeod), Gabriel, Walker (Kemp); O'Brien, Channon, Saul, Paine, Sydenham.

Portsmouth: Milkins; Hand, Ley; Munks (Pointer), Youlden, Harris; Storrie, McCann, Hiron, Bromley, Jennings.

Referee: Mr. D. R. Nippard (Bournemouth).

Attendance: 10,145.

Men with many years of service to soccer meet on the centre spot at The Dell last night. Portsmouth skipper Harry Harris wishes John Sydenham (Saints captain for the night) all the best watched by Bournemouth referee Douglas Nippard.

Aldershot equal record

Below: *The Echo* relishes Saints' 2-0 Carling Cup win over Pompey in December 2003.

Carling Cup: Saints 2 Portsmouth 0 — Tuesday, December 2, 2003

MAKING THEIR POINT: Harry Redknapp, Jim Smith and Gordon Strachan.

RACE IS ON: James Beattie sprints past Arjan De Zeeuw.

Derby wait is well worth it

AFTER seven long years without a derby, the south coast was keyed up for a real cracker – but in the end it was no contest.

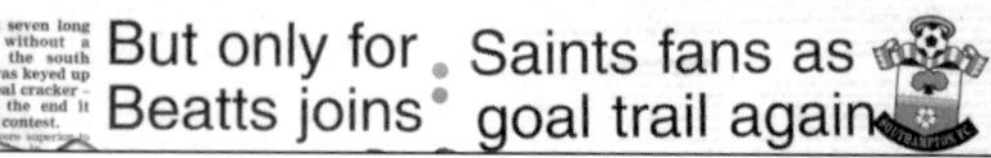

But only for Saints fans as Beatts joins goal trail again

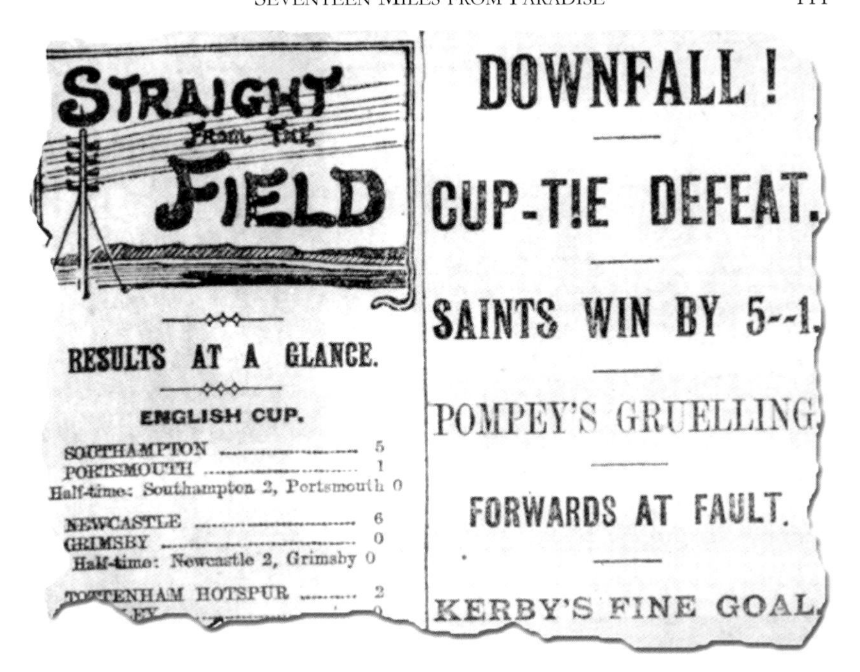

STRAIGHT FROM THE FIELD

RESULTS AT A GLANCE.

ENGLISH CUP.

SOUTHAMPTON 5
PORTSMOUTH 1
Half-time: Southampton 2, Portsmouth 0

NEWCASTLE 6
GRIMSBY 0
Half-time: Newcastle 2, Grimsby 0

TOTTENHAM HOTSPUR 2

DOWNFALL !

CUP-TIE DEFEAT.

SAINTS WIN BY 5--1.

POMPEY'S GRUELLING.

FORWARDS AT FAULT.

KERBY'S FINE GOAL.

Cutting from the Portsmouth *Football Mail* highlighting Pompey's demise in the January 1906 Cup-tie.

Pompey striker Mark Hateley contests a ball with Saints defender Mark Wright.
They would play together for England in the 1986 World Cup.
(author's collection)

Grainy image of the two teams lining up at The Dell to applaud Jimmy Dickinson onto the field for his 750th League appearance for Pompey. *(The News)*

THE FOOTBALL FIELD

SUPREMACY OF THE SAINTS.

RECORD "GATE" SEES POMPEY BEATEN.

RAWLINGS SCORES TWO GOALS.

The many supporters of the Southampton Football Club who attended the match between their favourites and the Po...

The Evening News cutting from the crucial 1922 Third Division (South) match.

Southampton Football & Athletic Co.

Official Team Card, Saturday, Oct. 8th.

PORTSMOUTH R.A.

(SOUTHERN LEAGUE).

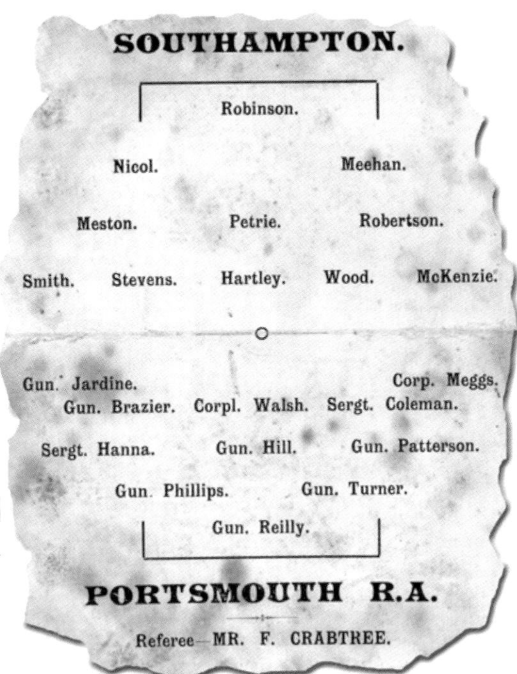

SOUTHAMPTON.

Robinson.

Nicol. Meehan.

Meston. Petrie. Robertson.

Smith. Stevens. Hartley. Wood. McKenzie.

Gun. Jardine. Corp. Meggs.

Gun. Brazier. Corpl. Walsh. Sergt. Coleman.

Sergt. Hanna. Gun. Hill. Gun. Patterson.

Gun. Phillips. Gun. Turner.

Gun. Reilly.

PORTSMOUTH R.A.

Referee—MR. F. CRABTREE.

The cover and teamsheet from the Southampton v RA Portsmouth match in October 1899. Saints won 4-1. *(Chris Gibbs Collection)*

Pompey's Richie Reynolds beats Steve Middleton – who would later play at Fratton – but hits the bar. Saints won 4-0 at The Dell in September 1975. *(The News)*

URDAY, MAY 6, 197

Saints' 7-0 farewell to Milkins

By REG BETTS

In a sentimental way it was a pity that Southampton came across to Fratton Park last night on a neighbourly mission for goalkeeper John Milkins' ten-year testimonial fund, and wound up by massacring Pompey 7—0.

But, quite rightly, there should be no sentiment when playing in front of paying ... nd for Milkins.

Teams and hundreds of admirers lined up to applaud Milkins from the pitch he has graced for ten years — and ... would like to ...

before O'Neill unerring arrowed his shot past Milkin It was a goal in a million.

Pompey's defensive defici...

Saints beat Pompey 7-0 in John Milkins' testimonial at Fratton in May 1972. Pompey players hardly did their best for their distinguished goalkeeper, according to *The News*.

Spectators flocked to The Dell as Saints reached the First Division, as seen here, queuing outside the ground in February 1967. *(source unknown)*

DAVID CROWNS SAINTS!

Super Pompey shame Keegan

Pompey 2, Saints 1

David Crown finally showed his Brentford form for Pompey last night – and old rivals Saints were bounced unceremoniously out of the new Hampshire Professional Cup at Fratton Park.

Crown has chased the form which twice devastated Pompey's defence as a Brentford player since moving to the South Coast two months ago.

By MIKE NEASOM

But in this first competitive meeting between three Hampshire neighbours since 1976, he revelled in the space allowed by a careless and undisciplined Ivan Golac.

He crashed the Pompey's first goal a minute before half-time to instantly wipe out the lead Mike Channon's unspotted run he created and then early in the second half punished Golac's defensive negligence by setting up a sharply taken winner for Jeff Hemmerman.

So he for one will derive a considerable amount from the inaugural match of a far from significant competition . . . and so should Pompey's entire team.

For this victory was well earned; Saints were at full strength and yet, slick though some of their one-touch midfield football was, they were never able to look two divisions above their hosts.

So Pompey, who have endured an ordinary first half to the season, should walk that little taller come Saturday when Bristol Rovers come for a match of greater reality.

And that was the point Frank Burrows made in his fleeting visit to the post-match inquest.

"It's nice but it will count for nothing if we don't beat Bristol on Saturday," was his sole comment.

His opposite number, Lawrie McMenemy, was more expansive but equally pointed.

"In most respects we got what we wanted from tonight: after all the problems with the weather we needed a good match without any injuries — the only injury was to our pride.

"[illegible] live with that. [illegible] not be a [illegible]

●GOAL! Mick Channon runs onto a free kick and steers the ball past Steve Aizlewood.

● NO WAY THROUGH . . . Mike Channon is guarded by Steve Aizlewood and Steve Bryant as he tries to force his way through the Pompey penalty area and ends up on the ground.

The News reports Third Division Pompey's shock 2-1 win against First Division Saints in December 1981 in the Hampshire Professional Cup.

Pompey misfit striker and ex-Saint Ian Baird shakes hands with Saints' Kevin Bond and future Pompey coach at the end of the first Division One derby in 1987. *(The News)*

Future Saints head coach Steve Wigley in the Pompey colours he wore 1989-92. *(Chris Gibbs Collection)*

Plus: COUNTY SUCCESS FOR TOTTS · SEE SPORT ON MONDAY

JUST PITIFUL

Saints turn in dismal derby performance

JUST PITIFUL.

That was the general summing up of Saints' performance in yesterday's south coast derby to forget.

Saints were beaten 1-0 by a second-half goal from Yakubu to suffer their first defeat on Pompey territory since September [illegible] and only their third ever at Fratton Park.

The nearest Saints came to an undeserved point was when Kevin Phillips, pictured, lashed a last-minute shot against a post.

The dismal defeat left Saints boss Paul Sturrock promising changes for next Saturday's [illegible] match with Tottenham.

Sturrock blasted: "I felt this was going to be a cup tie but one team played it in a cup tie spirit and another team played it as a league game.

"I don't know whether we've got a comfort zone where we feel we can saunter out the season now.

"But the important thing for players to appreciate is that some of them have to make sure they're regulars in Paul Sturrock's team.

"And the only way to do that is to do what Paul Sturrock says, and some of them will lose their place because of it next week."

● Derby coverage: See Sport on Monday pul[illegible]

The Echo sums up Saints' showing at Fratton Park as Pompey won 1-0 in March 2004.

Saints' Matt Le Tissier and Pompey's Paul Walsh during Saints' 3-0 FA Cup win in January 1996. *(The News)*

Saints and Pompey in action at Fratton Park, looking towards the Fratton End, in this September 1907 Southern League fixture. Pompey won 3-0. *(source unknown)*

The Saints' team was the sa... that which ousted Norwich City fro... the Cup. The teams lined up in char... of Mr. H. E. Gray (of London) as follow...

SOUTHAMPTON.

ALLEN

HOUGH KEEPING

SHELLEY HARKUS WOODHOUSE

HENDERSON ROWLEY TAYLOR MURPHY

RAWLINGS

COOK WATSON HAINES MACKIE GOODWIN

MOFFAT FOXALL DAVIES

McCOLGAN CLIFFORD

McPHAIL

PORTSMOUTH.

An open-air musical festival preceded the match. First there was the Pompey ...olo player blowing a lone solo in ... then ... Royal A...

The Evening News' cutting discusses Pompey's 3-1 win at The Dell in January 1927. Pompey were promoted to the First Division at the end of the season.

Saints' winger Terry Paine was an idol at The Dell. *(source unknown)*

Huge crowds in Frogmore Road formed part of a 44,000 crowd inside Fratton Park for the FA Cup fourth round replay with Fulham in February 1968. *(The News)*

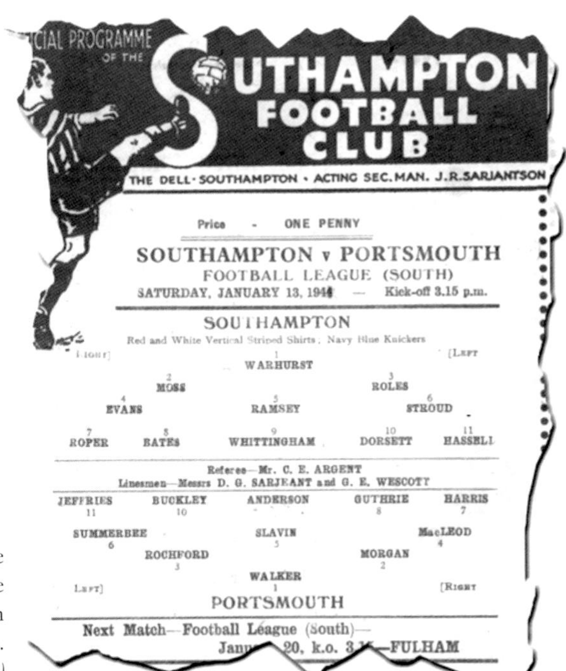

CIAL PROGRAMME OF THE
SOUTHAMPTON FOOTBALL CLUB
THE DELL · SOUTHAMPTON · ACTING SEC. MAN. J.R. SARJANTSON

Price - ONE PENNY

SOUTHAMPTON v PORTSMOUTH
FOOTBALL LEAGUE (SOUTH)
SATURDAY, JANUARY 13, 1944 — Kick-off 3.15 p.m.

SOUTHAMPTON
Red and White Vertical Striped Shirts ; Navy Blue Knickers

RIGHT] [LEFT
1 WARHURST
2 MOSS 3 ROLES
4 EVANS 5 RAMSEY 6 STROUD
7 ROPER 8 BATES 9 WHITTINGHAM 10 DORSETT 11 HASSELL

Referee—Mr. C. E. ARGENT
Linesmen—Messrs D. G. SARJEANT and G. E. WESCOTT

JEFFRIES 11 BUCKLEY 10 ANDERSON GUTHRIE 8 HARRIS 7
SUMMERBEE 6 SLAVIN 5 MacLEOD 4
ROCHFORD 3 MORGAN 2
WALKER 1
LEFT] [RIGHT
PORTSMOUTH

Next Match—Football League (South)—
Janu... 20, k.o. 3... —FULHAM

The Saints programme for a London War League game with Pompey in January 1945. *(Chris Gibbs Collection)*

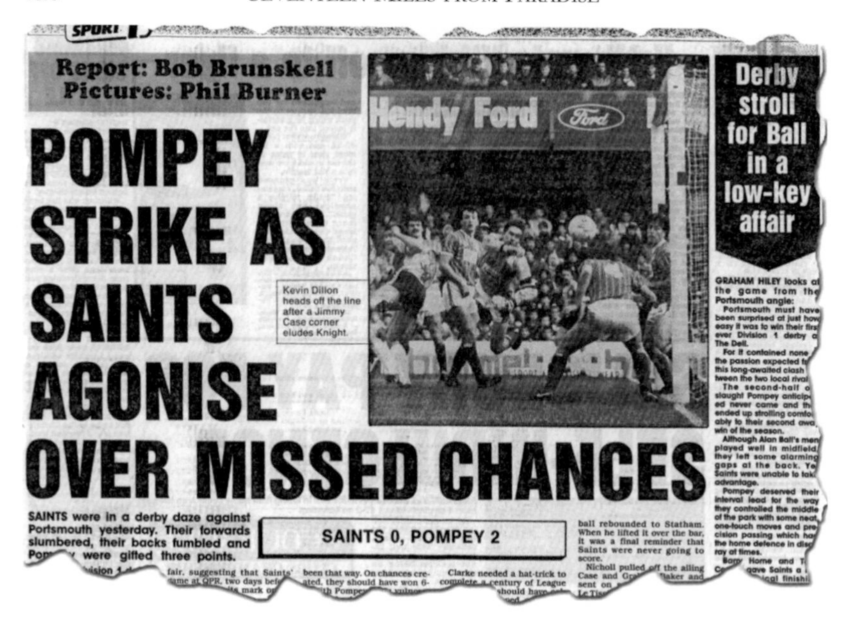

Report: Bob Brunskell
Pictures: Phil Burner

POMPEY STRIKE AS SAINTS AGONISE OVER MISSED CHANCES

Kevin Dillon heads off the line after a Jimmy Case corner eludes Knight.

SAINTS were in a derby daze against Portsmouth yesterday. Their forwards slumbered, their backs fumbled and Po[...] were gifted three points.

SAINTS 0, POMPEY 2

ball rebounded to Statham. When he lifted it over the bar, it was a final reminder that Saints were never going to score.

Derby stroll for Ball in a low-key affair

GRAHAM HILEY looks at the game from the Portsmouth angle:

Portsmouth must have been surprised at just how easy it was to win their first ever Division 1 derby at The Dell.

For it contained none [...] the passion expected [...] this long-awaited clash [...]tween the two local rival[s].

The second-half o[n]slaught Pompey anticip[at]ed never came and th[ey] ended up strolling comfo[rt]ably to their second awa[y] win of the season.

Although Alan Ball's men played well in midfield, they left some alarming gaps at the back. Ye[t] Saints were unable to tak[e] advantage.

Pompey deserved their interval lead for the way they controlled the middle of the park with some neat, one-touch moves and precision passing which ha[d] the home defence in disa[r]ray at times.

The Echo reports on Pompey's 2-0 win at The Dell in January 1988.

Colin Clarke, the former Saints striker who joined Pompey from QPR for a then record £440,000 in 1990.

Alan Biley fires over for Pompey in the January 1984 FA Cup-tie, which Saints won 1-0.

The opening paragraph of *The Echo's* report of Saints' 1-0 win at Fratton Park in the epic January 1984 FA Cup-tie fourth round tie.

PORTSMOUTH 0, SOUTHAMPTON 1

STEVE MORAN was the target of some crude jibes by the Portsmouth fans. And the Saints' pocket battleship silenced them with a stunning broadside at Fratton Park on Saturday.

The man who had dumped Nottingham Forest out of the third round broke thousands of Pompey hearts and sent Saints surging into the FA Cup's last 16 for the first time in three years.

As a player, Tony Barton was a wing-half for Pompey. He was then chief scout, assistant and caretaker manager at Fratton Park. He was also assistant manager at The Dell.

Right and Below: Programme cover for the critical game which Saints won 1-0, condemning Pompey to relegation in 1975-76. Saints' Peter Osgood, Jim McCalliog and Jim Steele missed the game after a breach of club discipline the night before.

POMPEY

Colours: White shirts with double vertical stripes, blue shorts

1 Phil Figgins
2 Chris Lawler
3 Bill Wilson
4 Jeff King
5 Paul Cahill
6 Keith Viney
7 Steve Foster
8 Norman Piper
9 George Graham
10 Chris Kamara
11 Mick Mellows
12

BALL DONOR

ANCO PRODUCTION
Anco House
Albert Rd
Southsea

Golden Goal Time:
W.B.A.
47.54

SOUTHAMPTON

Colours: White shirts with red stripes and black shorts

Ian Turner 1
Peter Rodrigues 2
David Peach 3
Nick Holmes 4
Paul Bennett 5
Jim Steele 6
Hugh Fisher 7
Mick Channon 8
Paul Gilchrist 9
Jim McCalliog 10
Bobby Stokes 11
12

Referee: P. R. Walters (Bridgwater)
Linesmen: M. K. Bevan (Yellow Flag)
D. R. Hughes (Red Flag)

John Mortimore had two spells as Saints' assistant manager, but failed spectacularly in his spell as Pompey boss during 1973-74.

The News reports on trouble after the January 1984 FA Cup-tie at Fratton Park, which Saints won 1-0.

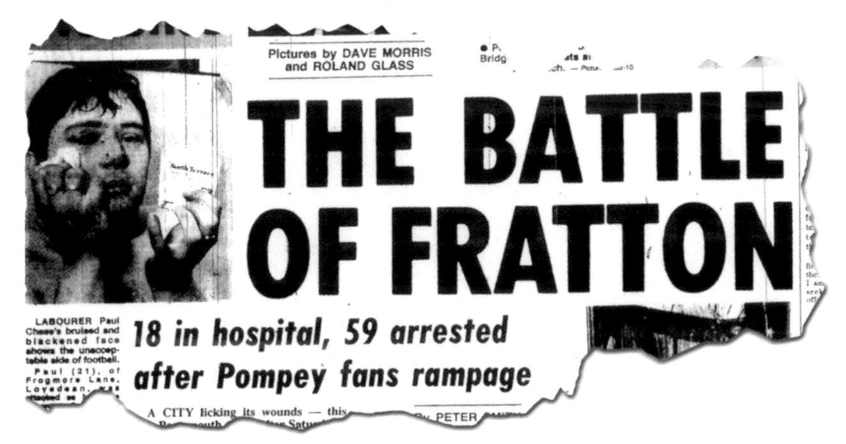

Pictures by DAVE MORRIS and ROLAND GLASS

THE BATTLE OF FRATTON

18 in hospital, 59 arrested after Pompey fans rampage

LABOURER Paul Cheese's bruised and blackened face shows the unacceptable side of football. Paul (21), of Frogmore Lane, Lovedean, was attacked as ...

A CITY licking its wounds — this ...

By PETER ...

The News captures Yakubu scoring the only goal at Fratton Park in March 2004. It secured Pompey's first home derby win for 41 years.

POMPEY IN THE PREMIERSHIP

Club owner Milan Mandaric shows fans the banner they have waited 15 years to see

Pompey chairman Milan Mandaric looks forward to his club surpassing Saints on the night that Pompey clinched promotion to the Premiership in April 2003.

Ted Bates: The mastermind of Saints' rise from the Third to the First Divisions.

The Echo sums up Saints 5-2 victory at Fratton in February 1966, en route to promotion.

Dean and Chivers snatch the goals to sink Pompey

By "Observer"

THE SAINTS beat Portsmouth by 5—2 at Fratton Park on Saturday because they were the sharper side in front of goal. The ample margin perhaps flattered them a bit, but there was no doubt they were the better side.

The game, fast, open and exciting, was one of the best between these Hampshire rivals for many years. It was played in good sporting spirit, with none of the bad feeling that has sometimes marred this "local derby." There were only about half-a-dozen fouls, and no bad ones, in the whole game.

The Saints' first goal. The ball goes in off Dean from Sydenham's cross.

Below: The Thornycrofts works team from Woolston line up at Fratton Park before their FA Cup-tie with First Division Burnley in 1919. *(source unknown)*

Above: The Pompey team which took part in the first ever FA Cup-tie with Saints in January 1906. *(Association Football and the Men Who Made It)*

Above: Pompey's Mick Tait wins out against David Armstrong and Frank Worthington in the 1984 FA Cup-tie. *(The News)*

BOMBSHELL AT THE DELL

Saints Without a Team

FOR MATCH WITH POMPEY

Pickford Cup Surprise

The biggest football bombshell in the history of Southampton burst at Southampton last night, when the Portsmouth team arrived at the Dell to play for the Pickford Benevolent Cup.

Fifteen of the Southampton players have refused the terms offered them and because they had not re-engaged for next season declined to play in the match, so that Southampton were left without a team to meet Pompey.

... view of the "pros." was that if they ...

The Evening News reports on the so-called 'Dell Bombshell' as Saints can't raise a side for a charity cup final in May 1931.

Ron Saunders, Pompey's centre-forward (left), challenges Saints goalkeeper Ron Reynolds during the first League meeting of the clubs in 33 years at The Dell in August 1960. *(The News)*

Saints' goalkeeper John Hollowbread beats Pompey's debut-making Ray Hiron to the ball in Saints' 3-0 win at Fratton in September 1964. *(The News)*

Bombed out by Ian Branfoot, ex-Saints midfielder Alan McLoughlin was a popular midfielder at Fratton Park.

Saints' Kevin Phillips steers a last-minute shot against a post, allowing Pompey to escape with three precious points in March 2004. *(The News)*

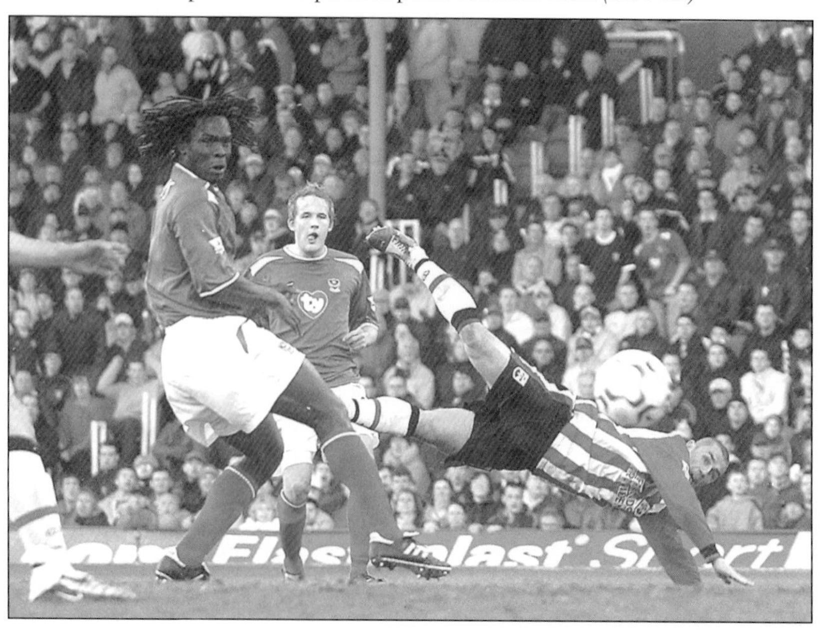

Whatever the truth behind the alleged banking 'scandal', it was stirred by the fact that similar accusations were not without precedent. Supporters of Accrington Stanley would never excuse the alleged part played by neighbouring Burnley and Football League chairman Bob Lord in that club's futile last-ditch bid to rescind their resignation from the Football League in 1962.

With regard to Portsmouth, however, clearly someone forgot to tell the Saints players. On 24th April 1965, Pompey's fate was as much in Saints' hands as in their own. The relegation equation required Saints to beat Swindon at The Dell, which would allow Pompey to escape, provided they could draw at already promoted Northampton. If Saints only drew, then Pompey had to win. Saints had nothing but fourth place to aim at, but aim for it they did, securing a 2-1 win thanks to goals from Huxford and Paine. Perhaps Terry fancied another crack at his old 'mate' Roy Lunniss after all. For Pompey, that was the easy bit. By a quirk of timing, their game at Northampton was scheduled for the Saturday evening, so at least they now knew what was necessary. On an emotion-charged night, with Dickinson making his 764th and final League appearance at the age of 40, Pompey held out at 0-0 until the 77th minute. The Cobblers were on a roller-coaster ride from the Fourth Division to the First and all the way back again, but tonight they got lucky when forward Johnny Gordon scored a bizarre own-goal. Pompey looked down and out, but found an unlikely saviour in veteran full-back Alex Wilson. Despite a record of just one goal in 250 Pompey appearances, Wilson popped up to level with six minutes remaining. Upon the final whistle the thousands from the south coast who had swelled the gate to more than 24,000 invaded the pitch and Dickinson was chaired all the way back to the tunnel.

The new 1965-66 fixture list decreed that Portsmouth would have an early opportunity to thank their neighbours in person. Saints' second home game brought Pompey to town, or more accurately 'city', as Southampton had been accorded that civic status in 1964. Saints manager Ted Bates was coming under pressure. Compared to Pompey, Saints had spent big money, but had yet to reach the First Division. However, two wins to start the campaign reignited optimism that this could finally be their year. Pompey, with their pared down sixteen-man squad, had no significant newcomers among their ranks. A pair of 4-1 results to start the season, the first won at home to Plymouth, the second lost at Preston, set the scene for an inconsistent campaign. In these circumstances the point gained at The Dell was good from Pompey's point of view, less so from Saints'.

The occasion was overshadowed by Pompey centre-half Vince Radcliffe's double leg fracture, following a harmless-looking challenge with Huxford after 28 minutes. Radcliffe was replaced by winger Tony Barton, who thereby became the first Pompey player to appear as a substitute, the

League permitting the practice for the first time. It was one of the more bad-tempered derbies. Referee Lowry took the unusual step of lecturing both teams in their dressing rooms at half-time about their conduct, but he might as well have saved his breath. Surprise, surprise, Paine and Lunniss were at it again, 'both guilty of silly petulance,' according to 'Linesman', but the Pompey man was booked for shoving Paine in the chest. Melia gave Saints a thirteenth-minute lead. Harris, covering for Radcliffe, headed against the bar before levelling a minute from the break with a 'sizzling 30-yard drive'. With the pace still fast and furious, Pompey keeper John Armstrong spilled Sydenham's cross and Chivers profited after 71 minutes, but the points were shared when McCann struck an angled shot high into the net three minutes later.

Despite their suspect defence, Portsmouth kept pace with their rivals until October, but then a run of seven defeats in eight matches – including a 2-8 surrender at Wolves on 27th November – ushered in the usual threat of having to ward off relegation. Ironically, Saints had been involved in their own September goal-fest with Wolves at The Dell, winning 9-3 with Chivers bagging four, a landmark already achieved by O'Brien a fortnight earlier in the 6-2 slaughter of Bury. Saints' promotion hopes were dogged by inconsistency before Christmas, however, several games being lost by the odd goal.

Coming into the return game at Fratton Park on 5th February, 1966, Saints were lying sixth, five points behind second-placed Coventry with a game in hand. There were also signs that they were rectifying their suspect away form, although a 5-3 win at Cardiff on 27th December was sandwiched by defeats at Ipswich and Huddersfield. Pompey were fresh from a 1-3 defeat at Plymouth – 'a miserable performance' according to manager Smith – which featured Lunniss's farewell appearance for the club. Shortly afterwards his contract would be terminated, after he was apparently accused of snatching a woman's handbag in Commercial Road. According to urban legend at least, he did so while wearing a club blazer.

Southampton fielded Norman Dean, a 21-year-old forward, who had finally broken into the first team. Despite giving a couple of inches in height to Frank Haydock – Pompey's £20,000 December signing from Charlton, as cover for the unfortunate Radcliffe – Dean mastered him in the air. The game turned on chances taken. Saints took theirs, while Pompey didn't. 'We took what was going,' observed manager Bates afterwards. For the *Echo*, 'Observer' agreed that Saints had been the sharper shooters, but had no doubts about the validity of the outcome: 'The ample margin perhaps flattered them [Saints] a bit, but there was no doubt they were the better side'.

There had been a touch of fortune about Saints' opener after 21 minutes, when Sydenham's cross-shot took a deflection off Dean and ended in the opposite corner of the net. Two minutes later, Saints were gifted a second as Armstrong fumbled Wilson's back-pass and Chivers pounced for his second goal of the season. By this time, Pompey's McClelland had already missed a sitter, but two minutes before half-time Lewis headed home a McClelland cross and the balance began to swing back towards the Blues. When McCann outsmarted Paine to fire home a second-half equaliser, it seemed the force was with Pompey. The Chimes boomed out as the home crowd found their voice, only for Pompey's defence to fall apart again. In the 70th minute Melia's miscued shot turned into a perfect pass for Dean, who scored easily. After that Pompey caved in. Dean completed his first hat-trick in League football, profiting as Armstrong dithered on his goal-line as he raced through. Then, late on, Haydock and his keeper blundered: 'For Armstrong the ball once again took on the qualities of petroleum jelly,' was Chris Newman's memorable description of the incident in *Match of the Millennium* (Bull and Brunskell eds 2000). The error gifted a fifth goal to Chivers, delighting the large travelling Saints contingent, which was mostly congregated on the Milton End. Armstrong's confidence was shattered, and with lurid tales of being 'led astray' by Lunniss, he would play just one more match that season. In his post-match report, 'Linesman' was far from upbeat about either sides' prospects. Of Pompey he wrote: 'Unless there is a general tightening up trouble looms just around the corner,' while 'weaknesses in defence, exposed, but not exploited at Fratton Park may well stop Southampton just short of the first division.'

Going into April, his assessment looked spot on. Pompey had duly tightened up – since the Saints game they had not conceded more than one goal in any match – while Saints had won just one game in six. With nine games left they were still sixth, five points short of a promotion place, although they still had that precious game in hand. Pompey were now about to repay the favour of the previous April. Three of the clubs above Saints – Huddersfield, Coventry and Wolves – were due at Fratton Park. Pompey duly beat the lot of them, and in front of attendances better than many at The Dell that month, as the Portsmouth public responded to the team's upsurge in form. Saints stepped on the gas themselves, six wins and two draws in eight games opening the door as they profited from their rivals' frailties.

On Monday, 9th May 1966 they travelled to Brisbane Road to face already doomed Leyton Orient needing a point to be virtually certain of promotion. It is estimated that anywhere between 12,000 and 15,000 Saints fans swelled Orient's usual gate to more than 19,000, but the occasion looked like going pear-shaped when Orient led through a first-half goal by Peter Allen. But Paine headed the equaliser after a defensive mix up to earn the priceless point and send the Saints contingent swarming onto the pitch at the final whistle. In actuality, a 0-6 defeat in Saints' last game at champions Manchester City could have denied them, but that calamity was avoided. Coventry, by now managed by the revolutionary visionary Jimmy Hill (younger readers please note this is not a joke), who later turned TV pundit, were left stranded a point adrift. One helping hand deserves another, and Saints could be grateful that Coventry had recently dropped two points at Fratton.

Not that Southampton decided to display their gratitude. Two days after the Orient game, Pompey travelled to The Dell for a testimonial for John Hollowbread. The former Spurs goalkeeper had been forced to quit at Christmas through an injury sustained earlier in the season against Coventry. The Saints players and manager Bates received a standing ovation before the start, and the first half was a competitive affair, the teams going in all-square after Hiron had cancelled out Dean's opener. After the interval, however, Saints scored five more goals without reply. Chivers netted twice, once from the spot, then Melia, Dave Walker and Dean added three in four minutes.

Pompey had a few hundred fans in the 10,000 gate, which was smaller than expected, although local folklore maintains that Saints supporters were still recovering from the Orient celebrations. The visiting fans stood unsegregated on the Milton Road End terrace and as the game drew to a close, the home crowd took to song, borrowing the refrain from Vera Lynn: 'We'll see you again / But we don't know when / Goodbye Pompey, goodbye'.

At the final whistle the crowd invaded the pitch and a promotion party – not quite a full-blown affair as the Maine Road game was still to be safely negotiated – got under way. Portsmouth's undisputed reign as south coast top dog, which remained more or less intact while both clubs were in the Second Division, was over. It was Southampton's turn to gloat.

Chapter 8

~ Parting of the Ways ... Again ~

(1966-76)

Southampton kicked off their great adventure in Division One in a similar vein to Portsmouth 39 years before – with a draw. Terry Paine fired home a cross-shot early in the second half to level against Manchester City at The Dell. The crowd, under 20,000, hardly indicated that the Southampton public were clamouring to see top-flight football.

Attendances at the respective clubs now became a real issue for both sets of supporters, particularly as chastened Pompey fans sought to claim that – irrespective of League standings – Saints should still know their place. In fact, Saints' gates were on the up, averaging around 25,000 as they attempted to consolidate their position. Their task was made easier by summer signing Ron Davies, a £55,000 capture from Norwich, who would end the season as the division's leading scorer with 37 goals in 41 matches. Eventually, Saints would finish fourth from bottom, although their 'goals against' column, 92, was the worst in the division.

It was the FA Cup that ignited the dispute about the potential support each club could muster. On third round day, 28th January 1967, Pompey earned a 1-1 draw at divisional rivals Hull, while Saints had to come from behind to draw 2-2 at Fourth Division Barrow. With the blessing of Hampshire Constabulary, both replays were scheduled for Wednesday, 1st February, and the respective turnouts were as much a talking point as the results. Saints sauntered past Barrow 3-0, watched by 24,697, in line with their seasonal norm, but at Fratton Park 33,107 clicked through the turnstiles, well over double the previous League gate. More significantly, that figure was almost 8,500 more than at The Dell.

The belief – or myth if you are of Saints persuasion – that a latent multitude existed, ready and willing to back a resurgent Portsmouth team, was born that night. The following day, the *News* rubbed in the fact that the crowd for Third Division Brighton's simultaneous replay against Aldershot also dwarfed that at the Dell. Pompey drew their game 2-2 and eventually prevailed 3-1 in a second replay at Coventry, where south-coast fans made up the bulk of an 18,000 gate. In the fourth round, Pompey took an estimated 15,000 to White Hart Lane to see them lose to a Jimmy Greaves-inspired Spurs, who would go on and win the Cup, while Saints too took a substantial backing to Bristol City, only to see their side subside 0-1 to their Second Division opponents.

With both sides having a spare Saturday on fifth round day, 11th March, what better than to arrange a friendly at Fratton. Saints were on a bad run that had brought just three wins in sixteen matches, dumping them on the fringes of the relegation scrap. Manager Ted Bates had acted, signing Blackpool midfielder – the days of 'wing-halves' were numbered – Hugh Fisher for £35,000. Having recovered from an ankle knock, Fisher played his first Saints game in the friendly, although Paine, John Sydenham and Tony Knapp were all out through injury. Both managers were elsewhere, too, Bates scouting in Scotland, Smith at an unrevealed location, but the attendance of more than 13,500 was respectable enough, in spite of moans in some quarters that charging full price – the best seats were 9s 6d (47½p) – was hardly an incentive. Both sides could take heart from the 2-2 draw, which saw Paine's understudy, eighteen-year-old local-born Micky Judd, open the scoring in the first half. Two goals in six minutes early in the second from Nicky Jennings and Harry Harris turned the game around, but Ron Davies finally escaped stand-in centre half Ron Tindall to head an equaliser after 64 minutes.

The result seemed to galvanise Southampton, who would pick up eleven points out of their final 22 available to avoid the drop with something to spare. Portsmouth, on the other hand, saw their season tamely deflate, with just one win in their last eleven matches, to eventually finish fourteenth.

'Tame' is not how the columns of the *Football Mail* could be described as a polemic erupted over the significance of those Cup attendances back in February. On 4th March, Mr H Clapper from Winchester set the ball rolling, citing Saints' 'superior' brand of football compared to that of Pompey. He added: 'Unfortunately for the "swinging city", [Southampton] The Dell has its limitations and a great many out of town fans will not always attempt the journey for fear of a lock-out.' The inference was that Pompey's gate against Hull was possibly enhanced by a proportion of Saints fans who thought they might not be able to get in at The Dell. Back came Mr G Cole of North End: 'As far as Saints are concerned, my advice to Mr Clapper is to forget about his superior football theme and face the hard facts. These are that there are bigger gates at The Dell because of the attractive visiting teams and above average gates at Fratton Park because of the honest endeavour of the home team.'

A running sore that would erupt at intervals ever since had been incubated, although for the moment, the last word must go to Saints fan David Brooks: 'Despite the unfair comments they [Pompey fans] make in this column I have nothing against them, though I admit I would not like my daughter to marry one.' Quite.

In the summer of 1967 both teams shuffled their squads. Saints finally signed Everton defender Jimmy Gabriel to shore up their shaky defence, while at Fratton, George Smith continued to mix and match promising young players – albeit signed from elsewhere – with experience. Former

England centre-forward Ray Pointer had joined from Coventry the previous February, and the additions of 21-year-olds left-back George Ley from Exeter and George Smith (no relation), a tough tackling midfielder from Barrow, gave Pompey's slender resources a more solid look than had been the case for several years.

Southampton started the 1967-68 campaign brightly, culminating with a sensational 6-2 win at Chelsea in early September. Davies showed he was still in the goal groove by bagging four that day. However, as Saints' good form faded, attention switched to Fratton Park, where Pompey opened up with a nine-match unbeaten run to take them to the top. Gates regularly topped 20,000 as the claim that the Portsmouth public would respond to a winning team seemed to be borne out. On 2nd December Pompey hosted promotion-chasing Blackpool, but few could have predicted the monumental 35,000 attendance – Pompey's biggest ever in the Second Division – which seemed to reinforce the trend.

Going into February it seemed Pompey were on course for promotion, sitting as they were in second place. By contrast, Saints' alarming slump after selling Chivers to Tottenham for £125,000 in December had the relegation clouds gathering. Following four successive defeats, under 21,000 turned out to see the 1-2 defeat by Stoke on 3rd February, 5,000 fewer than saw Pompey beat Derby 3-2 at Fratton the following week.

February also saw the FA Cup take centre stage. While Southampton needed a third round replay to overcome Fourth Division Newport, Pompey won 1-0 at disgraced Peterborough (condemned to relegation for illegal payments). In the fourth round Pompey forced a 0-0 draw at First Division strugglers Fulham, while Saints were also drawing 1-1 at West Brom. This meant another big night of Cup football as the two replays were scheduled for the following Wednesday, 21st February, but the plot was given a twist by the fact that the winners would meet in the fifth round. The south coast derby to end all derbies was tantalisingly close.

To add impetus to their promotion push, Pompey had forked out a record £40,000 for Everton forward Mike Trebilcock, a two-goal hero in the FA Cup final two years beforehand. Trebilcock scored the only goal of the game to take Pompey past Fulham. Once again the crowds flocked to Fratton Park, and for the first time since the early 1950s the capacity – although reduced to 46,000 – was pushed to the limit. More than 44,000 passed through the Fratton turnstiles that night, compared with 26,000 at The Dell, providing further ammunition for those who spoke loudly about Pompey's 'potential'. They would need something to cling on to.

Southampton suffered a disappointing night, despite an early goal from Frank Saul – signed as a replacement for Chivers – and the derby dream died with Saints' 2-3 defeat. In the fifth round, their conquerors West Brom claimed their second south coast scalp, winning 2-1 *en route* to an eventual Wembley triumph, but again Fratton Park was bursting with an all-ticket 42,000 crowd.

Free now to concentrate on promotion, Pompey did precisely the opposite. They would win just three more matches to end up fifth. Saints, though, quickly put their Cup defeat behind them and three successive wins saw them ease well clear of the drop zone at the final reckoning. Their upturn was due in no small part, yet again, to Ted Bates' skills at wheeling and dealing in the transfer market. Shortly after the West Brom defeat, John McGrath arrived from Newcastle to fill a vacuum at centre-back, while cultured right-back Joe Kirkup came from Chelsea as the makeweight in a player-exchange deal which took David Webb the other way. Saints were now becoming an established fixture in the First Division. The following, 1968-69, season would see them into the top half and strike their own blow in their bid for regional superiority by finishing high enough to bring European football to the south coast for the first time.

Saints had got off to a poor start, however, and in December 1968 fewer than 18,000 turned up for the visit of Nottingham Forest. A storming run in the New Year, including another spanking of Chelsea, this time 5-0 at The Dell in February, set them on the way to a seventh-place finish however. In those days that was good enough to qualify for the Inter Cities Fairs' Cup. No matter that fifth-placed Chelsea and sixth-placed Spurs were deemed ineligible, on the grounds that fourth-placed Arsenal had already taken 'London's' berth in the competition. Bizarrely, UEFA permitted only one team from any given city to compete.

On 17th September 1969 Southampton flew to Trondheim to play Rosenborg, although a 0-1 defeat by the Norwegian club was hardly an inspiring debut. In fact, in the late 1960s, to find any English team losing to a Scandinavian one was a shock. Any hopes Pompey might have built on the promise shown during 1967-68 quickly vanished. A year later they returned to a familiar fifteenth. Too good to go down, but without the strength in depth to mount a serious promotion campaign, Pompey seemed stagnant in mid-table Second Division mediocrity. The 1969-70 season had started even worse, and by the time Saints launched their European adventure, Pompey were already in the lower reaches of the table. Included in the Saints side which lost in Norway was eighteen-year-old winger Bobby Stokes, Paulsgrove-born and bred. Stokes had announced himself on the big stage with two goals on his debut in a 5-1 thrashing of Burnley at The Dell in April 1969. He had been rejected by Pompey as a young teenager as their youth policy was winding down. He had been allowed to sign for Saints and quickly earned England Youth honours. Stokes wouldn't be the last to get away.

Southampton overturned their first-leg deficit, winning 2-0, and then beat Portuguese side Vitoria Guimaraes 8-4 on aggregate. Third round opponents Newcastle United were more familiar foes, and were the defending holders of the trophy. Following a 0-0 draw at St James' Park, Saints were confident of progressing. The second leg marked Saints' third game against the Magpies inside a month – the FA Cup third round having also paired the sides and seen Saints emerge victorious by 3-0.

The second leg saw Wiltshire-born Mick Channon – who was now a regular, having made his debut in 1966 – break the deadlock. Ten minutes from time Ron Davies headed against the bar. Instead of being 2-0, the score was soon 1-1, when four minutes from time Bryan 'Pop' Robson ensured that Saints went out on the recently introduced 'away goals' rule. In the League, Saints' form was miserable. In almost any other season clocking up just six wins from 42 games and scraping just 29 points would have been punished by relegated, but seventeen draws just about kept Saints' heads above water. In fact, Saints were three points clear by the close, with an improbable 3-1 win over Leeds – chasing the title, FA Cup, and European Cup – in April ensuring survival.

Pompey fared little better. Although relegation was averted, a finishing position of seventeenth and an FA Cup third-round exit at home to Third Division Tranmere hardly met the expectations of fans for whom First Division football was now an eleven-year-old fading memory. The term 'sleeping giant' was now heard more and more frequently in connection with Pompey, it has to be said with some justification, as the club's immediate post-War dominance was still relatively fresh in footballing memory. A comparison with a present-day club like Nottingham Forest might be drawn. Despite a recent record which suggests that Forest are anything but a Premiership club, they still retain the kudos of being double European Cup winners within living memory and thus 'deserving' of better.

As that ultimately disappointing season – for both clubs – drew to a close, Pompey scraped a bit of jam from the bottom of the jar as they travelled to face Saints on 20th April 1970 for John Sydenham's testimonial. The winger was leaving The Dell after thirteen years' service and more than 10,000 turned out to pay tribute, but his former colleagues sold him short. Bob Lever in the *Echo* summed up the night from a Saints perspective: 'Pompey played in an attractive, forceful style, but Saints did not respond as a team, nor did they capture the mood of the night,' he wrote the following day. Mike Neasom, then Saints correspondent for the *News,* went further: 'Pompey handed Southampton a lesson in giving value for money … The Fratton Park men gave the paying customers a fair return for their cash. Bored, slap-happy Saints seriously short-changed them'.

The match facts are these: Brian Bromley fired Pompey ahead after 22 minutes with a crisp shot, only for Saints to respond within a minute with Gabriel – 'one of the few Saints in serious mood' – heading home a cross. After that, Pompey ran riot. Nicky Jennings restored their lead after 27 minutes, Hiron made it 3-1 in the 53rd, and the same player added a fourth with just under fifteen minutes to go. Channon pulled one back after 78 minutes, but it was too little too late. Local pride was Pompey's.

However, the crumbs of comfort such success brought Portsmouth needed to be offset against the bigger, unfolding picture. Two nights later Saints' 'A' team took on Warsash in the Hampshire Senior Cup at The Dell. The folly of Pompey's scrapped youth policy was there for all to see. In Saints goal was seventeen-year-old Portsmouth-born Steve Middleton and at right-back sixteen-year-old Steve Mills, likewise from the city and grandson of 1930s star Jock Gilfillan, who had kept goal for Pompey at Wembley in 1934. Pompey boss George Smith, who was about to hand over team affairs to Ron Tindall, was famously quoted as saying in terms of footballers 'there was nothing in Portsmouth but fish in the sea'. He was wrong.

For 1970-71, Ted Bates set about revamping his team, making midfielder Brian O'Neil from Burnley a record £75,000 signing. The Saints board also resisted overtures from Manchester United for Ron Davies. The previous season he had scored all four at Old Trafford as Saints recorded a stunning 4-1 win, and now, assisted by his goals – seventeen in 40 games – Saints finished seventh for the second time in three years to qualify for the Fairs Cup, now renamed the UEFA Cup. As had happened two years earlier, Saints needed a little help to 'qualify'. Although the 'one city, one club' rule had gone, Saints profited from Arsenal's League and Cup double, which had, in effect, freed an extra place for an English club.

Portsmouth also had the Gunners to thank for rescuing another mundane season. With neither relegation or promotion on the cards, it was left to the FA Cup to provide some excitement. Pompey's surprise 2-0 home win over promotion-chasing Sheffield United in the third round – the Blades had won 5-1 on their previous two visits – set up a fourth round home tie against Southern League Yeovil or Arsenal. In their delayed tie, the Gunners predictably prevailed and were on their way to Fratton. Interest was enormous, Trebilcock being frequently wheeled out for the nation's press to show off his (Everton) Cup winners' medal. On a damp January afternoon, Pompey looked dead and buried after Peter Storey's first-half penalty separated the sides going into injury-time. Then a slip in the Arsenal defence allowed full-back Fred Smith to cross. The ball squirmed through to Mike Trebilcock, who drove in the equaliser from close range. A close on 40,000 all-ticket crowd exploded with relief. Another chapter in the Portsmouth book of 'Big Attendances Despite Being a Mediocre Club' had been written. Pompey lost the replay 2-3.

Ted Bates' assistant manager since 1968 had been former Chelsea wing-back John Mortimore. Among the other short-listed candidates had been former Fratton favourite Jimmy Scoular, then boss at Cardiff, but in the summer of 1971 Mortimore had left Saints to try his luck as coach of Greek side Panionios, leaving Southampton as a club in transition.

Saints' 1971-72 UEFA Cup campaign went pear-shaped as Athletic Bilbao showed more resilience than their countrymen two years before, recovering from a 1-2 deficit from The Dell to win 3-2 on aggregate. In the League, Saints' defensive deficiencies were brutally exposed by Everton, 0-8, at Goodison in early November, then Manchester United, 2-5, a week later. Another humiliation, this time 0-7 at title contenders Leeds, in March left Saints teetering over the edge.

That nightmare performance was recorded for posterity by BBC TV's 'Match of the Day' and the closing minutes included a now clichéd sequence of unbroken Leeds passes, with no Southampton player getting near the ball. The footage ensures that any BBC retro football programme invariably makes happy viewing for Pompey fans.

Saints avoided the drop with three wins in April, but Pompey were in even worse shape. Another promotion bid was fizzling out by early November, as usual, and a miserable run following their fifth round FA Cup defeat at Birmingham meant relegation to the Third Division was barely avoided.

That season's Pompey curtain was brought down by a testimonial for John Milkins, deferred from the end of the previous season, which saw Saints head east on Cup final eve, Friday 5th May 1972. If Saints had dawdled for Sydenham two years earlier, Milkins' Pompey teammates contrived to go one worse, producing surely the most inept derby display in the entire history of the rivalry. Nearly 9,000 turned out to pay homage to Milkins, who had progressed through the youth ranks to give eleven years' sterling service, but by half-time they must have wondered why they had bothered. Inspired by Terry Paine, who was having none of this 'friendly' nonsense, Saints were up for it, and carved pathetic Pompey apart. After thirteen minutes Brian O'Neil put Saints one up with a clinical finish, then John McGrath, Davies and a quick-fire double from Jimmy Gabriel made it 5-0 at the break. After 68 minutes Davies made it six, and the goal-fest was rounded off by man-of-the-match O'Neil thirteen minutes from time. Hiron did get the ball in the net once, but even that consolation was disallowed for a Richie Reynolds foul on goalkeeper Eric Martin.

Poor Milkins rued afterwards: 'I will want to forget this match because it was bitterly disappointing from our point of view. Southampton scored some goals even Leeds wouldn't have stopped and while I would have liked the result to have been closer I hope the fans were entertained'. *Echo* reporter John Hughes summed up the night: 'The difference in class between the sides was embarrassing as Saints played with insolent ease.' The Saints travelling contingent in the crowd was concentrated under the South Stand and there were reports of scuffles and arrests after the match.

Portsmouth were a club on the precipice. The financial burden of building a team to return to the top flight was clearly beyond the existing board of directors. Gates at Fratton Park were at an all-time low. The final League match of 1971-72 had attracted fewer than 6,000 to see a 1-2 defeat to Burnley, and although the start of the new, 1972-73 campaign saw more than 16,000 turn out for a 'top of the table' clash against Huddersfield in late August, by October Pompey were down in the mire again. When Middlesbrough arrived at Fratton on 16th December 1972, Pompey were in the bottom two and just 4,688 clicked through the turn-stiles – the lowest League attendance in the club's history.

At one of the Portsmouth's darkest hours, however, a knight in shining armour was appearing over the horizon. Bramwell John Deacon, a Southampton-based property developer, had made a fortune from the boom in property values in the late 1960s and early 70s. He was keen to invest in a football club and, after overtures to Southampton had been rebuffed, he turned his sights on Pompey. The proposition was seductive: restore the club's fading glory and his place in the affections of the fans and the gratitude of the city was assured.

Introduced to current Chairman John Collett through his solicitor and Portsmouth Vice President Sir Alfred Blake, Deacon was granted a seat on the board from 27th December 1972 in return for an injection of capital which saw Ken Foggo from Norwich arrive, as well as midfielder Bobby Kellard, back for a second spell at the club, from Crystal Palace (Neasom 1984). The arrival of these two players steadied the ship and an eight-match unbeaten League run gathered enough points to stave off relegation, despite a late slump.

Southampton were also going through a relatively lean spell. Ted Bates was, by now, the longest-serving manager in the Football League, but although relegation was never a concern, gates were tumbling too at The Dell. During that 1972-73 season, sub-15,000 gates were quite common and for one game with Sheffield United, on 20th January 1973, just 12,125 turned up – Saints' lowest yet for a top-flight match and well-short of the reported 21,000 break-even figure they needed (Chalk and Holley 1988).

The plates of Hampshire's football geology were shifting. Ron Davies scored his last goal at The Dell – for Saints at least – to earn a 1-1 draw with the Blades, but by the end of the season he was unable to keep his place. Although Saints wanted to keep him, Davies was on his way to Pompey.

Of more pressing concern was 55-year-old Bates' future as manager. The resignation of assistant Stuart Williams provided the catalyst for change. In April 1973, Saints advertised in the *Daily Express* for an 'Assistant to the Manager/Team Manager Designate' (Bull 1998) to initially help, then take over from the man who had dedicated well over 30 years of his working life to Southampton FC. The cagey wording of the advert was perhaps to be expected. Saints' unprecedented run of success had been built on stability at the top. The leading candidate was John Mortimore, the Farnborough-born former assistant to Bates, who was ready for a return to the English game. Chairman George Reader was certainly keen, but the job title proved a sticking point. Mortimore recalled: 'Had Southampton said "team manager" I think I would have come. I'd had three years as assistant manager and coach and I'd done my apprenticeship' (in Bull 1998). Instead, persuaded by his old friend and former Chelsea teammate, Ron Tindall, who had become general manager, Mortimore opted instead to take the vacant manager's job at Fratton Park. Saints turned to another rising young manager, Lawrie McMenemy, who had guided Grimsby from Fourth to Third Divisions on a shoestring.

At Fratton Park, John Deacon rang the changes, his take-over complete as he became chairman. Ron Davies, almost 31, signed for a £40,000 fee. Within days, Wales full-back Phil Roberts shattered Pompey's record fee when arriving in a £55,000 deal from Third Division Bristol Rovers. It was a short-lived transfer record. In early May, Deacon forked out £100,000 to sign winger Peter Marinello who, with his flowing locks, had been dubbed the 'Scots George Best' when he arrived at Arsenal three years before.

Portsmouth's first game under the new regime was a testimonial for stalwart midfielder Albert McCann against West Ham. Marinello was mesmerising and Davies bagged a hat-trick in a 4-2 win. An astonishing 22,000 attendance – bigger than all but three of Saints' First Division gates – provided yet further evidence that Pompey were finally ready for lift off. With a new white-with-two-vertical-blue-stripes kit, 'new' Pompey in practice proved as fallible as ever. Even the arrival of a new central defensive partnership of Paul Went (Fulham) and Malcolm Manley (Leicester) for a combined total of £210,000 in December 1973 didn't help much, and Pompey finished sixteenth. A lot of money had been spent for a one-place improvement.

At least the Cup cheered, more than 33,000 packing Fratton for its first Sunday game on 27th January 1974 to see a 0-0 draw with Orient in the fourth round. Pompey eventually won a second replay but went out 0-1 at Nottingham Forest in the fifth, despite taking an estimated 15,000 fans to the City Ground. Saints also lost at the same stage, although their defeat at home to Third Division Wrexham was infinitely more disappointing. With McMenemy now installed as manager, Saints were sliding fast. Seventh in December, they now faced a spring battle against the drop, although the bank-breaking £275,000 arrival in March of Chelsea's temperamental, but gifted striker Peter Osgood was intended to pull them out of their slump. A run of just two wins in 21 games saw them marooned in twentieth place and relegated with a match to spare. This time the rules conspired against them: they became the first club to to suffer from the introduction of three up, three down between the top two divisions. Added to which, they became the first club from Division One since the War to be relegated with 36 points. There was much to be said for Saints' fans' lament that their team had been too good to go down.

By the standards of the period, the status quo had been restored. Somehow it seemed the south coast was never destined to enjoy two clubs in the top division together. Portsmouth could have laid down an early marker for the forthcoming 1974-75 season, as Southampton were at Fratton for a testimonial on Friday, 3rd May 1974 for Gordon Neave, a former Pompey player, trainer and now physio. Honours ended even, 0-0, Saints defender Paul Bennett taking the eye when preventing Mick Mellows and old-boy Davies from scoring. Unfortunately the headlines were made by a pitch invasion by 'scores of rival youths' and the front page of the *News* the following day reported nineteen people had been arrested – all from the Portsmouth area – and 87 ejected from the ground.

This was football hooliganism 70s-style; almost as much a part of the fabric of the game as silk scarves, stewed onions and stinking toilets. 'Experience has taught us to expect trouble whenever Portsmouth and Southampton meet and last night we were prepared. Last time the two teams met at Fratton was two years ago in another testimonial and we had comparable figures of fans ejected and arrested on that occasion.' That was the depressing conclusion of Police Superintendent A Feltham, in charge of security at Fratton.

Unfortunately it was only an appetiser. The first competitive meeting between the sides for more than eight years was scheduled for 14th September 1974 at The Dell, by which time both clubs were already in disarray. Saints had three defeats and three draws to their name, while Pompey were only marginally better off with a win and a draw in five matches. Going into the game the pair were nineteenth and twentieth respectively. However, a 1-5 midweek thumping by First Division Derby in the League Cup had shattered Pompey's morale, already close to rock-bottom after Mortimore was sensationally suspended on the eve of the home game with West Brom a week earlier. The new manager was already waiting in the wings, as former Liverpool forward Ian St John was primed to take over on Monday morning.

However, it was Ron Tindall who picked the side to face Saints and it proved to be a rumbustious affair on and off the pitch. With Treorchy referee Clive Thomas in charge, fresh from World Cup controversy after he disallowed Brazil's 'winner' against Sweden by blowing the final whistle as the ball was rocketing towards the net, both sets of players had been warned that they needed to be on their best behaviour. Although it was not a particularly dirty game, Thomas was a stickler for the rules. Five players were booked and Saints defender Jim Steele sent off, late on, for a second caution after he hauled down Marinello in full flight. By then, Southampton were 2-1 up, the class of Peter Osgood and Mick Channon making the difference.

Prior to kick-off, Davies had been given a standing ovation by everyone as he led Pompey out, but the bad blood between the two sets of fans was underlined by an ugly twenty-yard-wide concrete scar of terracing on the Milton Road End. Patrolled by a line of shirt-sleeved police, it separated the Portsmouth contingent, which had arrived early to set up camp in the heart of 'enemy' territory, from their counterparts. About 300 Pompey fans had never even reached The Dell, detained on a train heading west after some compartments were vandalised. The miscreants were held at the police station exercise yard at Southampton Civic Centre, and only freed once the game was well underway.

On the pitch, Pompey's spirit was no match for Channon's elusive running and Osgood's clinical finishing. On the stroke of half-time Osgood gave Saints the lead with a brilliant volley from a tight angle. During the interval, Thomas entered both dressing rooms to lecture players about their 'off the ball' conduct, but the niggling continued, Osgood lucky to stay on the field after his apparent 'elbow' left Richie Reynolds with a cut eye. When Ian Turner in the Saints goal manhandled Davies as he attempted to win a header, Thomas awarded a spot-kick, duly converted by the former Southampton striker. However, Saints sealed the points with twelve minutes to go when Osgood netted after a goalmouth scramble. Brian O'Neil's two-footed lunge at Norman Piper in the final minute provided the final booking of the afternoon, but at least that was the end of the ugliness. The two sets of fans dispersed relatively peacefully afterwards, thanks in part to a 150-strong police presence.

Despite the arrival of new manager Ian St John, by November Pompey were bottom of the table and Davies had departed, finally making his 'dream move' to Old Trafford in exchange for former Chelsea and Arsenal midfielder George Graham. Manchester United, lest it be forgotten, were 'slumming it' for a season in the Second Division and their visit provided Saints and Pompey with their biggest home gates of the season – 21,866 and 25,608 respectively.

By the time Saints arrived at Fratton Park on Boxing Day 1974 for the return, Saints were safely in mid-table, while Pompey were showing some signs of life, three wins in the month lifting them clear of danger. A win would have taken Pompey above Saints, but any hopes they could retrieve their lost local pride was undone in three second-half minutes. First, Osgood looped a header over Pompey keeper David Best from a David Peach corner in the thirteenth minute, then O'Brien and Bobby Stokes combined to send Peach away to beat the advancing keeper. That Pompey had hit the post after ten minutes and seen Turner make a wonder save from the rebound counted for nothing. Much huffing and puffing from the home side could only produce a late Piper goal, from a pass from Billy Wilson, and it was the Saints fans who were celebrating at the end with a rendition of their traditional 'Oh when the Saints…' anthem. Saints boss Lawrie McMenemy paid tribute to their vocal support: 'They made more noise than they have done all season.' Saints' Bobby Stokes, playing his first Fratton derby, savoured the moment: 'This was one match in which I had to play and winning here is like a dream come true,' he said, having recovered from an ankle injury to take his place. The match passed off peacefully inside and outside the ground, the morning kick-off and seasonal goodwill diffusing the tension. A lesson to be learned for the scheduling of fixtures in the current era perhaps?

Despite their defeat, Pompey's form continued to improve and in the end both sides were comfortably clear of the drop, finishing four places and four points apart, Saints the higher in thirteenth place. The teams met once more, on Tuesday 6th May, as Ray Hiron celebrated a well-earned testimonial, but a wretchedly small 5,000 gate at Fratton underlined the moribund state of south coast football. At least Hiron, released by the club, had the satisfaction of scoring two early goals, the first a header after 35 seconds, the second a nonchalant flick after Marinello's shot came back off a post. The second half was all Saints, but they only had Stokes' late diversion of Peach's free-kick to show for their dominance.

Advantage Pompey for the coming campaign? The optimists would have thought so, but a glance at the visitors' team-sheet underlined the reason why Pompey were about to fall apart. In addition to Stokes and Middleton, Emsworth-born Malcolm Waldron and Fareham-born Pat Earles were also in the Saints squad. Sadly, Portsmouth-born Steve Mills was not playing, having been badly injured in a car accident in February 1975, which would end his career. Pompey had resurrected their youth policy in 1972 and their reserve side in 1973, but a generation of talent had metaphorically, as well as literally 'gone west'. With Deacon's pockets now empty, Pompey were close to sporting, as well as financial, bankruptcy.

For Portsmouth fans the events of the first half of the 1975-76 season must rank as close to the worst the club had ever known. Pledges made to St John of money to buy players had proved illusory. Instead, he had to use his contacts north of the border to recruit young Scottish players on free transfers, as well as lure veteran Liverpool defender and former team-mate Chris Lawler. Put simply, the team was just not good enough. By 6th December they were cast adrift at the bottom with just one win to their credit and a club-record eight-match losing run in their debit column. On 27th September they had travelled to The Dell to play a reviving Saints side. Pre-match, Lawrie Mac said the right things by saying it would be a close match: 'It should be one heck of a game and I don't think there will be a lot in it at the close.' Wrong. Saints ended up 4-0 winners. The main difference between the sides was Mick Channon. After 40 minutes he angled home after Pompey keeper Graham Lloyd saved his first effort, then after 63 minutes an outrageous, swirling shot from the by-line found the top corner. ' I meant it,' Channon told a dubious press corps post-match. His unchallenged header from Peach's corner with ten minutes to go sealed a memorable hat-trick. Saints' other goal came nine minutes into the second half, when Peach's free-kick went in off a post.

Channon's final goal sparked an exodus of 300 Pompey fans, congregated on the Archers Road End, who intended to head off Saints fans leaving from the East Stand exits. More than 250 police struggled for a short time to contain a frightening situation. During the game frequent scuffles had broken out, but the violence was judged to be 'low key'. A police spokesman commented that the twenty ejections, 'several' arrests, and minor property damage was 'nothing more than usual for a home match'. As an illustration of the parlous state of football in this period, his assessment could not be better.

The match was also at the root of Pompey fans' perceived bias against their club – a belief that thrives to this day – by the Southampton-based broadcast media. 'Southern Soccer' was a periodic Sunday afternoon show on ITV during the 1970s. Their editing of this particular match chose to leave on the cutting room floor two shots by Reynolds, one which struck the post, the other the crossbar, at stages in the game when Pompey were pressing hard. Had either of those efforts gone in, things might have been different as St John rued afterwards: 'I thought we did well and to lose by four goals was absolutely ridiculous. In fact I think we had more efforts on goal than they did and ended up with nothing.' In retrospect, McMenemy's verdict, harsh though it was, was undeniably fair: 'Pompey did not try to shut things up. They tried to play good football but basically the difference was we had better players'.

Saints and Pompey were now set on sharply diverging trajectories. Following Pompey's 0-2 home defeat by relegation rivals Oxford in November 1975, the Monday headline in the *News* summed things up: 'On a clear day you can see division three'. Meanwhile, Saints were racking up five straight wins in December to move to the fringes of the promotion race.

That month also saw the course of history – in this part of the world at least – changed. Pompey's main problem was scoring goals, so a swap deal was engineered with Bobby Stokes 'coming home' while Paul Went moved to The Dell (Chalk and Holley 1988). The deal foundered as the Paulsgrove-born boy couldn't agree terms at Fratton Park. Good decision. Although Pompey's second half of the season was good enough that – had it been replicated in the first half – it might just have kept them up, the dreaded drop was looking unavoidable by 27th March 1976, after a 0-1 home defeat to promotion chasing West Brom.

Seven days later Pompey were due to host Southampton, but the game was rescheduled for the following Tuesday as Saints were otherwise engaged. Their promotion hopes had been undone by inconsistent form, a cause not helped by a blossoming FA Cup run. A third round 2-1 replay win at First Division Aston Villa completed a notable south coast 'double' as even wretched Pompey managed to win the previous night in their own replay at Villa's divisional rivals Birmingham. Blackpool were then undone by Southampton in the fourth round, before West Brom were scorched 4-0 in a fifth round replay. In the quarter-finals Saints were paired with the competition's surprise package Bradford City, but a classy finish by Jim McCalliog as Osgood flicked up a free-kick to be volleyed in put paid to the Fourth Division side's resistance. So, on Saturday, 3rd April 1976 Saints yet again found themselves one game from Wembley. Standing in their way were Third Division Crystal Palace, managed by the flamboyant Malcolm Allison, but late goals from Paul Gilchrist and a Peach penalty put Saints and their followers in heaven.

Three days later Southampton were at Fratton Park. Defeat for the home side would effectively extinguish their faint hopes of escaping the drop, despite there being five games to go. Saints' preparations were hampered by the post-Palace celebrations. Jim Steele, McCalliog and Osgood were all sidelined for a 'breach of club discipline', namely breaking a curfew at the club's hotel at Hayling Island on the Monday night. Before the kick-off Pompey's players had formed a guard of honour to applaud the their rivals' achievement as they entered the arena and the gesture racked the atmosphere up a notch as Mike Neasom's *News* report acknowledged: 'The Chimes boomed out to stifle the roar of marching Saints that greeted Peter Rodrigues and his much-changed side'.

Chances were at a premium throughout an evenly but fiercely contested game, but going into injury-time Saints' Paul Gilchrist crossed and Pompey's defence fatally hesitated, hoping for an offside flag. Pat Earles laid the ball back and Channon fired home off the post from fifteen yards, sending the red and white masses behind the Milton End goal into ecstasy. Within seconds, Pompey's hooligan fringe abandoned the Fratton End and circled the terracing, as you could in those days, to show their feelings with a flurry of fists and boots, but mercifully trouble outside the ground was minimal.

To condemn your most bitter rivals to relegation in such dramatic circumstances must rank highly in any 'memorable moments' poll. Those Southampton supporters present had travelled just seventeen miles and found paradise. But a little over four weeks later, some 20,000 of them, and many more who couldn't get tickets, would relish the most magical moment of all.

One common jibe by Pompey fans is that Southampton could not sell their entire allocation of Wembley tickets for the FA Cup final against Manchester United, scheduled for Saturday, 1st May. This is untrue, although the myth is given credibility by the fact that many Pompey fans queued along with thousands of others to buy tickets for the occasion. Some of them even went to Wembley to support Saints!

Another Saints claim – that around 250,000 people lined the streets when the team returned to the city the following day – is often rubbished by their rivals as a rose-tinted exaggeration. However, contemporary accounts had the police estimate of the crowds as exactly that. The fuss, incidentally, was generated in the first place by a bobbling 83rd-minute left-foot cross-shot, looking suspiciously offside, despite BBC TV commentator David Coleman's immediate assertion he was onside, which crept past United keeper Alex Stepney just inside the far post. It was the only goal of the game and it won the Cup against the odds – just like 37 years before – for the south coast underdogs. The scorer was Bobby Stokes. A Saints legend was born … in Portsmouth.

Chapter 9

~ Worlds Apart, but not for Long ~

(1976-83)

Southampton's status as holders of the FA Cup gave them an international fame and prestige that Portsmouth never enjoyed, not even in their glory, glory days. The television age was upon us and the Wembley final had been beamed live around the world to a global audience still in thrall to the oldest Cup competition in the world.

Victory also meant Saints would be back at Wembley in August for the traditional Charity Shield contest between the League champions and the FA Cup winners. Pompey had once had a share in the Shield, back in 1949, after a 1-1 draw with Wolves at Highbury, but Saints were unable to even match that, losing 0-1 to Bob Paisley's first great Liverpool side. It was an encouraging performance, however, for a Saints side that were short-priced favourites for promotion to the First Division. A pre-season win in the Tennant-Caledonian Cup, beating Glasgow Rangers 2-1 at Ibrox in the final, also hinted at better things.

So, Southampton's seven-match winless run to start the 1976-77 season was quite unexpected. Four straight wins, including a 6-2 thrashing of Wolves at Molineux steadied things, but by Christmas sluggish Saints were still in the bottom half of the table. But if Saints thought they had things bad, they knew nothing. Pompey's mounting financial crisis came to a head in September and for a few days the club teetered on the brink of bankruptcy. Backed by the *News*, supporters rallied round and raised more than £20,000 for the SOS Pompey campaign. On the field, a dreadful start to their Third Division campaign – just one win in their first thirteen games – was not arrested until Ian St John began pitching products of the club's youth policy to the fore. A 4-1 win at York on 18th December lifted Pompey out of the dreaded bottom four. On Boxing Day promotion-chasing Brighton were in town and again the Portsmouth public turned up in numbers. More than 32,000, helped by a sizeable Seagulls following, turned out to see David Kemp's early goal earn a famous victory.

Saints' gathering momentum in the European Cup-Winners' Cup compensated for their disappointing League form. The 4-0 thrashing of French giants Olympique Marseille at The Dell in September was, ironically, Saints' first win of the season. The second leg safely negotiated, Irish League Carrick Rangers were easily dispatched in the second round, ensuring a place in the quarter-finals in the spring. By then, McMenemy had demonstrated his knack of signing players who had a point to prove. He added Arsenal midfielder Alan Ball to his squad in December, to follow the signing of Norwich striker Ted MacDougall in September. Their quality transformed Saints' prospects. Twelve League wins after Christmas weren't enough to get back in the promotion race, but the foundations for the following season were laid. Saints' hold on the FA Cup was loosened, but only after two tremendous battles with Manchester United in the fifth round. Dreams of European glory were only extinguished by a 2-3 aggregate defeat by Belgian greats Anderlecht.

By contrast, Pompey's grip even on the Third Division remained in the balance. A 1-2 home defeat to fellow strugglers Grimsby on 30th April 30 1977, followed by a 0-2 loss at Mansfield 48 hours later, proved too much for Chairman Deacon, who suspended Ian St John and turned to club secretary and legend Jimmy Dickinson to step in to fill the breach. The last two of three vital points necessary to stave off relegation to the Fourth Division were gained only in the penultimate game of the season, at home to York, and in the euphoria that followed, Dickinson was persuaded to take the job full time.

Money was still tight at Fratton, but in March 1977 the club had somehow scraped together £5,000 to sign Saints forward Paul Gilchrist – the only money St John ever got – and in the summer of 1977 Dickinson also signed goalkeeper Steve Middleton, released by the Dell club. The new boss was also negotiating to bring home the one player who truly got away from Pompey, Bobby Stokes, who had spent the summer playing in the United States after being given a free transfer.

As Portsmouth's 1977-78 season got off to a reasonable start, Stokes was finally persuaded to put pen to paper and even scored on his debut in early September, as Chesterfield were beaten 3-0 at Fratton Park. That was the high point: it was downhill for him and Pompey from then on. Within a month Stokes was the target for the boo-boys, unforgiving of his role in Saints' finest hour, as he struggled for form, fitness, and confidence. 'I'm really choked; I'm desperately keen to do well for Pompey and yet nothing seems to be going right,' he lamented to the *Sports Mail.* Middleton was also in the firing line, his slip in October gifting Swindon a replay as Pompey tried to reach the fourth round of the League Cup.

While Portsmouth were sliding into oblivion, Southampton were in the thick of the Second Division promotion race. The loss of Mick Channon in the summer, sold to top-flight Manchester City to enable him to pursue his England ambitions, was offset by the signing of Phil Boyer from Norwich, while the arrival of grizzly defender Chris Nicholl from Aston Villa finally gave Saints an experienced core around which promising talents like midfielder Steve Williams could flourish. Unfettered by Cup runs, Saints were rarely out of the top four and, with three games to go, just three points were needed to ensure a return to the big boys. Two points were gleaned at Luton on 22nd April, and by a twist of fate Saints travelled to Brisbane Road, scene of their promotion glory twelve years beforehand, to play Orient – temporarily shorn of their 'Leyton' prefix. Once again 12,000 Saints fans swelled the gate to 19,000 and, to keep the coincidences going, Saints made their point drawing 1-1. Now, as then, it was a header, from another young forward, Tony Funnell, which did the trick. A win against Spurs in the final match would have delivered the title to Saints, but the London club secured a 0-0 draw and the point they needed to go up behind Saints in third place. That result meant Brighton, chasing a second successive promotion, missed out.

As Southampton marched proudly back into the big time, Pompey were planning for life in the basement. Seven wins from 46 games told its own story, the gut-wrenching performance at home to Plymouth, as Pompey surrendered 1-5 on 21st March, effectively opened the trap door. A 0-2 home defeat to Oxford a fortnight later meant they dropped through it. The speed at which the two clubs' orbits had diverged was breathtaking. By then, Stokes had left Fratton Park, to pick up the threads of his career in the States. With the relegation issue still in the balance, the club were understandably reluctant to extend his one-year contract, given his poor form, so in early March they parted company. A clearly gutted Stokes accepted the decision: 'I can understand Pompey's position; I'm the first to admit my time here has been a disaster. I hoped I might provide the spark Pompey needed and I haven't.' With Gilchrist out of form and out of the side too, at least Middleton was an ex-Saint who could still get a game, although he couldn't escape the jeers of the unforgiving sections of the crowd. Middleton's part in a cock-up with Paul Cahill over a thrown-in back-pass, which gave Plymouth a 2-0 lead in that fateful game, had put him well and truly back in the hot seat. His last game for the club was in a 0-2 defeat at Chester on 26th April. Three days later, sixteen-year-old Alan Knight made his debut in a rare 1-0 win, against Rotherham. A brighter future had been glimpsed.

If there was one thing Portsmouth could console themselves with, as they prepared for the start of the 1978-79 season in the Fourth Division, it was that they had never lost their first match in a new competition. The Southern League (first and second divisions), all three divisions of the Football League, the League Cup, and even the FA Cup had all been successfully, or at least not unsuccessfully, debuted. That proud record ended on 19th August as Bradford City counter-punched their way to a 1-0 win at Fratton Park, thanks to a first-half David McNiven goal. The attendance of 8,000 was highly respectable by the Fourth Division standards of the day, but the balance of football power had fundamentally shifted to the west. If Pompey fans thought things couldn't get any worse, the events of the following week proved them wrong. On the Tuesday, a first win of the season looked likely as they led 2-1 at York City, only for three goals in eight minutes by the home side, and a sending off for Peter Ellis, to contribute to a 3-5 defeat. This truly was the nadir. Pompey were only kept off the bottom of the entire Football League by virtue of the fact that new-boys Wigan Athletic had scored even fewer goals in their equally catastrophic start. The ultimate ignominy – Portsmouth FC, proud Pompey, twice champions of England, 92nd and last – was only averted by a goal five minutes from time by Steve Davey, a striker signed from Hereford in the summer, to earn the first point at Hartlepool.

The fixture list also underlined the new reality. 'Derby days' now meant trips inside a week to Aldershot and Bournemouth at the end of September. Although Southampton lost 1-3 on that same opening day, against Norwich – these were the pre-Premiership days when all four divisions started simultaneously – a draw with Bolton, then a home win against Middlesbrough, followed by a 5-2 thrashing of Birmingham at St Andrews in the League Cup, soon had Lawrie McMenemy's blend of youth and experience firmly ensconced in mid-table.

By this time, too, the hapless Paul Gilchrist was finally able to end his Pompey nightmare as Swindon signed him for a nominal fee. On leaving, he offered a few insights into the burgeoning bitterness and distrust Pompey fans seemed to reserve for ex-Saints: 'Things didn't go too badly at the start, but then the crowd didn't help. They weren't prepared to forgive me for coming from Southampton. I knew there was tremendous rivalry between the two clubs and their supporters but I didn't realise it went so deep. Look what they did to Stokesie – and he was a Portsmouth lad.' He was soon followed out of the club by goalkeeper Steve Middleton, whose time at Fratton Park had apparently been so traumatic that in October 1978 he retired from playing professional football altogether to run a pub in the city. Adding to the irony was the fact that Emsworth-born Malcolm Waldron – another one of Pompey's who got away – was forming an impressive partnership with Chris Nicholl at the heart of Saints' defence.

Although Southampton continued to scuffle around the lower reaches of the First Division, relegation was never really a threat – so inept did Chelsea, QPR and Birmingham prove to be that season. Instead, now bolstered by the cosmopolitan touch of Yugoslav full-back Ivan Golac, Saints were on their way to Wembley in the League Cup, qualifying by beating Leeds in a two-leg semi-final. Having earned a 2-2 draw in the snowy wastes of Yorkshire, Terry Curran scored the vital goal at The Dell. The icy grip had extended even this far south, but relented enough to allow the game to go ahead.

McMenemy was quick to use the team's success to put pressure on Southampton City Council to help develop the antiquated Dell. By now the ground had a capacity of 26,000, half of the lower tier of the East

Stand having been converted into seats. Talks had been on-going with civic officials for three years, the stumbling block being the financing of any development, put at anything between £6 million and £12 million. Vague talk of completion of a redeveloped site by 1987 was mooted, success on the field or otherwise. McMenemy would be long gone, come back and left again, before this particular nut would be cracked. Whether Southampton needed a bigger stadium – better undoubtedly, but larger? – was a moot point and the old chestnut of the respective support on the south coast was given another airing.

Many Saints fans will concede that in the late 1970s their away support was far from impressive. For instance, only 500 made the trip to Elland Road for the semi-final in January 1979. Admittedly it was the worst winter for sixteen years, but Pompey took considerably more than that to Wigan – a longer journey – a few weeks later for a Fourth Division match. That didn't stop the battle being joined in the columns of the *Sports Mail*. Ian Darke – yes, that Ian Darke of Sky Sports fame – an exiled Pompey fan in Blaby, Leicestershire lit the flame, citing his 'amusement' at The Dell being referred to as a 'rabbit hutch', adding 'I would have thought this was being distinctly unkind to rabbits. I am told hutches are warm, comfortable and (for rabbits) spacious. The Dell is none of these things.'

Southampton's return to the big time had seen gates average 21,000, a figure Saints fan Dawn Chase used to strike back, claiming this was 'good', while ridiculing Pompey's average of around 11,000. Among others, the prevailing mood of Pompey fans was summed up by Steve Burgess, of Hilsea: 'Does she really think Southampton's average home gate is "decent" when one considers their success over the past three years? I think it is appallingly low. Her attempts to ridicule Pompey's home average is equally misplaced. Let us not forget what has happened to Pompey in those same three years … I conclude we have some of the most loyal supporters in the league. If the fortunes of the two clubs were reversed, I doubt very much if the difference in gates would be as close as 10,000 per match'.

The spat, predictable and parochial perhaps, serves to encapsulate a school of thought which runs deep, particularly in the generation of Pompey supporters who grew up during the 1960s and 70s. For them, Pompey had the history and the stadium – all that was lacking was a decent team. With that, they insisted, the Portsmouth public would come thronging back in huge numbers. The case 'for' would cite 32,000 people who saw the game against Brighton in the Third Division on Boxing Day 1976, or a similar number who had turned out for the humiliating FA Cup replay exit against Charlton earlier that year. By such reasoning, Saints were a small-town team with an inadequate ground and small-time support. If Pompey were halfway up the First Division and at Wembley, Fratton Park would be packed to the rafters – went the theory – and for many, that record is still stuck in the same groove 25 years on. The fact that Saints still had a 'reasonable number', according to club secretary Brian Truscott, of their 30,000 ticket allocation for sale less than a week before their 1979 League Cup final against Nottingham Forest was also considered evidence for the prosecution.

A criticism frequently levelled at the Blues by the Reds is that Pompey's bitterness towards their neighbours is based on simple jealousy of Saints' success. Not exactly. Many Pompey fans, in fact, don't regard Saints as being 'successful' at all. 'Success' is measured by titles, not finishing seventh. If anything, the so-called bitterness is fuelled more by that marvellous German word *schadenfreude* – the taking of pleasure in the misfortunes of others – or, in this case, the absence of it. What many Pompey fans would really like to see is Saints suffer. Not relatively, like losing a derby match or finishing below Pompey in the League, but truly suffer like Pompey has over the past 40 years or so. Only then, they maintain, would the true depth of Saints' support, or more likely lack of it, be revealed.

Southampton eventually lost the final, with a full complement of fans, 2-3 to Forest. McMenemy was continuing to build a side which would, as no one of Blue persuasion could deny, transform Saints into the great entertainers of the First Division. Lawrie Mac pulled off another of his transfer coups back in December, recruiting former Arsenal star Charlie George from Derby County in a club-record £350,000 deal. Injuries would hamper the start to George's Dell career, but his signing was a prelude to what remains one of the most sensational transfers of all time, in February 1980.

But we are getting slightly ahead of ourselves. In the week following their Wembley defeat, Saints saw another Wembley trail go cold, as they drew with Arsenal on the Monday, then lost 0-2 at Highbury two days later in an FA Cup quarter-final replay. The ice and snow had forced a fixture pile up which would also contribute to an ultimately disappointing season for Portsmouth. After their traumatic start to life in the basement, Pompey had perked up, and were in the running for promotion until the spring when their form fell away, rusty after playing just one League game in six weeks between December and February. They also had to ride the blow of manager Jimmy Dickinson suffering a massive heart attack after a 1-1 draw at Barnsley at the end of March. At the end of the season Frank Burrows replaced Dickinson. Pompey's most loyal servant would recover, although never completely, and he died in November 1982.

With Saints now firmly established back in the top flight, the new man at the helm at Fratton Park had a simple task: to prevent Pompey becoming an established 'Fourth Division' club. The pressure to deliver wasn't helped by the fact that Saints now had new 'rivals' in the shape of Brighton and Hove Albion, 60 miles along the coast in Sussex, who had recovered from their last-day disappointment in April 1978 to clinch promotion to the First Division for the first time. Incredible to relate, sandwiched between them, Portsmouth were in the Fourth!

With half a new team, financed by the sale of centre-half Steve Foster to Brighton, Pompey made a start to 1979-80 which was little short of sensational, racking up 40 goals and twelve wins in the first fourteen League matches. That run climaxed with the visit of Bradford City on 23rd October. City were no slouches themselves, with ten wins and a draw in thirteen matches. Almost 24,000 turned up at Fratton – the biggest Fourth Division attendance since the early 1960s, and better than several in the First – to see Pompey romp to a 4-1 win. The victory was thanks in part to a brace of goals from Phil Ashworth, who four weeks beforehand was playing for Rochdale reserves. Ashworth remains, statistically at least, Pompey's most prolific forward ever, with four goals in two starts, plus a substitute appearance. The fact that that attendance exceeded The Dell's for the visit of Leeds seven days later was not lost on those vociferous Pompey fans of a certain generation mentioned above.

At least, Saints could argue they were now playing to full houses every week. Capacity had been reduced to 24,000 as the lower tier of the West Stand had undergone the same treatment as the East Stand the previous summer. And their own start to the season had been almost as impressive, a 4-1 win over Crystal Palace in early October lifting them to third place. Prodigal son Mick Channon had been re-signed from Manchester City and, in partnership with Phil Boyer, the goals flowed. Wrexham went for eight over two legs in the League Cup, Spurs were beaten 5-2 and Derby 4-0 at The Dell. The first Hants-Sussex First Division derby had ended with honours even, as Saints and Seagulls drew 0-0 at The Goldstone. In late October Saints wobbled. Three straight defeats prompted McMenemy to find £350,000 to end former Sunderland and Manchester City defender Dave Watson's nightmare spell in Germany at Werder Bremen. Signing a current England international was something of a coup, but McMenemy's contacts would shortly deliver something better still.

Southampton's form continued to dip in November, and skipper Alan Ball, now 35, bore the brunt of the terrace frustration, although it was Waldron who paid the price with the manager, losing his place when Chris Nicholl regained fitness. Consistently unpredictable, Saints rallied and were fourth in the League by the New Year, at the heart of the race for a European place. Pompey saw out 1979 with a 6-1 annihilation of Northampton which left them short-priced favourites for promotion – if achieved it would be their first since 1962.

Both McMenemy and Burrows sought to strengthen their squads at this crucial time. How they did so underlined the chasm that now existed between the two clubs. Frank Burrows' ability to persuade central defender Alan Garner to step down two divisions from Watford to join Pompey's bandwagon might have captured the headlines any other week. However, McMenemy well and truly trumped him. Fresh from a 5-1 thrashing of Brighton, underlining Saints' undoubted southern superiority, came a staggering announcement on Monday, 11th February 1980. Twice European Footballer of the Year and European Cup winner with Liverpool, Kevin Keegan, would be joining the Saints from German club SV Hamburg on the expiry of his contract in the summer. The news caused a sensation. How did the most amazing of transfer coups ever come about? According to Lawrie, he'd got talking to Keegan about getting hold of some special wall lamps, which were manufactured in Hamburg, for his house. 'So everything's ended well. I've got my lamp and his signature,' he quipped at the press conference to announce the deal to the stunned local and national media.

Keegan's arrival was timed to coincide with yet another Council meeting to try to secure an alternative site to The Dell. Not for the first time, nor the last, agreement couldn't be found and Southampton would now face the problem of how to fit a quart into a pint pot. With 18,000 season ticket holders already, Saints were not in a position to welcome the floating fans who were drawn by the prospect of seeing one of the great players of his generation. At 29, Keegan was not far off his prime. Ticket prices, too, would rise, with a 50 per cent increase announced as supporters, in part, picked up the tab for Keegan's arrival. A stuttering end to the season also meant the high hopes of Keegan assisting Saints in Europe had to be put on hold.

Portsmouth, too, suffered end of season agonies, as failure to put away bottom-four sides Hereford and Crewe at Fratton Park kept their promotion hopes on ice. Only on the last day, as Pompey won 2-0 at Northampton, while Bradford City lost 0-1 at Peterborough, was the once seemingly inevitable promotion clinched. Pompey were back. Well, on their way back, at least. The local rivals even had occasion to play one another at the end of the season, Southampton putting out a first team for Duggie Reid's testimonial. Having retired as Portsmouth groundsman, 11,000 turned out to salute one of the true Pompey greats. Saints reinforced the huge gap in class by winning 4-2. Steve Williams gave them the lead, then Steve Perrin levelled. Malcolm Waldron converted a penalty after eighteen minutes, only for Perrin to square things again. Goals from Mick Channon at the end of each half ensured the local pecking order remained undisrupted.

With Kevin Keegan aboard, McMenemy had high hopes his side could push on and establish themselves as one of the 'big' clubs, although the limited facilities at The Dell would remain a constant brake on such lofty ambitions. However, the start of the 1980-81 season promised much. Saints were second by mid-September, although that start also included one of those bizarre results which make football the wonderful game it is. Having defeated Graham Taylor's Second Division Watford 4-0 at The Dell in the second round of the League Cup, the return was seen as a simple formality. Think again. In an incredible evening's football, Watford hit back to force extra-time at 5-1, then scored twice more to record an improbable 7-1 victory. Pompey fans – 18,000 of them – streaming out of Fratton Park having witnessed their own giant-killing act as Second Division Oldham were beaten on away goals, exulted in the result.

Saints ran out of steam in the League, too, and were languishing in mid-table by November. A packed Dell, which had seen Manchester City beaten 2-0 on the opening day, thanks to a brace from Channon, was attracting fewer than 19,000 by the time their unbeaten home record was surrendered to Stoke in October. Meanwhile, Pompey were in the process of proving their supposed pulling power, by averaging 15,000 as the momentum of the previous season's exploits propelled them toward the head of the Third Division. In late October Pompey took the best part of that number to Anfield, to face reigning champions Liverpool in a fourth round League Cup-tie on a Tuesday night. They might have lost 1-4, but Pompey's reputation for travelling away in large numbers – complete with ticker-tape welcome when the players' ran out – was forged that night.

On the field, McMenemy was also rebuilding, selling Phil Boyer to Manchester City as young-gun Steve Moran showed that Saints' talent-spotting knack hadn't deserted them. The Warsash-born striker made an audacious start to his senior career with 21 goals in 36 League and cup appearances in 1980-81. Saints dragged themselves up the table in the New Year, eventually securing a UEFA Cup place, thanks to their seventh place finish. This was a fine team, underlined by the fact that in their 1-0 win over Manchester United in March Saints fielded four England captains – Channon, Watson, Ball and Keegan (Chalk and Holley 1988). Saints might even have finished fourth, but for taking just two points from their final four games. Over at Fratton, Pompey's promotion hopes stayed alive until April, but an Easter defeat at Reading killed them. Pompey fans also had the consolation of glimpsing a brighter future when their youth side beat Saints 4-2 at Fratton Park in the third round of the FA Youth Cup in January, watched by 1,700.

During the summer of 1981, Saints had acted to address the capacity issue at The Dell, demolishing the old Milton Road End, chocolate boxes and all, and erecting a new two-tiered stand. This maintained the ground's unusual claim of being the only one in England with an uncovered 'upper' terrace. The new stand provided an additional 1,000 standing places, increasing the capacity to 25,500.

Despite Southampton's flying start to the 1981-82 season, with five straight home wins, The Dell's new capacity was never tested and the gate even dropped below 19,000 when Notts County arrived in October. Yet more disappointing were the attendances for Saints' latest excursion into Europe. First up were League of Ireland's Limerick, ironically player-managed by an old Pompey favourite – Eoin Hand. In the away leg, Saints killed the tie by winning 3-0, but that cannot excuse a gate of fewer than 13,000 for the return, which ended 1-1. Nor did it smack of huge latent attendances bursting to get into The Dell. It was a similar story in the second round. Saints staged the first leg against high-profile Sporting Lisbon, but not even 19,000 turned out. Saints' 2-4 defeat also put paid to hopes of progressing.

In the League, though, Southampton were thriving, prompted by veteran Alan Ball, back for a second spell at The Dell after a stint as player-manager at Blackpool ended in relegation and the sack. By the beginning of December 1981 Saints were second and McMenemy must have been dreaming of bringing the championship to the city for the first time. Reacting to criticism that his team was ageing, he explained: 'We must always be looking to make progress and to get better so now we have got to try to win the first division and who is to say we can't do that?' Saints' class was emphasised when they had a chance to go top for the first time in their 96-year history by beating European Cup winners Liverpool at Anfield, then Manchester United at The Dell in successive weeks. All that stood between them and the summit were struggling Brighton, who came to The Dell on a chilly December evening. Former Pompey favourite Steve Foster, born and bred in Portsmouth, skippered the Seagulls. He was imperious that night, displaying the form which would earn him a place in the England's 1982 World Cup party for Spain six months later. Saints' dreams were dashed, temporarily at least, by a 0-2 defeat.

Defeat by Brighton only delayed the scaling of Everest by six weeks, when Kevin Keegan's sharply-taken goal at Middlesbrough on 30th January carried Saints two points clear at the top. But by then a curious entry in the register of matches between Saints and Pompey had been made. Down at Fratton Park, Pompey fans had no choice but to grin and bear Saints' success, particularly as their own team was dropping perilously close to the relegation zone. Following Saints' defeat by Brighton, the weather intervened, wiping out crucial matches. Desperate for match practice, McMenemy seized on the semi-final of the newly reinstalled Hampshire Professional Cup, scheduled for Tuesday, 22nd December against Portsmouth at Fratton Park. His opposite number, Burrows, similarly frustrated by Pompey's postponed game at Swindon, was equally up for the occasion. So, with barely 24 hours notice, the match was upgraded to a clash of first teams.

Pompey fans wanted an early Christmas present and Santa obliged when David Crown finally earned praise from a critical Fratton crowd with a fine equaliser on half-time, cancelling out Channon's opener. Midway through the second half, Crown – a former Brentford winger swapped for Chris Kamara in October – crossed for Jeff Hemmerman to flick home the winner. Magnanimous McMenemy even praised the Pompey crowd, as 7,000 had been persuaded to turn out for what was, in effect, a friendly. 'Tremendous. I'm constantly surprised by what's going on here on the south coast, here, at The Dell and at Brighton. There's not many places you'd have got a crowd like that, on a night like this, for a match like this.'

Once the weather relented, Southampton's march towards the title gathered momentum. After going top, they stayed there, although the 'full house' signs were yet to be seen at The Dell. Saints' lofty pretensions survived a 2-5 tonking at title rivals Ipswich. As Pompey slipped even lower, following a 0-3 surrender at Burnley on 27th February, Saints' second home win in a week – 3-1 against Birmingham – carried them four points clear, although the chasing pack did have games in hand.

March 1982 looked like being decisive, both for the season and, in retrospect, for our tale of two cities. For Portsmouth, things took a turn for the better. Three wins and two draws lifted the spectre of relegation, even though Burrows was a casualty of Chairman John Deacon's frustration as the season tamely ebbed away. Burrow's replacement was former Pompey wing-half Bobby Campbell.

For Southampton, a spate of injuries, notably to striker Moran, had left them short in attack. The signing of Oxford's Keith Cassells on transfer deadline day could not fill the breach, and two points out of twelve took the wind out of their title sails. A 2-3 defeat to Spurs on 20th March, inflicted by a hat-trick from Pompey and Saints reject Graham Roberts, knocked them off the top. That Saints were deposed by Swansea City, at the apex of their roller-coaster journey between divisions, suggested that this was not perhaps the classiest First Division field of runners. A 0-3 home defeat in early April to mid-table Aston Villa, the defending champions – managed by former Pompey winger and chief scout Tony Barton following the resignation of another old Pompey favourite Ron Saunders – realistically terminated their hopes. By the close, Liverpool had sprinted through the pack on the back of a sixteen-match undefeated run to clinch the championship. Saints rallied sufficiently in April to secure seventh place and another crack at the UEFA Cup, but the sense that a golden opportunity had been scorned could not be ignored. Saints would come closer to the title two years later, but 1981-82 has to go down as the big chance that should not have slipped away.

What a League championship for Southampton, coupled with a drop for Portsmouth back to the basement, would have done for the respective fortunes of each club is a matter for speculation. Certainly it would have destroyed Pompey's boast of an illustrious past that Saints could never quite match.

Instead, inspired by Bobby Campbell, and helped by Deacon throwing another huge – by Third Division standards – wad of cash at reviving the club's fortunes, Portsmouth ensured that the gap with their rivals would narrow. During the summer of 1982, Pompey signed Reading's precocious midfield talent Neil Webb, a snip at £87,500, Fulham centre-half Ernie Howe, and persuaded former Burnley, QPR and England winger Dave Thomas to sign under freedom of contract from Middlesbrough.

On the eve of the 1982-83 season, Campbell showed he too had McMenemy's gift for the theatrical, unveiling First Division Everton striker and Rod Stewart look-a-like Alan Biley. The fee was a cool £100,000, and Pompey, for so long spoken of as a 'sleeping giant', began to stir. The Third Division didn't exactly crumble at their feet, but from Christmas onwards Pompey were a cut above the rest. They survived an unexpected jolt from Fourth Division Aldershot, who dumped them out of the FA Cup in the second round. That season Biley weighed in with 26 goals and his sidekick Billy Rafferty nineteen, but it was the audacious deadline- day signing of Birmingham's Kevin Dillon for £200,000 – after a bid for Alan Curbishley was thwarted by City boss Ron Saunders – which made the biggest splash. The only sadness was the untimely death of Jimmy Dickinson in November, just as the club he had served loyally for almost 40 years was about to re-awaken. Towards the end of the season even the crowds came flooding back to Fratton, with more than 22,000 there to see the Third Division title clinched against Walsall – a gate bigger than any at The Dell that season, save for the visit of champions Liverpool.

By the summer of 1983, it would be Southampton, incredibly, whose high profile was being threatened by the single-minded and at times abrasive Campbell. The 1982-83 season had seen a slump in Saints' fortunes. Nor could salvation be found in Europe. An away-goals exit in the first round to Swedish part-timers Norkopping, coupled with headline-making, if ultimately unsubstantiated, sex allegations involving Mark Wright and Steve Moran, added to the sense of anticlimax at The Dell.

McMenemy's touch with recruiting older stars, and coaxing one last hurrah out of them, was still intact. The defensive qualities of Ipswich, England and former Pompey youngster Mick Mills, and the still razor-sharp reflexes of England goalkeeper Peter Shilton – two more oldies-but-goodies snapped up by McMenemy – couldn't inspire Saints to any higher than twelfth. In October, Saints were even rooted in the bottom three, put there by two maulings – 0-6 at Tottenham and 0-5 at Liverpool.

But the footballing power balance along the coast was shifting. Brighton, under disco-dancing, former Saints winger Jimmy Melia, had come close in extra-time to winning the FA Cup – '… and [Gordon] Smith must score …' – remains in the top ten of famous last words uttered by TV commentators. Brighton subsequently lost the replay to Manchester United 0-4, having already lost their battle to stay in the First Division, and would now be facing Pompey in Division Two the following season. With Portsmouth's inspired signing of Coventry and England Under-21 striker Mark Hateley, for a knockdown transfer tribunal agreed fee of £190,000, Campbell ensured that Pompey were now grabbing their share of the limelight nationally, as well as locally.

Southampton's key signing in the summer of 1983 was classic McMenemy. Frank Worthington was a wayward football genius. Despite his bright-lighting, womanising, Elvis-impersonating lifestyle, he had stayed near the top of the First Division scoring charts and now was unfurled at The Dell. With the emerging and maturing talents of Moran, Danny Wallace, Wright and Steve Williams – soon to be a full England international – blending with the old heads of Shilton, Worthington, Mills and David Armstrong, this was arguably the best Saints side ever. They would 'prove' it by finishing second in the League, an elevated position secured by a powerful finish to the season. Reigning champions Liverpool were always in pole position, however, so comparisons with the Saints team that really could have won it in 1982 will remain the stuff of debate for many years to come.

Oddly, the Southampton public were reluctant to turn out to support their side, with gates in the autumn of 1983 averaging around 18,000 – not dissimilar to Pompey's as they consolidated their new-found Second Division status. However, in many ways this season turned on the events of lunchtime, Monday, 9th January 1984, when the balls in the velvet bag at Football Association headquarters at Lancaster Gate clicked and clattered before the announcement, in hushed tones: '… Number 24, Portsmouth, will play Number 27, Southampton …' For the first time since 1906, the Hampshire rivals had been paired together in the FA Cup. It was time to settle some old scores and, as events would turn out, create some new ones.

Chapter 10

~ TOGETHER AGAIN ~

(1984-87)

The scramble for tickets for what was billed as 'the match of the decade' across the south coast and beyond began almost at once. Not surprisingly, Hampshire Constabulary had ordered the match be made all-ticket on security grounds. Fratton Park's capacity was still an impressive 36,000, but with Football Association rules dictating that the visiting team was entitled to 25 per cent of tickets available, the split meant Pompey had just 27,000 to sell to their own fans, while Saints received 9,000. Whatever system of distribution employed by Pompey's secretary, Bill Davis, there would be deserving cases who missed out.

However, the club managed to create a public relations disaster, first by increasing the price of terrace admission from the normal £2.80 to £3 – not 'profiteering', but a 'nice round figure', according to Chairman John Deacon – and then by allowing individuals to buy unlimited numbers of tickets but only on personal application to the club's ticket office, which in those days doubled up as its reception area. Postal applications, other than for season-ticket holders had been ruled out. Distant supporters, unable to travel all the way to Portsmouth, felt rejected, while queues snaked their way round Fratton Park for days as fans struggled to get their hands on the precious bits of paper.

Inevitably, loyal regulars missed out, while band-wagon jumpers and touts filled their boots. The policy also ensured that many Saints fans got their hands on tickets for the Portsmouth sections of the ground, creating a potential security headache. Things were not quite so frantic at The Dell, but when the day came for 1,500 seats to go on sale, queues started forming from 6am, despite the rain, and the allocation was quickly snapped up. To accommodate the travelling Saints contingent, Pompey allocated them the entire Milton End terrace, plus the standing enclosure under the South Stand to the Milton End of the tunnel, and the seats in Section D of the South Stand.

To his credit, secretary Davis acknowledged the problems and also drew praise from some quarters for turning up personally to open the club's offices at 5.45am – an hour and a quarter early – to start selling the tickets as long queues formed. However, his biggest nightmare was no doubt the prospect of a replay. The Safety at Sport Grounds Act (1975), which had reduced Fratton's 46,000 nominal capacity by 10,000 in ten years – not to mention disfiguring the stadium with ugly perimeter fences around the pitch – had also bitten at The Dell, which was down to a 24,000 capacity. Meeting the inevitable demand with just 6,000 tickets at his disposal was truly the stuff of sleepless nights. In the end he needn't have worried.

In the build up to the Cup-tie, old derby hands were wheeled out to give their views. Mick Channon, scourge of Pompey in 1976 with that last-minute winner and now at Norwich City, played down the game: 'I've played for Southampton against Portsmouth, for Manchester City against United, and Norwich against Ipswich, but those matches never really meant anything to me. They are just another game, but that doesn't mean to say I don't appreciate how other fans feel about them.' He added that, while he thought Pompey had a good chance, 'Portsmouth will have to watch they don't get caught on the break.' We can see how Channon made a career as a top racehorse trainer with betting insight like that, for his assessment would prove to be spot on.

David Armstrong, a boyhood Sunderland fan and a former Middlesbrough player, so no stranger to intense derby days, said: 'The games do tend to mean more to the supporters than the players, but it is because the players don't want to let the supporters down that they are not always classics. You can tend to become a little over-cautious because you are so anxious not to make mistakes.' Armstrong said he knew how the Pompey crowd could back their side from his days at Boro. He recalled the 1-1 draw with his side at Fratton back in 1980, when Pompey were a Fourth Division club: 'Once they equalised we really had our backs against the wall, because the crowd got behind them'.

Frank Worthington, too, was looking forward to his first south coast derby: 'The Southampton players, like myself, who have not been brought up here didn't realise the extent of the rivalry until this match. It is obvious that it is very, very intense. I know their fans will be making a heck of a lot of noise, but we will have a lot of fans too and our away support this season has been marvellous'.

The only player born in either city on show that day would be Saints midfielder Nick Holmes, who admitted that the Cup-tie had come a bit too soon for his liking: 'It's a pity we have to face Portsmouth now as really I would have liked both clubs to go all the way. I am not one of those people who thinks they automatically have to think the worst of Portsmouth. I always look for their results and I am delighted when they do well, because when the teams are doing well it gives the whole area a lift'.

For Pompey, Alan Biley was also overwhelmed by the passion evoked by the match: 'I thought Mersey derbies were a bit special,' said the former Everton striker, 'but not any more. Matches against Liverpool were always built up a lot, but I have honestly never known anything like this. From the moment we came out of the hat against Saints, people have wanted to talk about nothing else. It's fantastic!'

Saints defender Mick Mills, who had been rejected by Pompey as a youngster, also gave solace to his old club. 'In fairness I had not really shown anything by then [1965, when he was released] which would suggest I would achieve all I have been lucky enough to do in soccer.' He added that shortly after his departure, a trial at The Dell had also proved inconclusive and he eventually moved to Ipswich. An FA Cup winners medal and 42 England caps later, the veteran full-back, now 35, would have the task of shackling Pompey winger Alan Rogers.

Neither side was tearing up any trees in the League in the run up to the big game. Mid-table Pompey, whose hopes of a blindside promotion run were fast evaporating after a four-match winless run, ground out a 0-0 draw at Middlesbrough, before being held 1-1 at home by Cardiff. Meanwhile, Saints lost 2-3 at Manchester United before losing 0-1 at home to Nottingham Forest on the Monday before the Cup-tie. That game with Brian Clough's side was initially scheduled for 14th January 1984, but postponed due to the unfit Dell pitch. It was hastily squeezed in when it was realised that Steve Williams' two-match suspension, due to start on 16th January, would have ruled him out of the Pompey game. Instead, he had now served his punishment, having also played at Old Trafford, and was free to play.

It's hard to imagine modern-day top club managers, in thrall to the financial imperative of staying in the Premier League, making such a sacrifice. Saints were fifth in the First Division at the time and although a title bid looked a long shot, UEFA Cup places, which sometimes stretched down as far as seventh, were up for grabs. In 1984, the FA Cup had lost none of the glamour that it has today. The hype surrounding the tie was whipped up even further by national tabloid *The Sun*, which proclaimed in sensationalist back-page terms: 'SCUM HATE RECORD FURY.' The target of their attack was Portsmouth folk singer-cum-DJ Shep Woolley, who had gently ribbed Saints on the city's Radio Victory in a single called 'Pompey Rock'. Never let the facts get in the way of a good story.

Matchday was cool and cloudy, although by kick-off a watery, winter sun was poking through. The referee was Lester Shapter, the Torquay official who had incensed McMenemy back in October 1976, when he had sent off George Best on his Fulham debut against Saints at The Dell. Lawrie Mac felt the wayward star's reputation had determined the matter, though he felt obliged to write a grovelling apology when presented with a transcript of the exchange between player and referee.

Both teams were near full strength, with Pompey boss Campbell preferring the width that Rogers provided, keeping 'super sub' Nicky Morgan – hero of the previous round – on the bench. McMenemy omitted defender Ken Armstrong, with Holmes moving back to partner Mark Wright, allowing Steve Williams to take his usual central midfield role. As the teams ran out, the crowd, packed in like sardines, roared as they had never roared before. In those pre-Premiership days any pre-match entertainment was more likely to be RAF dog handlers than micro-skirted dancers. But on this day myriads of balloons were sent spiralling into the air in a competition sponsored by Townsend Thoresen ferries.

Up in the television gantry, Match of the Day cameras were set to preserve the match for posterity. But after all the hype, most of the footage ended up unseen. The tension of the occasion, as David Armstrong had warned, created a nervy, tetchy encounter that wouldn't live long in the memory. The exception was two key incidents which shaped the match. Attacking the massed Saints ranks in the first half, Pompey created only one chance, plus a penalty appeal turned down, when Reuben Agboola clattered into Mark Hateley. That chance came from Pompey's first corner, in the 32nd minute. Full-back John McLaughlin floated the ball to the near post, Mick Tait back nodded on, only for Biley to head over a gaping goal. In the second half, Saints finally got to grips. Mills forced Alan Knight into his only proper save of the game, and shortly afterwards Williams curled a shot inches wide after a swift break by Danny Wallace. Pompey weathered the storm and with five minutes to go fashioned another chance to ease the worries of the increasingly tense Pompey secretary, as a dreaded replay loomed ever larger. Biley, on the corner of the six-yard box, screwed his shot high into the Fratton End. The die seemed cast, the game would end goalless, and minds could turn to squeezing a quart into The Dell's pint pot in three days' time.

However, the decisive moment was yet to come, in stoppage time added for an incident by the corner of the North Terrace, close to the no-go zone which separated the warring factions. The more unsavoury elements among Portsmouth's support, who had tarnished the club's reputation on many an away trip as the club see-sawed through the divisions, had congregated as close as possible to their detested rivals. Periodically the police had waded in to confiscate potential missiles, but whenever a Saints player got within range, he was the target for whatever small change could be mustered. More regrettably still, bananas were hurled in the direction of Saints' black forward Danny Wallace, as the more sinister neo-Nazi element – which lent its overt support to the self-styled hooligan 'crews' of the era – made their sickening point. Pompey's 'crew' were the '6:57', so called after the supposed departure time of the train from Portsmouth used to travel to away games.

Shortly before Mills had forced that save from Knight, an object – later confirmed as a 50 pence piece – had struck Saints' left-back Mark Dennis on the head. The game had to be halted while the prone player was attended to. There was later a suggestion that the notorious 'bad boy' Dennis had made a meal of the incident – several players and both linesman had alas been hit without collapsing – but to be fair, that is not really in character for Dennis and, anyway, it is hardly the point. The time referee Shapter added was enough for Saints to win the match. Worthington was the instigator, with a cross-field pass to Armstrong, who scuttled down Pompey's seriously under-manned right side. His cross was met at the far post by Steve Moran, who along with Wright was the butt of many a Fratton End taunt after the previous season's 'Swedish scandal'. Moran showed his poacher's instinct by hitting a bouncing ball inside Knight's near post. Poetic justice? Quite possibly, as the majority of the stadium was stunned into silence, while the rest exploded into unconfined joy.

There are Saints supporters present that day who insist that other pockets of fans around the ground, including some in the Fratton End, also erupted as the ball went in. This was doubtless true, the chaotic ticketing arrangements saw to that, but for most Pompey fans the abiding memory is of an eerie stillness which seemed never-ending.

After the match, McMenemy typically tried to play down the manner of the victory. 'We've got a good result, £4.50 in loose change and two pounds of bananas, so we're happy.' Moran too, saw the funny side of the incident, having been hit himself several times: 'They were mostly two pence pieces being thrown, but Steve Williams had a five pence piece land near him, so he picked it up and tried to bribe the referee.' As a 'local', he had felt the pressure of expectation more than most and was delighted to have scored the winner: 'Nick Holmes and myself probably felt the pressure more than anyone else ... We've lived most of our lives in the middle of Pompey and Saints fans, so we knew how much the game meant to both sets of supporters. The feeling I had when the goal went in is hard to describe. I felt tremendous and was relieved we didn't have to go through it all again in a replay'.

For Pompey's part, there was wounded pride, not only at the result, but also at the comportment of a sizeable minority of its fans. The watching FA official and the referee exonerated the club from blame for the incident, and the club were also pleased to receive a letter of support from the Saints Travel Club for the way the match had been stewarded. But Chairman Deacon was irate, threatening life bans for any culprits identified. His dismay was compounded by the racial overtones of the incident. 'There are couple of players we are interested in at the moment who are very talented but black – could we risk exposing them to that kind of reaction from their own fans?' he mused.

Later that year, Deacon's words would resonate, as newly-signed West Indian defender Noel Blake told the tabloids of his 'Pompey hell' at the hands of the boo-boys. In mitigation, Blake's discontent had more to do with home-sickness and the barracking he endured was sparked more by a string of defensive gaffes which had made Pompey the own-goal kings of the country than by any overt racial overtones. Blake would in time become one of the most popular Pompey players of his generation.

For Portsmouth, the rest of that 1983-84 season was a write off. Out of the Cup, concentrating on the League meant treading water in mid-table. Any remaining hopes of getting into the promotion hunt were quashed a week later, on 4th February, by Newcastle United, inspired by Kevin Keegan, who had left Saints the previous summer to become a Geordie messiah. 'King Kev' was leading the Magpies back to the promised land and single-handedly destroyed Pompey in the mud that afternoon, 4-1, scoring twice and making two for his partner in crime Peter Beardsley. Talk about rubbing salt in the wound.

Just one home League win in ten matches from New Year's Eve left Pompey uncomfortably close to the drop zone, although the arithmetical possibility of relegation had actually vanished with three games to go. Not even the signing of former Saints centre-back Malcolm Waldron – another 'local' coming home – could shore up a dodgy defence, which conceded 64 goals that season, half of them at Fratton. Waldron had left the Dell for Third Division Burnley the previous summer, but did not settle and was delighted to move back south for £45,000. A crunching tackle in the first minute of his debut, at home to Carlisle, helped endear him immediately: 'I wondered how I might be received because I understand the feelings of the people here, but they were tremendous. I heard just one comment all afternoon, when I went to take a throw in, but you'll always get that.' At least the one home win in that miserable run had been spectacular, 5-1 against Brighton, completing a double over the Seagulls. Their fans were left penned in for twenty minutes in the rain after the final whistle, and were forced to listen to repeats of Pompey's five second-half goals over the tannoy. However, the overall outcome of the season – missing relegation by just two points – was not what Deacon had had in mind, and manager Bobby Campbell paid the price. His replacement would raise a few eyebrows, to say the least.

By contrast, Southampton's 1983-84 season was well and truly up and running. The selection of Steve Williams and Mark Wright for the England squad to meet France – Williams was forced to withdraw with injury – reinforced the feeling that Saints had a team for the future as well as the present. By piling win upon win, Southampton kept the points board ticking over, and kept leaders Manchester United more or less in range. Further victories in the FA Cup over First Division Blackburn and Sheffield Wednesday – the latter in a Dell replay – had put Saints in the semi-finals for the first time since 1976.

Southampton's 2-0 win over title rivals Liverpool, including a sensational overhead kick by Wallace, in front of a national TV audience – this was the first season that domestic League games were shown live –

rammed home the point, for any Pompey fans who hadn't quite got the message. This Saints side was serious ... about winning things. In the run up to the semi-final, the dropping of eight League points out of nine realistically ended their title hopes. Nevertheless, confidence was high that semi-final opponents Everton – who had been in the doldrums until they'd got out of jail in a Milk Cup quarter-final at Third Division Oxford – were there for the taking.

Oddly, and it remains strange even twenty years on, the Southampton public seemed intent on proving their Portsmouth detractors right. Gates of 16,000 and 17,000 to watch a team playing some of the best football the south coast had ever seen must have caused consternation for the club's board of directors. A semi-final is always a useful tool for mining latent support – as Pompey would discover eight years later – and 20,000 supported Saints at Highbury. Their hopes were shattered in extra-time by Adrian Heath popping up with the only goal. It took Everton to their second Wembley final of the season, to meet Watford.

The sense of 'what might have been' was emphasised three days later when Saints beat, you've guessed it, Everton, 3-1 at The Dell in a rearranged League fixture. Fewer than 17,000 turned out as Saints newfound friends melted away again. Six wins – including an unlikely 8-2 victory over Coventry – and three draws in nine matches crammed into four weeks kept the League championship theoretically alive until early May. Saints would finish runners up – three points adrift of Liverpool – their highest League position ever. From Saints' perspective a very good showing undoubtedly; from Pompey's, still not quite good enough.

By this time, Portsmouth had parted company with Bobby Campbell. Arriving in his place, as caretaker at least, was Alan Ball. The carrot-haired, squeaky-voiced World Cup winner of 1966 had retired from football following his 726th League game in October 1982, missing a penalty as Saints beat Everton 3-2. After a spell playing in Hong Kong, Campbell had recruited him as youth team coach, while giving him scouting tasks – 'part of his education as a manager' – according to Campbell. Little did he realise that learning curve was going to be quick, culminating in Ball replacing his mentor.

Ball's 'caretaker' spell lasted one game, which saw Pompey thrash doomed Swansea City 5-0 – it was only two years since the Swans had wrestled the leadership of the First Division from Southampton, but it must have seemed a lot longer as they plunged headlong into the Third. Ball was given the job permanently a fortnight later. His appointment was hardly met with universal approval. If his Saints connections weren't bad enough, an eight-month spell in charge of Third Division Blackpool had ended in the sack, relegation, and his return to Southampton. Hardly a track record to inspire confidence.

And Ball's first task was unpopular, if inevitable. Mark Hateley's 26 goals had attracted the attention of England manager Bobby Robson. On their South American tour, the lanky striker became the first Pompey player to represent England since 1956. Better (or maybe with hindsight worse), he scored in the Rio's Maracana Stadium as England beat Brazil 2-0. (If Hateley's goal is largely forgotten today by the public at large, John Barnes' is not.) Italian giants AC Milan were hooked on Hateley, and a £1million transfer fee was too good to turn down.

Flush with money available, Ball set about building the team to fulfil Chairman Deacon's aim of restoring Pompey to the top. Crystal Palace defender Billy Gilbert, Middlesbrough's centre-back Mick Baxter and midfielder Mick Kennedy all arrived in a whirlwind three weeks, along with Manchester United striker Scott McGarvey. Apocryphal wisdom has it that the choice was between McGarvey and Mark Hughes …

Lawrie McMenemy, too, was wheeling and dealing, with 35-year-old Frank Worthington shown the door on the expiry of his contract, on account of an alleged sexual liaison in the team hotel before a game at Stoke. In his autobiography, *One Hump or Two …?* (1994), Worthington claimed it was all an innocent misunderstanding, but McMenemy was having none of it and sent him packing. In came a comparative youngster – only 32. Former Leeds, Manchester United and Scotland star Joe Jordan ended a three-year exile in Italy at AC Milan and Verona by joining Southampton for £150,000. Substituting Worthington with Jordan was akin to replacing a rapier with a sledgehammer.

As the 1984-85 season began to take shape, Portsmouth were suddenly among the leading pack in Division Two after a five-match unbeaten run. By contrast, Southampton were winless and bottom of the First Division. At least Saints could look forward to a possible UEFA Cup run, but even that evaporated as – watched by 19,000 – SV Hamburg forced a 0-0 draw at The Dell, then won the return 2-0. In the League however, Saints revived, and by the time Pompey hit top spot on 13th October, a six-match unbeaten run had bounced Saints into the top half of the table.

Both sides had the wind in their sails. By December Pompey were still in the top three, and Saints were back in their by-now customary top six. Pompey's anticipated promotion sparked speculation about the pair finally locking horns in the top flight. As an 'appetiser', Pompey's re-election to the Football Combination after an absence of eighteen years brought with it a reserve-team clash. Saints' 3-0 win at Fratton on 20th November served notice that they weren't quite ready to give up their south-coast supremacy just yet.

Portsmouth's rise posed an interesting test of their public. For the best part of twenty years, the cry had been that Pompey just needed the promise of First Division football to get the supporters rolling in. In fact, they did anything but. An average of 13,000 by the end of November was hardly the stuff of so-called 'sleeping giants' awakening. Fratton's £3 terrace admission was one of the highest in the whole Football League, but this barely constituted an excuse. When Pompey had last been in such an elevated position – in the autumn of 1967 – gates had been 7,000 higher on average, and even five years beforehand, in the Fourth Division, the typical gate was significantly better.

To a certain extent Pompey's, and for that matter Saints', poor performance at the turnstiles could be explained by the fact that football, as a spectator sport, was in general decline. Rampant hooliganism, or at least its perceived threat, had alienated many prospective fans. That particular issue was about to touch the depths with the Heysel Disaster and the riot by Millwall 'fans' at Luton the following spring. The visit to Fratton of leaders Oxford on 22nd December 1984 finally persuaded some fans out of their armchairs, and a 22,000 crowd saw victory snatched from the jaws of defeat, as two goals by Biley, in time added for a pitch invasion by someone dressed as Santa Claus, propelled Pompey into second place.

It was hard to believe that the previous week Pompey fans, or a section of them in the Fratton End, had been chanting 'Alan Ball's a Scummer'. Ball's crime had been to replace popular Nicky Morgan with Bobby Doyle as Pompey trailed 1-2 to Huddersfield. Another ex-Saint, Waldron, had done the damage with an own-goal. For the record, Pompey rallied to win 3-2, but Ball's hopes on his appointment that he would come to be known as a 'lovely Scummer' looked remote.

An anonymous Pompey player was quoted in the *Sports Mail* the following week: 'What are that lot going to be like when the going gets tough?' He had a point. If Ball was delivering the best Pompey team in a generation, and some fans still couldn't forgive or forget where he came from, what would change hearts and minds? Terrace flak had also all but taken August signing Noel Blake – a replacement for the unfortunate Baxter, stricken by cancer – to the brink of a transfer request. Myopic? Bitter? Ignorant? Take your pick, but their self-proclamation of being among the best fans in the land could be taken with a pinch of salt at this time.

It was also around this time that cracks in McMenemy's hegemony became apparent. Starlet Mark Wright had already handed in a transfer request and had publicly quarrelled with his boss. Then, on the eve of a home game with Newcastle, another jewel, Steve Williams, fell out with the manager and was axed. Joe Jordan, too, had been firing blanks and his place in the side was increasingly going to a young striking prospect called Ian Baird, but more of him later. By the end of December, Williams was on his way in an on-off, but eventually 'on' £500,000 transfer to Arsenal. His departure coincided with four straight defeats, that saw Southampton tumbling to mid-table, but with Jordan finally finding his scoring boots the team were soon back in the thick of the hunt for UEFA places. Or they were, until a shock home defeat in a weather-delayed FA Cup fifth round tie by Second Division Barnsley. The transfer deadline capture of Jimmy Case, another veteran with a point to prove, shored up the midfield and Saints squeaked into the UEFA Cup places, indebted to a last-day win over Coventry at The Dell.

On that same day, Portsmouth were missing out on promotion to the First Division in heart-rending style. Their 2-0 win at Huddersfield was rendered useless by Manchester City's 5-1 thrashing of Charlton, although the death of 56 people in the Bradford City fire that same afternoon put matters into proper perspective. On Easter Monday, following a 3-1 win at Fulham, Portsmouth's promotion had looked assured, but April home defeats to Manchester City and Birmingham had irreparably damaged their cause. The renewal of derby hostilities would have to wait another season at least.

The summer of 1985 was turbulent for football in general and Southampton in particular. The tragedies of Heysel and Bradford had the authorities gunning for English football – and not without reason. Scenes of Juventus supporters being crushed to death as Liverpool fans charged them before the start of the European Cup final had shocked the world, and UEFA acted. All English clubs – blameless Saints included – were banned indefinitely from European competition. Saints, for whom assistant manager John Mortimore had departed for a second time to take charge of Benfica, also lost McMenemy, who opted to try to revive the 'sleeping giant' that was Sunderland. A tall order, but made taller still by the fact he was a Geordie. In his place at The Dell came Chris Nicholl, who returned to the club after a distinguished playing career and serving his managerial apprenticeship at Grimsby.

Over at Fratton, Alan Ball also shuffled his pack. Failure to gain promotion saw emerging talent Neil Webb move to Nottingham Forest for £250,000. His replacement would add another touch of controversy. Ball had already eyeballed his Scummer-jibing critics by signing former Saint Ivan Golac in January 1985 on a three-month loan. In that time Pompey climbed from ninth to third. But Ball's capture of 37-year-old out-of-contract Norwich striker Mick Channon looked confrontational, to say the least. In fact it was a masterstroke. Or almost.

Channon was typically forthright on his arrival: 'Forget I ever played for Saints. That's in the past and doesn't count for anything now. I'm a Pompey player and that's all that matters. In this game you have two loyalties. To yourself and to those who pay your wages. I know about this thing Pompey's fans have with Saints, although I can't understand it, but I know if I do the business for them, that's how they'll judge me.'

Channon and Pompey 'did the business' all right. Eleven wins and two draws in their first fourteen games of 1985-86 sent Pompey seven points clear at the top. The first of those wins, irony of ironies, was a 3-0 humiliation of Sunderland at Fratton Park. Typically, McMenemy took the terrace banter in good part. By contrast, his successor Nicholl's baptism was one of fire. By now accustomed to challenging for honours season-in, season-out, Saints found themselves scrapping down among the relegation candidates and the possibility of the two clubs swapping places was very real – an appalling prospect for the red and white half of Hampshire in their club's centenary season.

In the end, Saints had enough about them to keep their heads above the drop zone, although a final placing of fourteenth was not quite what they were accustomed to. Their fans were rewarded with another Cup run, though, terminated only by another semi-final extra-time defeat in north London, this time at White Hart Lane. On this occasion two Ian Rush goals for Liverpool shattered dreams of a Wembley return. The disappointment was exacerbated by Mark Wright being stretchered off in the first half with a broken leg.

But if Southampton fans were feeling sorry for themselves, they only had to peer a few miles east to cheer themselves up. In April 1986 Pompey's season imploded, perhaps not quite as spectacularly as Saints had done in 1949, but impressively nevertheless. For the second successive season promotion had seemed assured, especially after an Easter Monday 3-2 win at Brighton. With just seven games to play, Pompey were seven points above the fourth-placed team. Yet four defeats and a draw, coupled with Charlton and Wimbledon's relentless surge, left Pompey clutching at straws as they finished fourth. Dreams of a return to the promised land were put on hold once again. Perhaps even worse, the heart had been ripped out of the ground, the upper tier of the Fratton End falling foul of stringent safety requirements.

Ball toyed with resigning, but to his credit he girded his loins for a third stab at promotion. Channon's contract was unsurprisingly not renewed, although his 40 appearances, six goals and undoubted know-how had provided good value. In his place came another England veteran Paul Mariner — with not a Saints connection in sight – to finally find the blend which would take Pompey up.

Southampton were in full transition. Colin Clarke had been plucked from the obscurity of Bournemouth and would weigh in with some useful goals as Nicholl's side flirted again with relegation in 1986-87. Never out of the bottom half, a run to the League Cup semi-finals – where Liverpool again ended Wembley hopes – was more of a distraction. League safety was only assured after a run of just one defeat in eleven games in March and April.

Pompey's elevation was hardly vintage, but fired by goals from Mick Quinn – a deadline-day signing from Millwall in March 1986 – Pompey were top at Christmas and Easter. Despite a stutter which gifted the title to Derby, it would take an almighty collapse for Pompey to be denied promotion. Typically, the team put their fans through the mill, losing to a late Ian Wright goal at Crystal Palace on May Day. 12,000 fans had made the trip hoping to witness the point that would take Pompey up. But Shrewsbury's win over Oldham the following night did the trick and a reduced capacity 28,000 turned up to see the last-day party pooped only ever-so slightly. 'Scummers, Scummers, here we come!' was a common refrain as the pitch was swamped on the final whistle and the players took their plaudits from the directors' box. For the first time in history, Southampton and Portsmouth would be in Division One together.

Chapter 11

~ TIME OF CHANGE ~

(1987-89)

The publication of the 1987-88 fixtures in mid-June set the date for the first League meeting of the two Hampshire clubs in the First Division. And the pair wouldn't have to wait long to lock horns – 22nd August – Portsmouth's first Saturday home game. Contrary to popular belief, Pompey invested significantly for their first stab at the top flight in almost 30 years. Terry Connor, the Brighton striker, cost £200,000 and Barry Horne was plucked from Third Division Wrexham for £60,000. But the biggest outlay was again controversial, as Alan Ball decided to confront once more the Portsmouth prejudice against former Saints. A tribunal set the fee of £285,000 for Leeds striker Ian Baird, and Pompey had never paid out more.

Not only was Baird an ex-Saint: five months earlier a careless, but non-abusive, hand gesture to the Fratton End – as the taunts rained down on him while playing for Leeds – had him hauled up before the Football Association. His disciplinary record, which had seen the former England schoolboy international's career drift off course at The Dell, until he was sold to the Yorkshire club in March 1985 for £100,000, meant he would sit out the first two games of the season. During Pompey's pre-season tour of Sweden, playing mainly amateur outfits, Baird had accumulated three more bookings to put him in reach of another suspension. Baird and Pompey was not a marriage made in heaven; and that's not hindsight talking. However, with gifted but lazy midfielder Mick Fillery secured on a free transfer – the consequence of an administrative error at Loftus Road – Ball was confident he had the resources to keep the club up.

Indeed, on paper, Ball looked to have a stronger squad than Chris Nicholl, his counterpart at The Dell. Southampton had former Fratton favourite Tony Barton now installed as assistant manager, while for their part, Portsmouth's youth coach was one-time Saints record buy Peter Osgood. With Saints' star centre-half Mark Wright still angling for a transfer and Peter Shilton having moved on, Nicholl was high on the list of managers tipped by the tabloids to be out of work soon. In the pre-season build up both sides had remained unbeaten, but when the real stuff got under way it was Southampton who showed they still had what it takes, earning a 2-2 draw against Manchester United at The Dell, thanks to a brace of goals by the irrepressible Danny Wallace. That was followed by a 1-0 win at Norwich on the Tuesday, the goal coming from Kevin Moore. Moore had been a smart bit of business. Nicholl signed the centre-back from Oldham for £125,000, having known all about him at his previous club, Grimsby.

Portsmouth's start, by contrast, was catastrophic. The loss of defender Noel Blake a week before the curtain raiser with a bad knee injury threw Ball's defensive plans into chaos. Paul Mariner, whose only prior defensive experience was as a makeshift centre-back when Pompey were down to eight men before half-time at Sheffield United the previous December, was drafted in as emergency cover. And he scored the own-goal to decide that match. Now Mariner lined up alongside Billy Gilbert against Oxford United at the Manor Ground and was ripped to shreds by a streetwise Billy Whitehurst, prompted by former Saints Martin Foyle and Trevor Hebberd, not to mention a young Ray Houghton. Oxford won 4-2, and when Chelsea thrashed Pompey 3-0 at Fratton Park three days later, the long-anticipated derby was now being looked at with some trepidation at the eastern end of the county. Saints, on the other hand, fancied their chances, so long as Mariner continued his 'defensive' duties.

The game proved to be a cracker, so it was a shame only 20,000 were there to see it. Obviously Pompey's dreadful start could have been a factor, but this game had been anticipated ever since the fixtures were published. Pompey's fans, with last-minute defeats to avenge from Saints' last two visits to Fratton, had been licking their wounds for a long time.

Instead, much of the blame for this poor attendance – and for that matter, at all of Pompey's pre-Christmas home games – could be laid fair and square at the door of Hampshire Constabulary, which insisted any 'big match' was made all-ticket. It is worth remembering that in those days people were still in the habit of turning up to a game of their choice and paying on the turnstile to get in. Unlike Southampton, whose restricted capacity and winning ways in the late 1970s and early 80s had encouraged their core support into the season-ticket habit, Pompey sold very few by comparison – especially for the terraces. Having to make two trips to Fratton Park to see one game, even if eventually the club experimented with selling tickets through the *News*' branch offices, took its toll. Saints' numbers were also limited by the Milton End now being split into three pens, with the smaller two in each corner used as buffer zones. Pompey had also erected new perimeter fences. Those flimsy barriers that had been swept away by the post-Sheffield United pitch invasion were replaced with ugly, thick-posted grills which were impossible to see through. The term 'Fortress Fratton' had very different connotations back in the late 1980s. Football then, either at Fratton Park or The Dell, was not the 'must-see' leisure accessory it is today.

The weather was seasonally pleasant. Portsmouth gave a debut to Baird, and Saints to left-back Derek Statham. Referee Ray Lewis – who hailed from surely the most apt town any official could come from, Great

Bookham – led the teams out side by side in an attempt to diffuse pre-match hostility on the terraces. The players undermined the goodwill. Within a minute Mariner had clattered another one of Nicholl's old Grimsby favourites, Gordon Hobson, and received a yellow card. That had the effect of calming things down and at last the football flowed. The first real chance came in the fifth minute. How different might Baird's Pompey career have been had he converted Mick Kennedy's floated free-kick, rather than volleying over the bar? It was end-to-end stuff though, and first blood went to Pompey after twenty minutes. It was a slightly bizarre goal. Another of Ball's summer recruits, full-back Clive Whitehead, humped the ball forward. Statham hesitated as goalkeeper Flowers came off his line, only for Vince Hilaire to nip in and lob the hanging ball over the keeper's head and with one bounce into the net, behind which the 2,500 Saints fans were massed. It was the first competitive goal against, or conceded by – depending on your point of view – the 'auld enemy' since December 1974.

The home fans' delirium was short-lived. Five minutes later, Glenn Cockerill played the ball into the box and Colin Clarke's shot deceived Knight and found the corner of the net, under the noses of the Fratton End, its upper tier still closed. Now the balance swung the other way and Gilbert was forced into a desperate hack on Clarke which earned him a booking. From the free-kick Andy Townsend saw his shot blocked.

The second half was no less frantic. Southampton took the lead within three minutes, when future Pompey coach Kevin Bond's high free-kick was nodded down by Clarke, who ran on to an instant return pass to fire a shot across Knight and in off the far post. Within seconds, Knight denied Clarke a hat-trick with an athletic save. Now it was Pompey's turn to hit back. Baird saw a far-post header saved by Tim Flowers – who had replaced Shilton as goalkeeper – as was a long-range effort by Lee Sandford. Substitute Kevin Dillon went into the book for a crude foul on Cockerill. Then, with sixteen minutes remaining, Dillon played in Kenny Swain down the right. His cross to the far post was nodded down for Baird and Whitehead scrambled the ball home. 2-2.

Honours even. Pompey were satisfied by their first point of the season, while Saints could feel their 'natural' superiority had been preserved. After the game, Nicholl rued Knight's save just after Clarke had given Saints the advantage: 'If that had gone in it would have finished the game, but all credit to Pompey for getting back.' Inside Fratton, the game passed off peacefully on the terraces. Outside, any satisfaction was muted by reports of serious disturbances as Pompey fans attempted to ambush their counterparts on Goldsmith Avenue. These unsavoury episodes prompted the Conservative MP for Portsmouth South, David Martin, to rail against Portsmouth FC, and not for the first time. In 1987, footballing matters won no electoral votes. With no arrests in the stadium, however, Pompey pointed out they had fulfilled their need to protect public safety. What anyone does on the streets afterwards may well reflect badly on the club's image, but ultimately law and order is not, and never can be, a football club's responsibility.

Portsmouth also countered tabloid claims that former Saints' boss Lawrie McMenemy was about to descend on Fratton and form a 'dream team' with Ball. After his two-season stint at Sunderland had ended in relegation to the Third Division, 'Big Mac' was out of a job. The speculation was wide of that mark, although the partnership would eventually see the light of day.

If Pompey thought their first League point meant they had turned the corner, they were wrong. Despite shoring up their defence with Malcolm Shotton from Oxford, a 0-6 mauling at Arsenal saw Alan Knight embarrassed by his future boss, Graham Rix, who nicked the ball off him to set up Alan Smith for the first of his three goals. The result prompted some Sunday tabloids to nominate Pompey as the worst First Division team ever. That was not the case, and a 2-1 win over West Ham two days later lifted the pressure. After eleven games, with just one defeat in the last six, Pompey were up to eleventh – out of 21, as the First Division slimmed down in stages – six points above Saints, who languished third from bottom, albeit with two games in hand.

Chris Nicholl was under pressure. Still without a home win to celebrate – their worst Dell start in 50 years – Saints fans were restless, especially after newly-promoted Second Division Bournemouth, managed still by Harry Redknapp, bounced them out of the second round of the Rumbelows Cup, 3-2 on aggregate. Only 13,200 witnessed the fateful second leg, which Saints could only draw 2-2, despite a goal from the youthful Matt Le Tissier's first start of the season. Supporters were calling for the manager's head even before the match. It was tough on Nicholl, who was obliged by the board to slash the wagebill. Redknapp expressed sympathy for his opposite number, knowing he could use the Dell crowd to Bournemouth's advantage: 'I feel sorry for Saints and I don't like to see Chris getting stick. We've all got a job to do and it's hard for him at the moment. It was important we didn't let Saints get an early goal. We knew their confidence would be short after Saturday's 4-0 defeat against Everton and I was conscious the crowd would turn if we didn't let them get a breakthrough.'

Despite their mid-table position, things were not so rosy in the Pompey garden either. Ball, too, was feeling the heat from the terraces after his side's 2-6 aggregate humiliation by Third Division Swindon in the same competition. 'These things happen. What I can't understand is how a section of the crowd seem to collapse completely because we've lost a match.'

The Pompey crowd – or at least its critical elements – seemed to have judged the side pretty accurately. By the time the second derby came around in early January the team would be fighting for their First Division lives. By then, edging closer to the Fratton exit door was controversial Ian Baird. His expulsion against Charlton in September had landed the striker with another suspension and an injury to his instep didn't help matters. The terrace knives were out and not even his first (and only) League goal for the club, against QPR on 24th October, could get his season going. His former club, Leeds, scented the chance to buy him back at a knock-down price. They would have to wait until March to do so, for £185,000, but by then the most ill-starred transfer of an ex-Saint to Fratton had already run its course. Alan Knight's abiding memory of Baird, expounded in his autobiography *Legend* (2003) was of the disconsolate striker shuffling round the stadium repeating to himself the refrain 'What a shithole ...'

By contrast, Southampton's season picked up after their earlier embarrassments. A Danny Wallace goal gave them their first home win on 17th October against Watford, and five wins and three draws in their next twelve games had Saints pushing mid-table after the New Year programme. In the same period, Pompey had enjoyed just one League win and were third from bottom, one point behind Oxford, but seven shy of Saints, who also had a game in hand.

The derby was scheduled for Sunday, 3rd January 1988, with a noon – 'high noon' – kick-off at the insistence of the Hampshire Constabulary. Pre-match, Ball appealed for peace ahead of Pompey's first trip to The Dell since September 1975: 'I want this to be one of those occasions when people lucky enough to have been there can look back in years to come and say, "Do you remember when ..." The first match at Fratton was one of those, an open match with constant goalmouth action at both ends and lots to keep people on their toes and occupied.' The match would certainly be remembered, although less for the quality of the contest – both the *News* and *Echo* agreed 'low-key' summed it up – than for the result.

Chris Nicholl's Saints were still shell-shocked from a 0-3 chasing at QPR two days earlier on New Year's Day. He now reinstated Wallace after a groin strain. Alan Ball, cursing a missed penalty at 1-1 by Kevin Dillon in the closing stages of their home game with Arsenal, decided against recalling ex-Saint Baird, who had been struggling again with injury, this time a calf strain. Baird stayed on the bench. Up front were Terry Connor, finally justifying his fee after a nightmare start with injuries, and Mick Quinn, out of favour when Baird arrived, but now showing he was still capable of knocking them in. The referee, to keep it in the southern family, was a Sussexman, Alan Gunn, from Burgess Hill.

In many ways the match hinged as much on the chances Southampton missed as the two Portsmouth took. Before Barry Horne gave Pompey a sixteenth-minute lead, drilling home Hilaire's cut-back, Kevin Bond had thumped a header against the Pompey bar and Clarke had chipped over with only Knight to beat. Within seconds of Saints falling behind, Cockerill and Graham Baker opened Pompey up, but Wallace – short of match-sharpness – could only flail a leg and the chance went begging. Suddenly it was 2-0 to Portsmouth. Baker was again at fault, miscontrolling a pass. Quinn nipped in and sent the breaking Connor away to fire across John Burridge – the eccentric Workington-born keeper signed by Nicholl in October as cover for Tim Flowers. It was Connor's third goal in as many matches.

There were ecstatic scenes on the Archers Road end, packed with 4,500 Pompey season-ticket holders who had been the fortunate ones to get hold of tickets. Portsmouth's last League victory over Southampton had been back in February 1964, 24 years earlier. Suddenly, another win seemed tantalisingly close. Saints continued to miss the unmissable, this time Clarke slicing wide just before the break.

It would get no better for the home team in the second half, but Pompey might have killed the game eight minutes into the second period when Hilaire and Dillon set up Quinn, whose cheeky back-heel was saved by Burridge. At the other end it was turning into a comedy of errors. Clarke's mis-control inadvertently set up Wallace. The home fans, tearing their hair out behind the Milton Road end goal, had another tug when Wallace's effort landed amongst them. Le Tissier was sent on midway through the half, but his first contribution was to surrender possession to Hilaire. Saints finally realised it wasn't their day with ten minutes to go when Statham saw Knight block his shot, then ballooned the rebound high and not very handsome. For Pompey fans, they too had travelled seventeen miles to find paradise.

News journalist Mike Neasom, a veteran of covering Saints before starting the Pompey beat in 1974, aptly summed up the outcome: 'As dear old Ted Bates is fond of saying, "It's not what you make, it's what you take which counts". That message might well be hung on the dressing room wall at the Dell to greet Nicholl's squanderers as they come in for a week's daily dose of shooting practice.' Nicholl concurred: 'We have two scorers in the top-ten list – Clarke and Wallace – who are usually good finishers, but they didn't get it right today. They are disappointed with that. In that respect we let the fans down.'

For Alan Ball, however, it seemed like a turning point: 'Now perhaps people will start to believe what I've been saying – that we're not a bad side and we're in a false position. These people here [at The Dell] are supposed to be having a good season, yet we're only four points behind them.' Ball reserved special praise for his skipper Mick Kennedy, praise tinged with bitter regret as it would quickly emerge: 'In the last two matches he's taken on Steve Williams [of Arsenal] and now Jimmy Case and neither of them's done anything. That's why we're doing so well.'

As Kennedy took the field, however, a £300,000 move to Second Division Bradford City had been paved by Chairman Deacon, desperate for funds to stave off a looming financial crisis at Portsmouth as disappointing matchday revenue failed to keep up with expenditure. Midfielder Kevin Dillon had already been touted around earlier in the season, although he turned down the chance to join Watford.

Matters would come to a head in February, when a fire protection company filed a petition for a winding up order. They were quickly joined by the Inland Revenue over unpaid VAT bills. Bankruptcy was avoided, but the damage had been done, both in terms of team morale and in terms of Deacon's control over the club. It was an open secret now, Pompey were up for sale. Ironically, the players and Ball rose to the challenge, at least initially, with the best run of the season. A 2-1 win over Derby on 6th February put them up to fifteenth, six points clear of the drop zone, and just three behind Saints. FA Cup wins over Blackburn and Sheffield United, then Bradford City in the fifth round, set up the club's first quarter-final clash since 1952.

That was as good as it got. Unbeaten Liverpool rolled into town at the end of February, finally attracting a 28,000 capacity gate to Fratton, and departed as 2-0 winners. Two weeks later Luton, Saints' conquerors in round four, ended dreams of Wembley, and Pompey would win just one more match all season.

While Portsmouth were slip-sliding to relegation, Southampton were consolidating, bouncing back from their derby defeat with a 2-0 win at Old Trafford, ending Manchester United's unbeaten home record in the process. Saints felt comfortable enough to introduce teenage striker Alan Shearer for the home game with Arsenal in April, and his three goals in a 4-2 win – at seventeen he was the youngest player to record a First Division hat-trick – had him already marked down as a future great. Pompey's relegation was confirmed by a 1-2 home defeat by Newcastle on May Day, Bank Holiday Monday, the Geordies fielding the precocious young talent of Paul Gascoigne.

For many Pompey fans, however, dismay at relegation was blunted – in some case more than that – by managing to get one over on their old rivals. That result spawned a fanzine title – 'January 3, '88' – tee-shirts and a spate of smug small ads in the *News* and the *Echo*. In some ways this was a curious reaction, given that Saints extended their, by now, 28-year record of finishing higher than Pompey in the League.

For those who cherished beating Southampton more than anything else, the need now was to beat Bournemouth and Brighton – both in the Second Division for the 1988-89 season. Otherwise Pompey would slip to fourth place in the south-coast pecking order. For three months, Pompey threatened to bounce back at once. Deacon sold out to former QPR Chairman Jim Gregory, who set about throwing money at the team — Ball brought in Warren Aspinall, Mark Chamberlain, Warren Neill and Graeme Hogg for around £800,000 – and also at the ground. A whirlwind summer saw the old stadium gutted and re-clad. The redundant upper tier of the Fratton End was demolished and a replacement promised. On the pitch Pompey led the way with three wins in their first three games. The last was a 4-0 demolition of Leeds, who had former favourites Blake and Hilaire in their line-up, not to mention Baird. Baird's second yellow card, after a tangle with Hogg, earning a dismissal, was one of the more popular seen at Fratton and would have done little to change his opinion of the place, whatever the cosmetic surgery in progress.

Southampton, too, were on the up, temporarily at least, a 2-2 draw with Arsenal on 17th September leaving them second only to Norwich. Both sides maintained their momentum that autumn, but their seasons peaked simultaneously on 19th November. Saints confirmed that their top-five placing was no fluke with a 2-2 draw at Manchester United: Pompey went back to the top of the Second Division with a 3-0 win over Barnsley. Success wasn't matched by public interest, however: Pompey's gates scuffled along at under 12,000, while Saints' were not much higher.

By the end of January, the end of the season couldn't come quickly enough for either side. Four straight defeats, coupled with a replay defeat at Swindon in the third round of the FA Cup, left Pompey increasingly ill-equipped to chase a play-off place. Ball was sacked in January and replaced by coach John Gregory. Meanwhile, Saints were in freefall. Their FA Cup ambitions also ended at the first hurdle, after a replay, with a 1-2 defeat against Derby at The Dell, while hopes of another Rumbelows Cup semi-final were ended that same month by another 1-2 replay reverse at home to Luton. More serious was a sixteen-match winless run in the League, which dumped Saints into the relegation zone, at which point Newcastle, one place worse off, came to town on 1st April. Saints' end-of-season brinkmanship, which would become a familiar experience, had arrived.

To shore up their midfield, Southampton had turned to a controversial source, just before transfer-deadline day. The recent history of transfers between Saints and Pompey had been largely one-way. Saints players past their prime had usually ended up at Fratton Park trying to live down their past, while failing to live up to their reputations. This one was different. A club-record £700,000 bid was too tempting for Pompey to resist, and Barry Horne – a bargain-buy from Wrexham who had made a big impression the previous campaign in the First Division – was on his way back to the big-time at The Dell. Talk of the move had been around for some weeks. A cash-plus-player deal involving Colin Clarke, who had lost his scoring touch, was touted – but denied. Even new boss Gregory, wet round the ears maybe, was aware of the potential pitfalls of the transfer. Horne was one of Pompey's most popular players, in a side on a slide almost as steep as Saints': 'It had become increasingly difficult to keep Barry happy and it had reached the point where it was time to part. I felt this move was in the best interests of both this club and Barry,' said Gregory, before adding: 'I'm not sure how the fans will see it though …'

'A kick in the teeth,' was a typical response, expressed in the columns of the *Sports Mail* by L Male of Fratton (a disheartened season ticket holder of 25 years). Horne, a university graduate who was now looking to develop his international career with Wales, became the first player to move 'westwards' since Bill Rochford in 1946. This wasn't the first time Saints had paid a record fee for a Pompey player though, the transfer of centre-half John McIlwaine in 1930 having already broken that taboo.

Horne was a reluctant mover, too: 'I wanted first division football, but I admit I'd have preferred it to be with a club further north, because that's where my roots are, but that didn't happen and Saints have given me the chance to further my career.' Hardly a ringing endorsement of his new employers, although perhaps he was showing he had the brains to be diplomatic. Horne's new boss, Chris Nicholl – having also brought in defenders Neil Ruddock and Micky Adams – was in no doubt what his new acquisition would provide: 'I have been after him for quite a while, but now he is a Southampton footballer I am very pleased with that. Barry is here to help us stay in the first division and go on to better things. I like his strength, his aggression, his passing ability and I like his attitude.'

But there was that small matter of staying up. Horne's debut had seen Saints slump 1-3 at home to Arsenal. In the 90th minute the following week against Newcastle, the 0-0 scoreline was doing neither side any favours. Then Danny Wallace's surge into the box, seemingly away from danger, was ended by a collision with the Newcastle keeper and a penalty was given. Neil Ruddock thumped it home and Southampton's first League win since 12th November provided the launchpad for a run of just one defeat in nine games which saw the drop comfortably avoided.

For Portsmouth fans again there would be no *schadenfreude*, only more heartache as six straight defeats saw Brighton sneak above them into nineteenth place on goal-difference. With Bournemouth safely in mid-table, Pompey were for the first time second not only to Saints, but behind the Cherries and Seagulls too.

However, the most significant event of that spring was played out far from parochial jockeying for positions on the south coast. On Saturday 15th April 1989, 96 Liverpool fans were crushed to death in the pens of the Leppings Lane end at Hillsborough at the start of the FA Cup semi-final with Nottingham Forest. More than twenty years of conventional wisdom, that football supporters were no better than animals, came to its grisly dénouement. 'Safety' fences had become mincing machines. It was an event that would shape the future of football – a future to which Southampton were to prove far more adaptable than their neighbours.

Chapter 12

~ So Near, So Far Away ~

(1989-93)

Post-Hillsborough, as the safety of football grounds became a public priority, Portsmouth's board had a handy excuse for shelving the planned rebuilding of the Fratton End. With gates now below 7,000, raising capacity was hardly at the top of the club's agenda and the board said as much. The main summer transfer was top scorer Mick Quinn, who exercised his freedom of contract by joining newly-relegated Newcastle, managed by Jim Smith, for £750,000. Southampton, without any significant summer strengthening, would become – and would stay for years – bookies' favourites for the drop. The loss of striker Danny Wallace, for £1.2 million to Manchester United, weakened their resources further, but in another refrain that would become all too familiar, the player had been 'de-stabilised by his agent', according to Nicholl.

However, if any club was going to go down that 1989-90 season it was Pompey. New boss John Gregory, in his first job, was out of his depth trying to cope with the grizzled pros he had inherited from Ball. A New Year 2-3 home defeat to Leicester ended his tenure, by which time Pompey were in the relegation zone. Seventeen miles away, Saints defied the odds and were third on 21st October, following an astonishing 4-1 demolition of leaders Liverpool at The Dell, inspired by Matt Le Tissier. By the time caretaker Pompey boss Frank Burrows, who had re-joined the club the previous summer as a coach, reignited the season with a 2-1 win at Alan Ball's Stoke on 13th January, Saints were still fourth. They were also into the fourth round of the FA Cup after a 3-1 win at Spurs, as Pompey lost 1-2 in the last minute at First Division Crystal Palace. A Neil Ruddock header took Saints past Oxford at The Dell in the fourth round, but any Wembley dreams were halted by Liverpool, who exacted revenge with a 3-0 drubbing at Anfield at the next stage. Saints' League form barely faltered, and it would take two defeats in the last two games of the season, at Arsenal and Spurs, to end hopes of a UEFA Cup place, now that English clubs' post-Heysel exile was about to end. Seventh place was a fine and unexpected achievement.

Portsmouth, too, could be content with a mid-table finish after their catastrophic autumn. The publication in spring 1990 of the Taylor Report into the Hillsborough Disaster recommended that all Football League clubs should become all-seater. With Pompey's proposed re-location to the Goods Yard already a non-starter, plans to re-vamp Fratton Park were also on hold. Fans were desperate for the Fratton End to be rebuilt, to restore some atmosphere to a moribund stadium, but the report provided yet more useful breathing space for the board. With the team having apparently recovered from their worst post-War start to a season in 1990-91 – two draws out of six matches — plans were finally announced in late-October 1990 for a new 6,000-seater stand, although with gates still struggling to reach five figures consistently, it looked an over-optimistic scheme. So it would prove.

Both clubs harboured high hopes for the 1990-91 season. Pompey had even turned to an ex-Saint to provide the goals for a promotion bid, £440,000 being splashed out on QPR and Northern Ireland international Colin Clarke, who had been so profligate on that January 1988 derby day. By December, however, both clubs would be struggling at the wrong end of their respective divisions and it would be the Cups which provided the scraps of consolation. Saints, buoyed by Le Tissier's goals and the filling of the gap left by Danny Wallace by his brother Rod and Alan Shearer, reached the quarter-finals of the Rumbelows Cup, losing 2-3 at Old Trafford in a replay. Nottingham Forest accounted for them in a fifth round FA Cup replay.

That was also the round in which Pompey wheeled out their 'sleeping giant' credentials, yet again, by attracting 26,000 to see two second-half goals by an irrepressible Paul Gascoigne overturn the lead given by Mark Chamberlain. The big talking point on the south coast, however, was speculation that Chris Nicholl was fighting for his job. With a clutch of young talent coming through the ranks, in the shape of Le Tissier, Rod Wallace, Shearer and Jason Dodd, more was expected than being seventeenth in the table by late February. Another relegation battle loomed, but a characteristic late run turned things around. Nevertheless a final placing of fourteenth meant Nicholl was on his way out.

It was all change at Portsmouth, too. Frank Burrows shocked everyone by resigning in March, with the club deep in the relegation mire, but under caretaker Tony Barton – appointed by Burrows as his assistant the previous summer – a run of five wins and a draw in the final nine games saw the drop into Division Three avoided on the penultimate Saturday. Barton was to be disappointed when thinking the job was his permanently. At the last moment Chairman Jim Gregory changed his mind and handed the task of reviving Pompey's fortunes to the 'Bald Eagle' Jim Smith.

Southampton's replacement for Nicholl would prove to be more controversial, as little-known Crystal Palace coach Ian Branfoot found himself in the hot seat.

Jim Smith's first big decision was to rid the club of the big-name, high-wage under-achievers signed by his predecessors, and blood perhaps the richest seam of talent seen at Fratton Park since the youth policy was re-introduced in 1972. Winger Darren Anderton was the jewel in the crown.

Southampton-born, thus reversing the trend of the late 1960s and 70s, Anderton had already come to notice, winning a Barclays (present sponsors of the Football League) 'Young Eagle' award the previous season. However, the team that was denied an opening-day win in 1991-92 in the last minute at big-spending Blackburn also included Andy Awford, Kit Symons, and leggy striker Darryl Powell. The quartet had been at the core of the Pompey side which reached the semi-finals of the FA Youth Cup in 1990 and they didn't disappoint as they made the step up. An unbeaten home run and just four defeats in seventeen games had Pompey in the play-off places by November and suddenly the talk was not just of promotion, but the real possibility that they would be swapping places with Saints come the end of the season.

Poor old Ian Branfoot's attempts at re-structuring his squad were going badly. While Pompey were thrashing promotion rivals Middlesbrough 4-0 at Fratton Park on 28th December to go within two points of the top of the Second Division, Saints were losing 1-2 at Aston Villa to go bottom of the First. Enter the FA Cup – a competition which would significantly alter the complexion of both clubs' seasons.

The third round of the trophy threw up a fascinating contest for Portsmouth. Away to Exeter doesn't seem too exciting on paper, but throw in the fact that Alan Ball was now manager at St James Park, Steve Williams, now 33, was pulling their strings in midfield, while old-time Pompey scourge Steve Moran was in their attack, and the match took on a different hue. A typically chipper Ball acknowledged the fact: 'It's got all the ingredients: a couple of Scummers with a point to prove and a couple of Pompey old boys in Vince Hilaire and Paul Wimbleton wanting to do the same,' he chirped. 'And then there's me. I've got a little point to prove to a certain Mr Gregory as well.'

When Moran levelled the scores for Exeter in the 54th minute with a glancing header, to level Guy Whittingham's opener, the Third Division side sensed a shock. Pompey weathered the storm and secured their passage with a late goal from Warren Aspinall.

Saints boss Branfoot, booed along the touchline before, during and after the 1-2 home defeat to Everton on New Year's Day, saw the return of Le Tissier inspire a 2-0 win over QPR and relieve some of the pressure, although the screws were well and truly turned the following week as a 2-4 home defeat by fellow strugglers Sheffield United left them five points adrift of safety. A place in the promised land of the Premier League, to be inaugurated in August 1992, as the rich clubs decided they wanted to get considerably richer, was looking forlorn. Gates were at an all-time low for First Division football at The Dell. Fewer than 13,000 saw that Sheffield United match, while on the Friday night before Christmas, only 11,000 saw the 1-1 draw with Notts County. At Fratton, while not exactly booming in terms of gates, hope was now translating into expectation. For the return with Moneybags Blackburn, now managed by Kenny Dalglish, 20,000 saw a last-minute Whittingham goal earn a 2-2 draw. But it was the FA Cup that was the driving force. Almost 17,000 saw Anderton's two-goal televised salvo see off Leyton Orient in round four, then more than 18,000 saw the 1-1 draw with Middlesbrough in the fifth round.

The Cup – two cups to be precise – was coming to Southampton's, and Branfoot's, rescue too. An FA Cup fourth round 0-0 home draw with League leaders Manchester United, in front of a near full house of 19,500, was followed by an even gutsier 2-2 draw at Old Trafford in the replay.

It is useful to put attendances into context in the early 1990s, as there were only 33,000 inside Old Trafford for that game. Most of those would have been mortified to see unfancied Saints prevail 4-2 in the penalty shoot-out, introduced that season in a bid to cut down on fixture congestion. By then, Saints had already booked a Wembley place. The Zenith Data Systems Cup was the final incarnation of the Football League Full Members' Cup, initiated in the wake of English clubs' ban from European competition. Having won at Bristol City and Plymouth, Saints made the Southern final by beating West Ham 2-1 at The Dell. A 6,000 gate indicated that this wasn't a competition which had much public appeal. In the Southern 'final', Saints thrashed Chelsea 5-1 on aggregate to set up a Wembley confrontation with the Northern winners, Nottingham Forest, at the end of March. A Wembley date always pulled in the punters and Saints duly took around 30,000 to see their side claw back a 0-2 deficit, only to lose to a late goal. In that final, Saints wore their controversial 'blue' away kit, with red trimmings, which sort of made them look like Pompey circa 1972. Whichever marketing guru suggested it would be a good idea to clad Saints in these colours whenever there was a clash, clearly didn't understand football and its parochial rivalries. Whatever next, a red and white striped Pompey away kit?

The fifth round set up Southampton's trip to Third Division Bolton. Two goals from centre-half Richard Hall had seemingly avoided a banana skin, only for two replies in the last ten minutes to force a replay at The Dell, on the same night that Pompey travelled to Ayresome Park. It was to prove a thrilling night of football, reminiscent of some of those dramatic Cup nights in the late 1960s. At the end of it, the talk on the south coast was about a possible semi-final, or even Wembley, meeting of the old rivals. Saints, though, had looked on their way out, as Bolton led 2-1 going into the second minute of injury-time. Then, former Pompey midfielder Barry Horne fired in an unstoppable shot from long range to force extra-time. A home tie with Norwich awaited the winners, and it was Horne who ensured it was Saints who prevailed with a winning goal twelve minutes before another penalty shoot-out beckoned.

'Anything you can do …' goes the old song, and Portsmouth, perhaps not trumping Saints for drama, surely outdid their performance. Not that the game at Ayresome was dull. Far from it. Twice Pompey trailed – Paul Wilkinson scoring two goals in nine first-half minutes, sandwiching a Clarke equaliser – on a ground where Pompey had won just once in 40 years. Clarke levelled before half-time, then Anderton swung over a corner in the 58th minute which sailed into the far corner of the net to put Pompey ahead. Anderton added another before the end.

A quarter-final tie at Fratton Park with Brian Clough's First Division Nottingham Forest beckoned, and 26,000 tickets quickly disappeared. The 'sold out' signs were up at The Dell too, but Saints muffed their chance of a semi-final place. Glenn Cockerill missed a sitter, although the goalless draw with Norwich at least offered another bite at the cherry. Pompey, however, needed just one gulp as the ever-erratic Forest keeper Mark Crossley made a characteristic error, dropping a cross from John Beresford's free-kick, and midfielder Alan McLoughlin pounced from close range.

Ironically, McLoughlin was a Saints player at the time. The former Swindon midfield mainspring had been bought by Nicholl in December 1990, having made his mark by scoring against Saints eleven months before that in a Littlewoods Cup-tie. He cost the club a record £1 million, but struggled to make an impact in the top flight. Doubts about Nicholl's judgement went a long way to sealing McLoughlin's fate that summer. The more direct Branfoot style hardly suited the ball-playing attributes of the Republic of Ireland international, so a loan to Pompey, with a view to a £400,000 transfer in February 1992 seemed to suit all concerned, except perhaps, Southampton Football Club's accountants. Making, then taking a goal in the first eleven minutes of his debut against Tranmere went a long way to removing any anti-Southampton sentiment from the terraces and by 7th March he had already carved a niche into Portsmouth folklore.

In the Monday draw for the FA Cup semi-final were Pompey, Saints or Norwich, Second Division Sunderland or Chelsea, and Liverpool. Sod's law, for Pompey fans at least, meant it was they who got the mighty Liverpool, and from that moment hopes of a blindside run at automatic promotion, or even the play-offs, began to fade. In their first Cup semi-final since 1949, the only question was could Portsmouth cause as big an upset as that which saw Second Division Leicester knock out champions-elect Pompey in that game. By coincidence the venue was to be the same. Highbury. However, the venue was only decided once the other semi-final was sorted out. Sunderland upset another applecart, beating Chelsea 2-1 at Roker Park, but Saints couldn't keep alive the dream of an all-Hampshire final, as they heart-breakingly lost 1-2 in extra-time to Chris Sutton's strike for Norwich.

Unlike Portsmouth, the Cup run had inspired Saints' League form. Branfoot, for all his trials and tribulations, seemed to have found the right formula at last. Six straight wins in March and early April lifted Saints from bottom to seventeenth and, more importantly, eight points clear of relegation. Three wins and three defeats in the final six meant Saints would be proud, if relieved, founder members of the new Premier League.

Meanwhile, Portsmouth shifted their 17,000 ticket allocation for the semi-final in no time, despite a season's average gate of 11,000. Scores of coaches made their way to north London, although all but the most fervent of fans would have made the trip in hope rather than expectation. Liverpool, title winners in 1990 and a string of honours as long as your arm since the mid-1960s, were in transition as manager Graeme Souness unpicked the tangled threads which had prompted Kenny Dalglish to resign two years beforehand. They were still a class act, though. John Barnes, John Aldridge, Ray Houghton, Bruce Grobbelaar, even ex-Saint Mark Wright; everywhere you looked was a better player than even Pompey's fast-maturing crop could offer. On the day, anything can happen, however, and from the first whistle of the high noon Sunday showdown, it was clear that Portsmouth were more than ready to rise to the challenge. It was not the greatest of games, and in 90 minutes both sides could point to near misses.

The main talking point was a crunching, no, make that foul, tackle on Mark Chamberlain by Ronnie Whelan, which saw the winger stretchered off. The referee didn't see fit to punish Whelan. One of Pompey's key players was out of the game and the season. Extra-time came and the first period went. Then, in the 108th minute right-back Warren Neill set Anderton galloping away. With the Liverpool defence in hot pursuit, the twenty-year-old shot past Grobbelaar from the edge of the area. Pompey were twelve minutes from Wembley.

Saints fans will tell you there's nothing quite like an FA Cup final. Plenty still recall 1976 with obvious affection, while many more can tell you they were at Cardiff's Millennium Stadium in 2003. With the passing of time we will soon be able to count on one hand the surviving Pompey fans who were at Wembley in 1939. So, in this tale of two football clubs we are at a big moment. Pompey's glory, as many Saints fans were quite eager to point out, was behind them; a long way behind them. This was the moment that particular taunt came so close to being thrown back at them, possibly with interest. For the Wembley final would be against Second Division Sunderland, as it turned out, beaten once already that season by Pompey and half a table behind them in the League standings.

Even today, the thought that Portsmouth could have won not only the Cup, but found themselves in European football too for the first time, evokes tears of frustration. It would have been a massive achievement, putting Portsmouth in much the same historical bracket as their neighbours' efforts over the previous 25 years. Granted, there are plenty of 'ifs' and 'buts' in that particular theoretical equation, but few enough to have presented a real threat to Saints' recent hegemony. Of course, it didn't turn out that way. Four minutes remained when Andy Awford clattered Steve Nicol on the edge of the penalty area, Barnes curled a free-kick onto the post and the ball rolled agonisingly along the line for Whelan – who probably shouldn't have even been on the pitch – to tap home the equaliser. A good proportion of Southampton supporters must have heaved a huge sigh of relief.

Portsmouth took 19,000 fans to Villa Park for the replay, where they were served up with more of the same. Six minutes from the end of normal time McLoughlin hit the bar from eight yards. Close, but Saints fans might say, 'not close enough'. Touché. Extra-time failed to find a goal and Pompey wearily gave up the penalty shoot-out, missing three of their first four kicks.

Weary, too, was Portsmouth's forlorn pursuit of promotion. Nine games in 24 days took its toll and Pompey finished ninth, five points short of a play-off place. Optimism was high in 1992-93 that another promotion bid could be mounted, while Southampton, too, on the back of their latest great escape, could look forward to the riches of the new Premier League. Well, not quite yet. The financial chasm, which would open between the top flight and the rest of football, had yet to open so wide, but with a ground capacity of 20,000, Saints were still a selling club. Alan Shearer's fifteen League and Cup goals in a struggling side, and eleven in nine games for the England Under-21s, had alerted the talent scouts. Blackburn Rovers, back in the big time and with a stash of Jack Walker's cash burning a hole in Kenny Dalglish's pocket, took Shearer in a new record deal – £3.6 million – between British clubs. In his place came Kerry Dixon from Chelsea and David Speedie from Blackburn for a total of £1 million, while Arsenal's Perry Groves cost £750,000. Also on the move was ex-Pompey midfielder Horne, attracted by the lure of a so-called 'bigger club' in Everton.

In some respects Southampton and Portsmouth were not that dissimilar in this period. But whereas Saints were able to keep hold of at least one jewel, in Guernsey-born Le Tissier, Pompey were forced to lose two of theirs in the summer of 1992. Full-back John Beresford was all set to move to Liverpool, until the Anfield club pulled out of the deal following a medical, so he moved to First Division rivals Newcastle instead for £750,000. The greater loss was that of Darren Anderton, who became Pompey's record sale when going to Tottenham for £1.7 million. As a £400,000 makeweight in the deal came the 'misfit' striker Paul Walsh. It turned out to be good business.

The 1992-93 season proved to be a momentous one, for both clubs, and it which would go a long way to defining the next ten years of our story. Pompey's opening match in the newly-named Barclays 'First' Division, suggested things might be more exciting than usual. A 3-3 draw with Bristol City, thanks to a hat-trick by Whittingham, was refereed by Roger Milford, who as chance would have it, would also be in the middle for their last, more dramatic still, game of the season. Initially Walsh fired blanks, even if 'Corporal Punishment' Whittingham – he had been bought out of the Army for £400 – didn't. After being hauled off for the third match in a row, at Leicester, in his fourth goalless game, Walsh's arrival had all the trappings of an expensive boob by Jim Smith. A week later it was all smiles as he chipped home a classy goal in the 4-0 demolition of Birmingham, with Southampton-born former Pompey goalkeeper Gosney between the sticks. Gosney had finally decided, at the ripe old age of 29, that he was no longer prepared to play second-fiddle to Alan Knight. From then on, Pompey's season gathered impetus like the Flying Scotsman on a record-breaking run from London to Edinburgh.

In the new-fangled Premier League, it was business as usual for Southampton as their habitual grim battle to avoid the drop started in earnest from pretty much day one, when they drew a turgid game with Spurs 0-0 at The Dell. Dixon and Speedie failed to coordinate and by October the partnership was broken up, never to be reunited. Speedie had been reluctant to move south, preferring to commute from his home in the Midlands, and was placed on the transfer list. He would still have an unanticipated part to play in this season, though. Two goals (both from Dixon) and 21 appearances between them meant the pressure was mounting on Branfoot. Into the side came Iain Dowie, a £500,000 capture from West Ham the previous season, but he too was far from the fans' favourite, facing a torrent of abuse from the Dell faithful during a 1-1 draw with Leeds in September.

Not that there were many believers in those days. That Leeds game attracted a respectable 16,000, but as the grind of avoiding the drop took its toll, the late-October visit of fellow strugglers Oldham persuaded fewer than 11,000 through the turnstiles. It was Saints' lowest-ever Premier League gate, harking back to the bad old days of Division Three (South) in the 1950s. The fans were not happy either, despite a 1-0 win over Oldham, courtesy of a Hall header. A 'Branfoot out' banner was unfurled on the Archers Road End, while the manager needed a police cordon to protect him from angry fans.

If someone had suggested at the time that Southampton would be playing to 30,000 full houses week-in, week-out by the new millennium, the most kindly response would have been a dismissive 'wildly optimistic'. And that would be among fellow Saints fans. Another striker to get his chance, as Branfoot looked for a way to cover his £1 million blunder, was Portsmouth-born Paul Moody. Overlooked by Pompey, the 25-year-old 6' 3" blond forward had been handed a dream move from Southern League Waterlooville to the top flight the previous season. Branfoot had been pleased with the way he had worked on his game and gave him his debut against Wimbledon on 17th October, after Dixon failed a fitness test. Moody lasted less than an hour, with Saints scoring their two goals in a 2-2 draw after he had left the field.

An interesting diversion that season also saw Pompey finally play in Europe, although the Anglo-Italian Cup hardly set the pulse racing. It was conceived as a tournament for 'First Division' sides – as the Football League had controversially re-branded the Second Division following the birth of the Premier League – and their Serie B counterparts. A similar competition had been staged in the 1970s and Saints had played in a different version again in 1976 as FA Cup winners, losing 1-4 on aggregate to Napoli, their Italian counterparts.

It was again fated to be a brutish, ugly tournament, which lasted just two seasons and was watched by a handful of spectators. Having qualified by winning a domestic preliminary round, Pompey beat Cesena and Lucchese in front of sub-5,000 crowds, but a 0-3 defeat in the Stadio San Nicola in Bari meant they were knocked out of the group stage. That defeat was remarkable not so much for the fact that just 800 paying customers entered the 60,000-capacity stadium, but that 250 of them had travelled from Portsmouth, 100 having taken advantage of a special club charter flight. Less than a tenth of that number travelled to the redundant final fixture at Ascoli, which Pompey won 2-1.

As Portsmouth's promotion campaign stepped up another gear – surviving the loss of a 5-3 lead at Oxford in injury-time (it ended 5-5), Southampton too were getting their act together. Consecutive wins at struggling Nottingham Forest and at home to Arsenal hoisted them into lower-mid table by Christmas. Three defeats in four over the holiday period had the bottom three breathing down their necks again, but the spring of 1993 was to prove productive for both clubs. Eight goals – six of them from Whittingham, who now had 30 in all competitions – saw Pompey beat Bristol Rovers and Derby over Christmas, leaving them fifth, five points off an automatic promotion slot. A 0-1 defeat at Second Division Brighton in the third round of the FA Cup may have been bad for local pride, but the fabled consolation of being able to concentrate on the League suddenly came into its own.

Likewise, Saints were relieved of their FA Cup responsibilities at the first hurdle by Forest, but again the experience served only to revive fortunes in the League. Seven wins in the next ten matches banished fears (or in some Pompey cases, hopes) that the two clubs might change places at the end of the season. That issue settled, unseasonably early, our focus switches to Pompey's promotion push. A stutter at the end of February, including three points tossed away after very late goals were conceded (at home to Leicester, 1-1) and at Swindon (0-1), left Pompey in the play-off places. They were nine points shy of second-place West Ham and thirteen of runaway leaders Newcastle, managed by Kevin Keegan, who was verbally reminded of his Saints connections when 18,000 turned up at Fratton on a freezing February night to see Pompey win 2-0. Ten wins and a draw in the next eleven games carried Portsmouth briefly to the top of the table, following a 2-0 home win over Wolves.

Whittingham was still scoring freely, although he would readily admit that the catalyst for his prolific season was the craft of Walsh, whose combination of artistry and industry belied initial fears about his motivation. With two matches to go the equation was simple. Four points from the visit to lowly Sunderland and the visit of mid-table Grimsby would ensure promotion.

During the build up to the penultimate game, at Roker Park, Sky TV used England's Under-21 fixture against Holland at Fratton Park to test their camera angles for the following season's coverage. Vice chairman David Deacon, son of John, who inherited his father's place on the board as part of the deal which saw Jim Gregory become chairman in 1988, unveiled ambitious plans to build a futuristic 25,000-capacity stadium on Farlington playing fields.

Portsmouth were finally getting the crowds to justify it. Nearly 24,000 saw Derby beaten on Easter Monday and 23,000 saw the Wolves win. With Southampton's plans to relocate to Stoneham struggling to get past the planning authorities, Chairman Guy Askham contemplated rebuilding the West Stand at The Dell to ensure the stadium had a viable capacity once the recommendations of the Taylor Report were implemented. Pompey looked set to finally reclaim that which their supporters claimed was theirs by right. What could go wrong?

What indeed. Even with Portsmouth's irresistible surge in March, the worry was how to replace Whittingham or Walsh if either got injured or suspended. A knee injury in a reserve game in January had already ended Clarke's season and, as it turned out, his career. Manager Jim Smith was aware of the danger and, to pre-empt it, tried to sign Saints misfit Speedie. Smith was prepared to tolerate Speedie's long daily commute for the player's undoubted pedigree in the top flight.

Smith missed out, however, and Speedie joined West Ham instead. Now, with the transfer deadline looming, Pompey's boss turned his attentions to Bristol Rovers' John Taylor. £400,000 would have sealed the deal, but Jim Gregory, in ailing health, baulked at the price. Instead, enter 31-year-old George Lawrence on a short-term deal. Lawrence was a former

Saints apprentice who had scored twelve goals in 70-odd appearances for the Dell club in two spells there in the 1980s. He had also played for Oxford, Millwall and Bournemouth, but was presently on non-contract terms with Southern League Weymouth.

Lawrence was a player for whom the term 'unorthodox' was invented. However, his impact at Fratton was immediate, if limited. He was usually brought on as a late substitute with the team leading, his job being to waste time with the ball by the corner flag. In that 2-0 victory over Wolves, however, he ignored instructions and instead immediately sent over a decent cross that was headed in by Walsh. It was cult-hero stuff in a glorious blind-side promotion run. Or, at least, it would have been. But then Chairman Gregory's luck ran out, or probably more realistically, he paid for his parsimony. Pompey took 6,000 fans up to Sunderland. They saw Guy Butters sent off for punching the ball off the line and their team go 0-3 down early in the second half. Strange to say, with twenty minutes to go, their spirits were still up. There was still the Grimsby game to come, West Ham had a tricky-looking game at play-off contenders Swindon the next day, and besides, with Walsh and Whittingham you'd have to fancy Pompey in the play-offs. Then a linesman's flag alerted the referee to the fact that Sunderland defender Shaun Cunnington was in a heap. Walsh's frustration had got the better of him and his sly punch was red carded. He was eligible to play against Grimsby, but would be banned for the next three games. If Pompey went up, no matter, but if they had to settle for the play-offs ...

One lifeline was quickly cut. Glenn Hoddle was making his managerial way at Swindon who, now they were safely in the play-offs folded tamely to the Hammers, 1-3. The initiative was back with the east London club. The rules at this time stipulated that for teams level on points, goals scored took precedence over goal-difference. This could have ludicrous consequences, for goal figures of 90 for, 100 against, were better than figures of 89 for, 30 against, which flouted the principles of both goal-average and goal-difference. With only one game left to play, West Ham had two more in the 'for' column than Pompey. Whittingham's late consolation at Roker Park, which made it 1-4, could yet prove invaluable.

The equation was now simple. Portsmouth had to equal West Ham's result, but score two more goals in the process. The Hammers were at home to Cambridge, who had to win to have any chance of staying up. Almost 25,000 packed into Fratton and on an achingly tense day they saw their side concede the first goal to Grimsby, while the transistor grapevine informed everyone that West Ham were leading 1-0. The scorer? David Speedie! In the second half Pompey levelled through full-back Ray Daniel, before the grapevine sent out the ripple that Portsmouth-born, former Fratton Park apprentice Steve Claridge had equalised for Cambridge. In the pandemonium that ensued, the words of the radio commentator that Claridge's effort had been disallowed for offside were drowned out. Only slowly did the truth emerge. Whittingham scored his obligatory goal, his 42nd in the League and 49th in all competitions, but at 2-1 Pompey still needed a third goal. Another goal came, but not at Fratton. In the final minute Clive Allen wrapped up a 2-0 win for West Ham.

In the play-offs Portsmouth faced Leicester, the first leg at the City Ground, Nottingham as Filbert Street was being rebuilt. With his sidekick Walsh banned, Whittingham was impotent, and Julian Joachim's late goal gave Leicester – twelve points behind Pompey in the final reckoning – a slender advantage. That might have been overcome at Fratton Park, McLaughlin having levelled the aggregate scores, had referee Milford overruled his linesman, who did not flag for offside when Ian Ormondroyd levelled on the night. Lawrence's arrival from the bench was a futile gamble, the match ended 2-2, and dreams of a first Wembley (play-off final) appearance in more than half a century and, more importantly, the Premier League, were over. Saints could rest easy once more.

Chapter 13

~ Hanging in There ~

(1993-99)

In the summer of 1993 the prospect of another top flight derby may have been put on the back burner – for a good ten years as it turned out. But one thing united Southampton and Portsmouth in the build up to the start of the 1993-1994 season: their respective attempts to obtain planning permission for a new stadium. Pompey's grandiose scheme to build on Farlington Marshes was already, if not unravelling, then at least coming under pressure from a co-ordinated and slick NIMBY campaign. Scrapped already were the four 'domed' stand roofs. In their place, a more functional four-sided affair would become the blueprint for new stadia in the decade to come.

Southampton, too, were being continually frustrated in their attempts to create a coalition of planners from Southampton City, Eastleigh Borough and Hampshire County councils for an equally ambitious 'out of town' stadium at Stoneham. It was to be sited near railway, motorway and air links north of the city. These stadium stories would run and run, but the clock was already ticking. The legal requirement – post-Taylor – for all sports grounds in the top two divisions to become all-seater by August 1994 was beginning to bite. During the summer, Southampton had spent £800,000 converting the Archers Road End into a small covered stand, reducing capacity to 19,000, with the intention the following summer to turn The Dell into a fully-seated arena by installing seats into the Milton Road End. Capacity then would be just over 15,000. Inadequate certainly for a Premiership club, although it is worth remembering that in the early 1990s the public was not as enthusiastic for top-grade football as it is today.

For Southampton's opening game, lost 0-2 to Everton, just 14,000 turned up, a couple of thousand less than had come through the Fratton turnstiles to see Guy Whittingham's replacement – the veteran Nottingham Forest and Leeds striker Lee Chapman, not to mention husband of actress Lesley Ash – get himself sent off as Pompey slumped 1-2. Another summer signing by Jim Smith was former Saints and Swindon defender Jon Gittens, who cut short a miserable spell at Middlesbrough to return south. In that August came the sad news too that Tony Barton, former Pompey player, scout, assistant and caretaker manager, as well as assistant to Chris Nicholl at The Dell, had died following a heart attack. Renowned as one of the most decent men in the game, he had worked for a multiple sclerosis charity, after his rejection by Jim Gregory in 1991. He had quadruple heart by-pass surgery in the summer of 1992, from which he never recovered.

By the time Chapman had served his suspension he had left Pompey for West Ham, but by then hopes of another promotion drive had been hampered by a haul of just six points from 21. At The Dell things were even worse. Manager Ian Branfoot was feeling the heat yet again after eight defeats and just one win in the opening nine games left Saints with only Swindon below them. The £1 million spent on the combined strikeforce of Kerry Dixon and David Speedie the previous summer was acknowledged by Branfoot as a 'clanger dropped'. Another £550,000 was found to sign former England Under-21 international Paul Allen from Spurs and an old mate of Branfoot's, veteran midfielder Peter Reid, also arrived, but it made little difference. The decision to drop fans' favourite Matt Le Tissier hardly endeared the manager to them, nor would a disastrous Coca-Cola Cup exit at Third Division Shrewsbury.

A 3-3 home draw with fellow strugglers Sheffield United – a late brace by Jostein Flo salvaging an unlikely point for the Blades – unleashed a torrent of abuse from the Dell boo-boys. Throughout the match banners and jeers called for the manager's head, and one Saints fanzine was selling an issue with a picture of Branfoot and the headline 'Hope you die soon'.

At the final whistle, missiles, including pies and oranges, were hurled in Branfoot's direction as he made the lonely trudge from the dugout along the touchline to the tunnel at the corner of the stadium. Afterwards, Blades boss Dave Bassett had little time for Branfoot's tormentors: 'If there's any justice he'll get looked after, paid up and the club will go down. He's done nothing wrong. It was terrible what Ian was subjected to at the end by so many demented people … Some of them were swearing at him and if he swore back all hell would break loose.' No doubt those Saints fans implicated will point to the fact that the ultimate outcome that season 'justified' their actions. Branfoot's dismissal would be delayed, but only until January.

However, that episode removes some of the gloss from the 'superior' reputation Saints fans claim in relation to Pompey's. Those from the eastern end of the M27 are considered – so goes the school of thought – to lack 'class'. Despite the fact there is barely a smidgen of demographic difference between the two cities, according to the socio-economic indices available, people from Portsmouth – and by association supporters of its football team – tend to be more inclined to hooliganism, racism, crudity and fickleness. As with all good stereotypes, there is a grain of truth in this. Previous chapters of this book have highlighted the unsavoury nature of some of Pompey's support over the years, notably during the 1984 FA Cup clash between the sides. However, the treatment meted out to Branfoot in the latter days of his reign at The Dell suggest that some elements of

Saints' support are not averse to sinking close to the gutter, if not actually dropping into it. Fan-campaigns to unseat Portsmouth managers, notably Terry Fenwick and John Gregory, have been vociferous and long-running, not to mention successful, but it has to be said they never quite descended into the vilification of Branfoot.

With Le Tissier reinstated, Southampton rallied with home wins over Newcastle and Tottenham to lift the pressure, but it soon returned. A 1-2 defeat on 18th December at Swindon – who by the season's end would concede 100 Premiership goals – left Saints yet again with only the Robins below them and looking a short price to join them in the drop. Portsmouth, on the other hand, looked relatively buoyant. A Coca-Cola Cup run had given the season fizz, with a January quarter-final trip to Old Trafford on the horizon. Solid League form had also kept them in touch with the leaders, Tranmere and Charlton.

On the international front, Portsmouth had a player going to the World Cup finals for the first time since 1956, and it was an ex-Saint to boot. Alan McLoughlin had earned his place in Republic of Ireland folklore with the late equaliser in Belfast against the North, which ensured that Jack Charlton's men would be going to USA 1994. No matter that he would spend the tournament warming the bench.

The FA Cup draw had also given Pompey a tantalising prospect. On 8th January they would travel to Blackburn, second in the Premiership and on their way to buying the championship (the following season) with Jack Walker's fortune. In Rovers' side was Alan Shearer, the jewel in their crown. Shearer was subjected to the customary 'scumming' from the travelling Pompey fans. For the uninitiated, this requires any opposition player with one-time Saints connections to be jeered 'Scummer, Scummer', *ad nauseam* every time he touches the ball or ventures near the touchline. Whether this is moronic myopia or good-natured banter will depend on your point of view and, perhaps too, the disposition of the player on the receiving end. For Ian Baird, it was red rag to a bull. To Dave Beasant a chance to engage in a bit of repartee. However, Shearer responded to the stick in the only way he knows how, and smacked Rovers into the lead under the noses of those same taunting fans. Apocryphal testimony suggests that Shearer's smile was wiped off his face by a hurled meat pie that caught him on the side of the head as he wheeled away in triumph. The game swung to and fro, but it was McLoughlin's day as his last-minute scrambled goal earned a replay. Four days later two Walsh goals earned a 2-2 draw at Premiership leaders Manchester United in the Coca-Cola Cup, watched by 7,000 travelling fans. That was as good as it would get for Pompey.

Southampton hadn't quite reached their black hole. During the 1-1 third round draw with Second Division Port Vale, Vale's goal was set up by

Portsmouth-born and former North Terrace regular Paul Kerr, and it sparked another burst of spectator abuse aimed at Ian Branfoot. By the following Saturday he had quit, but his going split Saints' support to the core. At the heart of the 'Branfoot Must Go' campaign had been the Southampton Independent Supporters Association. Committee member Clive Foley summed up their view: 'This is a victory for people power. The fans wanted him out and it's the fans who have got him out. Branfoot has taken the team nowhere and it will take at least three years to return to the point we were at when he came.'

Not so, countered East Stand season-ticket holder Terry Powell, who hailed from the Pompey stronghold of Gosport: 'I didn't hold up red cards against Branfoot. I don't shout abuse at the man and I support what he's worked for. Now the fans have got Branfoot out, what are they going to do with the next manager? They seem to think they own the club.'

Both men could agree on one thing: everyone needed to get behind Branfoot's successor, whoever he turned out to be. Lew Chatterley and John Mortimore took charge of the team for the vital 1-0 league win over Coventry and the 0-1 defeat at Port Vale in the Cup replay. By then the name, or rather names, of Branfoot's replacements had emerged. It was back to the future for Southampton FC. The fact that Alan Ball had managed Pompey, and got them promoted back to the First Division, would be forgiven by Saints fans, especially as Lawrie McMenemy was also back, in his case as Director of Football.

Since being sacked as Portsmouth boss five years beforehand by Jim Gregory, Ball had had a spell coaching Colchester and managing Stoke – an unhappy association – before taking the Exeter City job. McMenemy had been out of work since the sacking of Graham Taylor in the wake of England's failure to qualify for the 1994 World Cup finals, having been implicated in the failure by being on Taylor's staff.

This new policy of harking back to Saints' true 'golden era' was a masterstroke by under-fire chairman Guy Askham, who in September had promised Branfoot three more years to get it right. Ball, too, was looking forward to the challenge and trod a delicate diplomatic tightrope – as far as Pompey and Saints fans were concerned – on his appointment: 'My heart is here [at The Dell] and I've always wanted to come back and manage a club where I was so happy as a player. There are only three clubs I would have left Exeter for. One was Everton, one was Southampton and the other, obviously, was Portsmouth, where I had some wonderful times. I am absolutely delighted to be back at The Dell. From the day you leave Southampton you look forward to the day you can come back. I call Southampton my home, the children still live here and it's great to return.'

Phew! Enough there to keep just about everybody happy, but little did Ball anticipate that he would be deploying the same juggling act four years later to uphold his undoubted reputation as being popular with both sets of supporters.

Ball and Lawrie Mac inspired Saints to a 2-1 win at Newcastle in their first match in charge, to lift them out of the bottom three, followed by a stirring 4-2 Valentine's Day massacre of Liverpool at The Dell. The players in Ball's squad then showed their recidivist tendencies. Three draws and four defeats in the next seven games, culminating with a 0-1 loss at home to fellow strugglers Manchester City on Easter Monday, left Saints four points clear of safety with just six games to play.

Two more derby days looked like being back on the footballing agenda for the following season, as Portsmouth's season had also nose-dived. Home replay defeats to Blackburn Rovers and Manchester United in both cups in January had knocked the stuffing out of the side. Not even the club-record £650,000 purchase of Celtic striker Gerry Creaney could spark a revival. A run of just one win in thirteen League games saw their play-off, let alone automatic promotion, hopes evaporate. Portsmouth would end the campaign with four straight defeats, three of them at home, gates were back in four figures, and a finishing position of seventeenth was bitterly disappointing.

All that was left to enjoy was Southampton's demise, except that Saints unexpectedly picked up. In early April, Ball's team's goose looked cooked as Chris Sutton put Norwich 3-1 up at Carrow Road ten minutes into the second half. Two goals from Le Tissier levelled things, only for Sutton to restore the advantage 60 seconds later. There were still only 63 minutes gone! Le Tissier gave another buff to his halo by heading home Jeff Kenna's cross. A famous hat-trick, but a point – even one as brave as this – was of little use. In the final minute Le Tissier's corner-kick found the head of Dutch defender Ken Monkou, who planted the ball into the back of the net. 5-4! Alan Ball's Great Escape (Mark I) was under way.

Two full-house home wins – over title-chasing Blackburn and Aston Villa – offset defeats at Spurs and Manchester United, and left Saints knowing that a point at West Ham in their final game should save them. Another brace from Le Tissier, giving him 25 for the season, and another from Neil Maddison, did the necessary, putting Saints 3-2 up. West Ham hooligans invaded the pitch, delaying play as they tried to get among the large Saints following. Play was held up for several minutes, racking up the tension. When Lee Chapman levelled for the Hammers there were still two minutes to go, but by then news of Sheffield United's last-minute defeat at Chelsea and Oldham's draw at Norwich had settled things in Southampton's favour. Ball's men were safe.

The changing nature of football was underlined by estimates that, in the new Sky Sports-driven Premiership, relegation would have cost them up to £3 million the following season. For a club facing up to the reality of a 15,000 capacity, it can be seen that this escape was more crucial to the future of Southampton FC than Pompey's last-gasp failure to come up twelve months beforehand had been to their prospects. Had Saints gone down, Le Tissier would have almost certainly been sold. Added to which, the three sides who did drop that year – Sheffield United, Oldham and Swindon – have yet to return to the Premiership. This highlights the fact that staying in the top flight is a sight easier than getting there in the first place.

Southampton celebrated their survival at, of all places, Fratton Park. Ball and McMenemy's arrival at The Dell encouraged long-serving Pompey goalkeeper Alan Knight to negotiate the visit of Saints for his long-overdue testimonial. The veteran of more than 500 League matches, spanning all four divisions, somehow persuaded Hampshire Constabulary that the game wouldn't end in World War Three. The only complication was a long-standing arrangement for Portsmouth to compete in a tournament in Greece. Saints insisted the testimonial was a 'first-team' fixture, but in the end Knight was able to cobble together a sufficiently strong Pompey XI. It comprised some first-team players allowed to delay their flights and a host of guests, including Mark Hateley, Darren Anderton, Paul Walsh – sold to Manchester City in March – and the centre-back pairing of Noel Blake and Billy Gilbert, both of whom were even older than Knight.

Not surprisingly, Southampton strolled to a 5-1 win, but Knight was the main winner with 17,000 in the ground. He scored his one and only Pompey goal from the penalty spot, and the second-half appearance of a portly Alan Ball drew applause from all sides. Le Tissier was able to show off his party tricks and have a wry smile at the North Terrace, which was taunting him about his proboscis. The less sensible end of Pompey's 'support' sounded the only sour note, although whether they were even in the ground for the game is a moot point. A wall was demolished afterwards, repair costs coming out of Knight's fund. Saints keeper Dave Beasant felt obliged to go and engage in banter with the 800 Saints fans facing an anxious wait before being escorted back to Fratton Station.

The brave new football world was taking shape. From August 1994, the Premiership season would commence a week later than its Endsleigh League counterpart, as the ragged edges in the tear in English football's fabric started to be patched. The 'family' of football clubs, envisaged by the founders of the Football League in 1888, was now truly split into the haves and the have-nots. The process would be completed by the summer of 1995, when four clubs would drop out of the Premiership, with just two taking their place, reducing it from 22 clubs to twenty. If there was a season to go up, or more importantly not to go down, this was it.

Southampton and Portsmouth both realised that a new stadium was vital to progress, but both clubs were seemingly thwarted at every turn.

Saints' proposed relocation to Stoneham, ideally located from a transport point of view – close to the Eastleigh junction of the M27 and Southampton Parkway railway station – had provoked outraged local opposition. Pompey had managed to get a stage further, the delicate party politics of Portsmouth City Council eventually finding a one-vote majority for the scaled-down Farlington scheme in October 1993.

The bad news was that the Environment Secretary, John Selwyn-Gummer, had decided to call a Public Inquiry. Evidence was heard over the summer of 1994, when the matter of the breeding grounds of Brent Geese at the nearby Farlington Marshes was raised. Apparently these sensitive birds are quite happy with a three-lane trunk road roaring by, but a football match every fortnight might upset them. In December 1994 it was announced that planning permission would not be granted. By May 1995 a fall-back plan to build a new Fratton End on the back of a Safeway supermarket, in the adjacent former Fratton Goods Yard, was in disarray after rejection by city planners. The sense of decline and decay at Fratton was palpable.

Although the gap between Southampton and Portsmouth remained a single division, and would stay that way, the two clubs were, at least in terms of media profile, on divergent paths. The next two seasons would do little to change that view. Encouraged no doubt by McMenemy, Ball had turned to a golden-oldie, eccentric former Liverpool keeper Bruce Grobbelaar, to reinforce his squad. Despite a dodgy start and another flirt with the bottom four in March, six wins in the last eleven matches propelled Saints to their best-ever Premiership finish of tenth. The only duff note was another one of those periodically spectacular collapses, 2-6 at home to Spurs in an FA Cup fifth round replay.

The key to Saints' success was the blossoming of Matt Le Tissier, given free reign by Ball. New England boss Terry Venables seemed to like the look of him too. Pompey, on the other hand, were more concerned with preserving their First Division status. The knock-on effect of the league re-structuring was that four teams would drop out of the Second Division, and by December Pompey were one of them. A slight upturn over Christmas was not enough for Martin Gregory. Jim Smith was sacked as manager, two days after a 0-1 home defeat to Leicester in the FA Cup. In his place came Terry Fenwick, a young and ambitious coach, who managed to steady the ship. A run of eight wins and four draws in the final eighteen matches avoided the unthinkable.

Any complacency Southampton might have felt was rudely shattered during the summer of 1995 when Ball departed to take up a better offer at Manchester City, now owned by his pal, former England international Francis Lee. In Ball's defence, he insisted he would have been happy to stay, but his request to renegotiate his contract – which had just a year to run – was met with a less than enthusiastic response. There was to be another twist yet in that particular tale.

For the start of the 1995-96 season, both Hampshire clubs had fresh faces at the helm. Dave Merrington, the former Burnley midfielder and Saints youth coach, made the step up at The Dell, while Terry Fenwick planned for his first full season in charge at Fratton Park. Saints were in their traditional position among the bookies' preferences for the drop. While their Stoneham stadium plans stuttered onwards, hopes of building a true Premiership club were on hold, as McMenemy acknowledged:

'Chairman Guy Askham and director Brian Hunt have been constantly meeting with people and holding talks to clear the way forward. In the old days we used to get crowds of 32,000 at The Dell, but that is in the past. Even if we played Barcelona every other week we could get no more than 15,000 in the ground, because that's all it holds now. We are as big as any club, although some have more financial power. We are a big club constrained in tight surroundings and there is no room for us to really develop our ground.'

Hunt remained 'optimistic' that the plans would be approved, but conceded that any completion date was unlikely before the turn of the century. So Saints had to soldier on in their shoestring way. Early on, it looked like their top-flight days really could be numbered this time. Just one win in their first ten matches had them rooted in the drop zone, finding goals hard to come by. Three wins in October and November hauled Saints clear of trouble, but going into the New Year, five draws and a defeat in six games, plus a shock Coca-Cola Cup exit at Reading, meant they were only a couple of points away from disaster.

Poor old Portsmouth were even worse off, with just three wins by the end of November seeing them rooted in the bottom three. Fans were also up in arms about the way Jim Gregory's son Martin, now in effect running the club in his ailing father's absence, was conducting things. A red-card protest at the home game with Huddersfield was staged against the backdrop of rumours about a northern-based businessman, Warren Smith, leading a takeover bid. Gregory junior was no chip off the block, in terms of his passion for football at least, and would happily have off-loaded the club if the deal were right. Optimism was clearly on the rise: Portsmouth won four matches on the bounce in December to haul themselves out of danger.

Following the first of those wins, 2-1 against Oldham on 2nd December 1995, the next day's FA Cup third round draw sent Pompey to The Dell. The scramble for tickets was no less frantic than in 1984, but the limited capacity restricted Pompey to just 1,500 tickets. The day before the game, fixed unsurprisingly for a noon kick-off on Sunday, 7th January, Warren Smith was telling the *News* that his takeover, still far from a done deal, was backed by a 'Far Eastern billionaire'. Certainly Pompey would need that sort of money if they were going to compete with the big boys in the Premiership.

Saints were a mediocre lot, to say the least, but that day they made Pompey look the First Division makeweights they were. The most striking thing was the physical difference between the teams. Saints looked heavier and taller than their counterparts. Graham Hiley's match report in the *Echo* summed up the occasion: 'There was only ever going to be one team coming out on top. Saints won because they were the better side and made absolutely sure they proved it on the day. They won because they were more incisive, rock solid at the back and scored at vital times. And they won because they wanted it more.' A damning, yet accurate indictment of a Pompey team of boys in blue who turned up to play men.

An early penalty shout, when mercurial striker Paul Walsh, re-signed from Manchester City in September 1995, tumbled under Jason Dodd's challenge, was as good as it got for Pompey and their fans, plus several thousand following the game on a big screen at Fratton Park. Referee Martin Bodenham was having none of it. That was in the eleventh minute and 60 seconds later play bounced to the other end, where Jim Magilton hooked home from ten yards. A minute after the interval Matt Le Tissier curled the ball into a crowded box, and when Alan Knight – a week short of his 600th League appearance for his only club – pushed the ball out, Magilton got the final touch to make it 2-0. Fenwick claimed post-match that the offside flag should have been raised. Neil Shipperley wrapped up the 3-0 win with a trademark strike, and Pompey were even denied a consolation when former Arsenal and Liverpool winger Jimmy Carter saw his shot come back off a post. It was as comprehensive a victory as Saints fans could have asked for and rid the mind of their team's abject surrender four weeks before at Elm Park.

There is also no doubt the Dell crowd lifted their team for the occasion. 'Saints fans? No passion!', is the typical response of their Pompey counterparts, but that accusation could not be laid at the Southampton public that afternoon. From the roar which went up to greet the teams coming out, to the late 'Bye-bye Pompey, Pompey bye-bye' bastardisation of the Chimes, the atmosphere never let up. Saints striker Gordon Watson acknowledged as much to the *Echo*: 'It has been said the south coast fans are not as passionate as those from the north but this proved that they can match them. I have played in derbies for Huddersfield against Bradford City which were pretty intense but nothing like this. It was something else. Sometimes the crowd can be a bit quiet but this time they were deafening and kept it up through the game. It was a terrific occasion.'

In truth, the 'passionless' Saints fan stereotype has always been a myth. While aspersions about their away following may have more credibility, at

The Dell they could rustle up an atmosphere as intimidating as most. It helped keep them in the Premiership after all, and Saints were at it again in April 1996. Title-contenders Manchester United blamed their hard-to-see grey second strip for allowing Saints to race into a 3-0 half-time lead. It was a vital win which once again allowed Saints to snatch safety from the jaws of disaster on the last day with a 0-0 home draw with Wimbledon. Had Manchester City scored a late winner at home to Liverpool – Alan Ball infamously ordered his team to waste time at 2-2, thinking a draw would do – then Saints would have gone down.

Pompey's squeak was even tighter. A run of just one win in eleven matches from 9th March, coinciding with the loss of the prodigal Walsh to injury, had tipped Pompey into the bottom three on the final Saturday. Warren Smith's takeover had gone quiet when Martin Gregory accused him of having empty pockets, leaving the club in a sorry mess. Relegation looked inevitable, but a 1-0 win at Huddersfield – Deon Burton scoring – coupled with Millwall's 0-0 draw at Ipswich, kept Pompey up, on goals scored. The result condemned Millwall – who topped the table in December – to the drop.

Football was changing rapidly from a sport into a business and both Southampton and Portsmouth were about to be exposed to a financial draught – with vastly differing outcomes.

The summer of 1996 saw football 'come home' for Euro 96. England manager Terry Venables was a penalty shoot-out against Germany in the semi-final from becoming a national hero. High-profile litigation meant he had already announced his resignation. Out of a job, and needing to earn a crust, his next port of call was Fratton Park. Ever since the Gregory family had assumed control, Venables' name popped up periodically in connection with the club. In early August he arrived, first as a 'consultant' – sharing the job with managing the Australian national team – then in February as chairman, replacing Martin Gregory. Venables famously announced he was buying the club (and its liabilities) for £1.

At Southampton, things were done in a far more businesslike manner, although the reverse takeover by Bristol property company Secure Retirement raised one or two ethical eyebrows. By May 1997, hockey-playing Rupert Lowe – who watched his first football match when Saints won 3-1 at Lincoln in a Coca-Cola Cup replay win in October 1996 – would be catapulted into the limelight as the new chairman of the club. He replaced Guy Askham. Southampton FC were now part of Southampton Leisure Holdings PLC and shareholders would be looking for a return on their investment. The new era was hinted at during the summer of 1996, when Dave Merrington's reward for averting relegation on a shoestring was the sack. As youth-team manager, Merrington had nurtured the likes of Matt Le Tissier, Alan Shearer and the Wallace trio, for all the good it did him. In his place came former Liverpool boss Graeme Souness, recovered now from the open-heart surgery which he underwent between the Pompey semi-final and the replay in 1992.

Souness's arrival didn't make much of a difference initially. Just two draws in the first seven games of 1996-97 had Saints bottom again by October. Despite a stunning 6-3 thrashing of Manchester United at The Dell, prompted by two-goal new signing Eyal Berkovic, Saints were still rooted at the foot of the table by April. Souness also had the embarrassment of being conned by a phone call offering Senegalese striker 'Ali Dia' – highly recommended by 'George Weah' – who he signed on the spot and placed on the subs' bench for the game against Leeds in November. When he came on, Ali Dia's incompetence was cruelly exposed, and it wasn't only Pompey fans who made hay at Saints' expense.

In the end it all came right. One of Souness's better striker additions, Norwegian Egil Ostenstadt, scored the winner at lowly Sunderland on 22nd April. That result paved the way for safety to be secured in the penultimate match – early by Saints' recent standards – against Blackburn. The 2-0 win, Le Tissier getting the second, did the trick.

For a period it looked like Portsmouth might be coming up. A blindside run, sparked by a seven-match winning League and FA Cup run from mid-January, had Pompey in play-off contention, not to mention the FA Cup quarter-finals. A 1-4 lesson doled out by Ruud Gullit's Chelsea at Fratton Park in March shattered the momentum and Pompey eventually finished two points shy of a play-off chance of squeezing into the Premiership via the back door. Lee Bradbury – like Guy Whittingham, bought out of the Army – bagged seventeen goals and earned England Under-21 international honours. He was partnered up front by Pompey's own Scandinavian ace Matthias Svensson, and the future looked brighter at Fratton than for some time.

Terry Venables had even got the ground sorted out. In August 1996, Pompey's plans to retain terracing until their Farlington scheme was dealt with meant the worst possible outcome. Capacity was slashed to 11,000 with a miserable seven rows of seats bolted onto the Milton End and North Terrace. Whatever atmosphere the ground retained after the loss of the Fratton End disappeared and gates dropped to the 6,000 mark. Venables recognised the problem and ensured extra seats were installed, so that by November a more viable capacity of 16,000 was achieved. As results improved, that capacity was even tested as Chelsea came to town. In May 1997 the bulldozers moved in and work finally began on a new 4,500-seat Fratton End. Its positive effect on Pompey's immediate future should not be under-estimated.

Meanwhile, the summer of 1997 was tumultuous at The Dell too, as Graeme Souness parted company to work in Italy, claiming the takeover of the club by persons uninterested in football had undermined his position. In his place came Stockport County boss Dave Jones, who had masterminded promotion at Edgeley Park from the Second Division to the First. He was also remembered, with mixed feelings, as the managerial brains behind Stockport's Coca-Cola Cup quarter-final win at The Dell the previous season.

Yet again Southampton started badly, finding themselves looking up at almost everyone else by late November. Le Tissier's magic, and the fact that Ostenstadt now had experienced striker David Hirst (brought from Sheffield Wednesday for a Southampton club record £2 million in October), to help grab the goals, meant that by May they would survive comfortably.

In January 1998 another twist to our tale arrived when left-back John Beresford – who had come to the fore in Pompey's 1992 semi-final team – joined Saints. In consequence, Saints' reserve left-back Matt Robinson moved to Pompey, who by now had Alan Ball back in charge. Wholesale summer changes had seen Lee Bradbury leave for Manchester City in a £3.5 million move, while Venables recruited a clutch of Australian players. Exploiting his inside knowledge as the Socceroos' national coach, he attracted internationals John Aloisi and Craig Foster, along with a host of lesser-known Aussies. The upshot of all these coming and goings was disastrous. When a 0-3 defeat by Manchester City on 12th January dumped Pompey at the foot of the table, Venables was history, reportedly negotiating a six-figure pay-off. Not far behind was his puppet, Terry Fenwick. In their hour of need, Portsmouth turned to the semi-retired Alan Ball to dig them out of trouble.

The catalyst for Ball's reappointment was the proposed takeover of the club by rock 'star' and Pompey fan Brian Howe – 'Bad Company' for a while, in case you're wondering – and his American business partner Vince Wollanin. Another prodigal back on board was on-loan Steve Claridge from Leicester. Portsmouth-born, but rejected after his apprenticeship ended in 1984, Claridge gave the attack much-needed punch, but it took a 1-0 win against Stockport on a chilly February night to get Ball's Great Escape (Mark II) up and running. On that night, Venables' one true legacy, the Fratton End, came into its own. From it, the fans urged on the team – winless since Boxing Day and six points adrift of safety – through a tense second half.

The final whistle marked the first of five wins in six games. These lifted the club away from the trap door, but another relapse – three points from the next eight games – left things in the balance with two games to go. Fratton was close to being full as Huddersfield were seen off 3-0 in the penultimate game. The equation was now simple. If they won at Bradford City, Pompey – celebrating their centenary – would be safe. Roared on by

3,000 travelling fans, win they did, condemning Ball's two previous clubs, Manchester City and Stoke, to accompany Reading down into Division Two.

With the Premiership now firmly established, Southampton's hopes to push on were continuing to be hampered by the confines of The Dell. So when Blackburn came waving a £7.5 million cheque to buy striker Kevin Davies, whose promising debut season in the top flight had been cut short by injury, Rupert Lowe could hardly resist. However, the foundations were being laid, if not yet physically, then metaphorically, for the move which could potentially shift Saints well and truly into the big time. Constantly frustrated by the inability to find a consensus on Stoneham, despite passionate deputations of fans addressing council meetings, the club were in delicate negotiations with Southampton City Council during the summer of 1998 over a vacant plot near the Northam gasworks. By March 1999 the club were given the go-ahead to build a 32,000-capacity stadium on the site. But the question was whether they could retain their Premiership status to make such a development viable, as Dave Jones's team was just one off the foot of the table with games running out.

If Saints thought they had problems, however, a sideways glance at Fratton Park would have cheered them up. With the death of Jim Gregory in September 1998, son Martin's 'moral' obligation to his father's passion was removed. Chaos ensued, players were sold for a song, and Portsmouth FC finally slipped into administration in January 1999. The prospect of professional football coming to an end in Portsmouth was very real. Contingency plans to establish a non-league club, playing at Alexandra Park, were formulated as a last-ditch option. Meanwhile the 'Portsmouth United' group looked to raise funds to set up a 'community club', along the lines of AFC Bournemouth, which had been similarly financially embarrassed a couple of seasons previously.

On the pitch, Portsmouth – like Southampton – were teetering on the brink of a catastrophic relegation which would have had severe ramifications for the club's future. Going into April, bookies fretted about a likely pay-out for a double drop. Such an eventuality would have meant our story taking a very different turn. Saints were still one off the bottom on 17th April, following a 0-0 draw at Derby, while on the same day Pompey were chucking away a 2-0 lead at West Brom. The 2-2 draw left them four points clear of trouble, but with three games left. A 3-1 victory over Stockport on 24th April secured First Division football at Fratton Park; then a fortnight later Saints took 12,000 fans to Selhurst Park to see their team carve their own escape route with a 2-0 win. A last-day Dell victory over Everton – with a brace from Latvian striker Marian Pahars, signed in the same week as the new stadium finally got the green light – ensured Premiership football again.

Within a year, the new Southampton ground, close to their St Mary's origins, would be taking shape. Meanwhile, in May 1999, after lengthy negotiations with the administrators, a Serbo-American businessman called Milan Mandaric, who had been running football clubs in the United States, Belgium and France for more than twenty years, was taking stock of his new purchase: Portsmouth Football Club. The south coast footballing landscape had changed again.

Chapter 14

~ Back to the Future ~

(1999-2004)

Like John Deacon and Jim Gregory before him, Milan Mandaric had been seduced by the challenge of restoring Portsmouth to their 'natural' position among the elite of English football. Introduced to the club through Deacon's son David – who remained in the new set up as managing director – Pompey's supposed 'potential' had been heavily played up. However, with just one season among the elite in 40 years, claims that this club was a sleeping giant really had to be taken with a pinch of salt. For 'sleeping' read 'comatose'. The reality was that by the new millennium, Portsmouth FC was, if anything, more naturally a 'second flight' club, with a stadium and, arguably, support to match. The bulk of their history had been spent at that level and the club hadn't attracted a League gate higher than 25,000 for over a decade.

If anything, Southampton's claims to be the natural 'top flight' club in the south had greater credibility. Since 1966, Saints had spent all but three seasons in the top division – eclipsing Pompey's 28-season stay – won the FA Cup, reached the final of the League Cup, and had stacked up a number of seasons in European competition. But for injury to leading scorer Steve Moran in February 1982, they might even have won the League that year. Mention 'Southampton' in the late 1990s to a supporter, say, of Olympique Marseille, and their 1976 Cup-Winners' Cup clash will likely come to mind. Mention 'Portsmouth', and the speaker would be met by a blank stare. Explaining that Portsmouth actually played in the Velodrome on tour in the 1950s wouldn't help much.

Saints' problem, though, remained The Dell, with its 15,000 capacity. Fratton Park's 19,000 – on completion of the new Fratton End in 1997 – could outgun Saints from time to time on attendances. Indeed, the new stand at Fratton Park had reinforced the idea that if a club provided the facilities, the public would come back in droves. Although the standard of football was often no better, sub-10,000 gates at Fratton were a rare occurrence these days, and the KJC Stand, as the Fratton End was now called, was invariably sold out.

As the Mandaric era got under way with a rash of new signings and a 0-3 friendly defeat at Southern League Dorchester, the Fratton faithful were still sufficiently encouraged to virtually fill Fratton for the opener against Sheffield United. Manager Alan Ball, handed a new four-year contract, engineered two wins out of three and Pompey were up in second place. Mandaric's dream must have appeared rather straightforward at this point. Southampton, too, started brightly, three wins in the first five games bouncing them into the top half of the Premiership.

Within a couple of months those balmy late summer days would be but a wistful memory. In late September Saints manager Dave Jones faced accusations dating back to his time when working in child welfare in the 1980s. He strenuously denied the charge, but was arrested by police and released on bail while inquiries continued. The club initially stood by their manager: 'We live in a country where people are innocent until proven guilty,' said chairman Rupert Lowe, while captain Francis Benali added: '[Jones] will get full backing from everyone, both on and off the pitch' (Holley and Chalk 2003).

After the announcement, Saints' form spiralled out of control. One win in four months meant the team were in familiar territory scavenging for scraps near the bottom of the League. A 1-0 home win over fellow strugglers Bradford City on 3rd January 2000, and another at Ipswich in the third round of the FA Cup, lifted the siege. But on 15th January Saints were sunk 0-5 at Newcastle and the following week Jones was given a year's 'leave of absence' – he didn't ask for, it should be recorded – to fight his looming court case.

True or not, there were those who thought that Lowe, sensitive about the club's image as he sought to hold together the package to finance St Mary's Stadium, decided to cut his losses. Into Jones's shoes – 'temporarily' – stepped former England coach Glenn Hoddle, who had been forced to stand down as the national coach in 1998 after ill-chosen remarks about disabled people and past lives. Ironically, Hoddle had reportedly been recently solicited for the Portsmouth manager's job, which had become vacant in December. Whether Hoddle rejected Pompey, or the club rejected him, fearing that he regarded it as merely a 'stepping stone' back to the big time, as Mandaric subsequently suggested, will remain conjecture.

The vacancy at Fratton Park was not unexpected. Alan Ball's second demise came about after a miserable November 1999, which saw five matches lost and just two points gleaned. On 4th December, record £1 million striker signing Rory Allen, bought from Spurs in July, fractured his left ankle on his comeback after three months out with an injury to his right. Portsmouth lost 0-1 and within the week Ball was once again part of Pompey's history. Rumours of player unrest – one unnamed source claimed 'morale was at rock bottom' – undoubtedly played a part in his going. A reportedly blistering verbal assault on his team after a 0-4 mauling at Crystal Palace in October was the beginning of the end for Ball, as he struggled to deal with a new, cosmopolitan, cash-rich generation of players.

However, Ball's stoic defence of the club through the anguish of administration, not to mention his record as the only manager to have got

Pompey promoted to the top flight in 60 years, ensures his continuing popularity in Portsmouth. Likewise, Ball commands affection and respect among Saints fans for his service as player and manager – despite the manner of his leaving in 1995 – making him pretty much unique in this rivalry. Ironically, one of Ball's last signings was a 'Scummer' – defender Scott Hiley, who had played for Ball at Exeter and had arrived at The Dell via spells at Birmingham and Manchester City. Hiley had recently found it difficult to establish himself in Saints' first team and a £50,000 move to Fratton suited all parties. As Hiley arrived, another ex-Saint was exiting, midfielder Alan McLoughlin heading to Wigan. Ball was trying, unsuccessfully as it turned out, to purge his perceived dressing-room critics.

Glenn Hoddle's impact on Southampton's fortunes was immediate. Three straight wins as January turned to February lifted the club clear of the dog fight. Despite a 2-7 mauling at Hoddle's 'spiritual home' Tottenham in March, consecutive wins against struggling Bradford City and doomed Watford in early April effectively ended relegation fears. By now, the St Mary's site had been cleared and the galvanised steel framework of the new stadium, which would transform Saints' prospects, was taking shape.

Portsmouth turned to Tony Pulis, whose resumé had seen him guide Gillingham from Division Three to Division One on a shoestring, only to be controversially sacked as a result of a feud with Gills' chairman Paul Scally. With Pompey rooted in 23rd place, Pulis's task was no mean one, but five wins in March were enough to keep the relegation wolf at bay for another season. Lee Bradbury was back, picked up cheaply in October. His club, Crystal Palace, had successfully courted the two Terries – Venables and Fenwick – and found themselves in administration for their pains. Bradbury formed a potent partnership with Steve Claridge.

Cowes-born Bradbury was an interesting case. From his arrival at Fratton in 1996, his Pompey-supporting credentials were highlighted, although many Island-based Pompey fans insisted the burly former soldier was, if anything, a Saint. Certainly, Cowes is the Saints bastion on the Island, unsurprising given the ferry which links it with Southampton. But the story is given a further twist by rumours, always denied by the player, that Bradbury also sported a Saints tattoo. Whatever, his contribution to Portsmouth, not only in terms of goals, but also the record £3 million plus received for his sale, meant it could never be said he didn't give Pompey full value.

By the end of September 2000 Dave Jones was consigned to Saints' history book. He agreed a severance package, while Hoddle signed a contract until December 2002. In December of that year the case against Jones collapsed, bringing a sorry story – with no winners and only losers – to a conclusion (Chalk and Holley 2003). Another slow start, this time to the 2000-01 season, saw Southampton down among the dead men following a 0-5 thrashing at Manchester United in late October. But nine wins in sixteen games saw them up to eighth, after a 1-0 home win over Everton on 17th March 2001.

Saints' winning ways were achieved without the talents of Le Tissier, whose role was becoming increasingly cameoesque. With James Beattie, who had arrived at The Dell in 1998 from Blackburn, and Marian Pahars forming an effective partnership in attack, Saints were always likely to score. However, it was their defence, marshalled by a Bosman free transfer the previous summer in Wolves' Dean Richards, which had turned Saints into a lean, mean, point-gleaning machine. The Everton win constituted Saints' seventh consecutive clean sheet, but Hoddle's 'Midas' touch, turning perennial strugglers into an effective Premiership side, had not gone unnoticed. When Tottenham came calling, Hoddle turned his back on Saints, eventually joining the north London club as manager at the end of the month, after an acrimonious battle to keep him at The Dell. Filling his shoes, temporarily, was coach Stuart Gray, who had served the club as a player towards the end of his career.

Managerial turmoil at The Dell was becoming an increasingly common occurrence, although the Saints still had some way to go to match Pompey's ability to shoot themselves in the foot. By October 2000 Tony Pulis had fallen victim to the same player-power which had ousted Alan Ball ten months before. Pompey's start to 2000-01, with £1.2 million record striker signing Lee Mills from Bradford City failing to set the scoring charts alight, was only average at best. When the axe fell, Pompey had just secured a couple of away draws. Although League attendances were holding up, a second round Worthington Cup-tie with divisional rivals Blackburn had attracted just 2,731 to Fratton, the club's lowest ever attendance for a mainstream competition. To be fair, Pompey were a pretty hopeless cause, having lost the first leg 0-4 at Ewood Park, a performance which prompted chairman Mandaric to offer those fans who travelled their ticket money back. Perhaps the most amusing aspect of the occasion was the Blackburn fan who pondered, without apparent irony, on one of the now-ubiquitous fans' internet message boards, why the gate was so low considering the attractiveness of the opposition. Not amusing in the least was the on-pitch fainting of Pompey's Southampton-born and bred goalkeeper, Aaron Flahavan, for the second time in a year.

The latest incumbent to the Pompey hot seat was Portsmouth-born Steve Claridge. He was given the player-manager role on a temporary basis, in tandem with coach Guy Whittingham and the recently retired Andy Awford. Three straight wins gave the 'dream team' the ideal start, but by the end of February Pompey were no better off – seventeenth and facing an uphill battle to beat the drop yet again. They were also out of the FA

Cup, beaten at home by Tranmere in round three. In the next round, Rovers were paired with Southampton. A 0-0 draw at The Dell, was a good result for the First Division side, but in the Prenton Park replay they trailed 0-3 with half an hour to go. A four-goal riposte, three of them from ex-Saint Paul Rideout, gave Pompey fans a rare field-day.

With relegation for Pompey a possibility, Mandaric again showed his iron fist and, in effect, axed Claridge ahead of a 0-2 defeat at West Brom. In his place came Graham Rix, the former Arsenal midfielder who was credited with having had a significant impact on the coaching of Ruud Gullit's Chelsea, the 2000 FA Cup winners. However, Rix was not whiter than white. An under-aged relationship had seen him imprisoned.

The irony of Rix's 'past' was not lost on Saints fans forced to endure ill-considered abuse by Pompey's over the unfortunate Dave Jones. In any case, both clubs had unproven men in charge and their inexperience showed. During the month of April 2001 neither Saints nor Pompey managed to win a game, but the effect on the Fratton Park club was more traumatic. Thanks to the points already banked under Hoddle, Saints' slide was merely cosmetic. They mustered just two draws from seven games before Gray roused his side to win their last two competitive matches at The Dell. That the scalps were champions Manchester United and runners-up Arsenal was impressive enough. A fairytale twist saw substitute Matt Le Tissier come off the bench to score the final and winning goal on the old ground in the last minute. You simply couldn't have made it up. It would take a hard-hearted Pompey fan to begrudge the moment.

Rix enjoyed an unbeaten four-game run, but three points from their next six put Pompey in the thick of the relegation battle. A win in their penultimate game, at home to Crystal Palace, would see them safe. Palace's own poor form, just one win in fourteen, had left them staring into the abyss themselves. For the first time in the League, Fratton's new 19,000 capacity was fully tested. If Pompey won, Palace would go down, relieving not only Pompey, but also Huddersfield and Grimsby in the process. Instead, Pompey reverted to their 1970s habit of screwing things up on the big occasion, gifting Palace three of their four goals with defensive howlers. Pompey could only manage two goals in reply.

On the final day, Portsmouth had to beat Barnsley and hope one of the other strugglers slipped up. Pompey did the necessary, winning 3-0. It was Huddersfield who eventually took the fall, as they lost 1-2 at home to Birmingham.

Portsmouth's game threw up another of those attendance myths which punctuate the south-coast rivalry. The gate was widely reported as just 13,064. Rather sorry, considering the importance of the game, taunted Southampton fans with some justification. Except for the fact that whoever phoned through the attendance to the news agency got it wrong. The actual gate was announced over the tannoy as 17,064 and reported as such in the *News* the following morning. Published match pictures reinforce the fact of there being very few spare seats in the ground that day, save for the sparsely populated visitors' section. Even the renowned Rothman's Football Yearbook has repeated the error.

With Southampton anticipating a move into 21st century facilities, the uncertainty over the identity of their new manager continued over the summer. Harry Redknapp, the Dorset-domiciled, recently fired manager of West Ham, was widely tipped as the 'obvious choice', although he ruled himself out by becoming Director of Football at Fratton Park. Instead, it was caretaker Stuart Gray who was offered the job, his appointment harking back to the old Saints tradition of appointing from within. Gray quickly spent £700,000 on Swedish international midfielder Anders Svensson. The Swede was not a conspicuous success and by mid-October Saints had just two wins to their name, offset by six defeats. The St Mary's jinx was also beginning to play psychologically, as neither of those two wins had been at home.

The angst was not eased by tales of Pompey-supporting construction workers having buried blue and white scarves beneath the centre spot, not to mention dipping bricks in acid to spell out the letters 'PFC' as the stadium weathered. Saints chairman Rupert Lowe had clearly been taking lessons on sacking managers from Milan. In the wake of a 0-2 defeat at West Ham on 20th October, Gray was dismissed and Gordon Strachan – sacked by Coventry six weeks earlier – was appointed in his place.

In all other respects the move to St Mary's had been a resounding success. Even the more optimistic Saints supporters had expected attendances to level out around the mid-20,000s. After all, it was getting on for fifteen years since gates of 20,000-plus watched Southampton regularly. Thanks to the club's canny marketing of tickets to its substantial membership list, the new average was a good 4,000 higher. In effect, Saints were mopping up the undisputed appetite for top-class football along the M27 corridor and beyond.

Not that Portsmouth were suffering unduly. In fact, the signing of the chain-smoking one-time Barcelona and Real Madrid playmaker Robert Prosinecki, made them a biggish draw in their own right. In mid-September 2001 Pompey went second in the table after a 4-2 win over Crystal Palace, one of the goals a trademark free-kick by the Croatian. Gates were as good as they had been at this stage of the season in more than 30 years, and two other summer recruits, QPR's beanpole striker Peter Crouch and wayward Celtic forward Mark Burchill, looked a lethal double act at this level. Within a week Burchill was ruled out for a year, victim of a freak training ground accident which wrecked his left knee. Another Pompey dawn would turn prematurely to dusk.

As it turned out, the dawn of the new season had already been pretty bleak. A week before it started, goalkeeper Flahavan, fresh from a batch of tests to diagnose his fainting problem, had watched Pompey beat Premiership Leicester in their last pre-season friendly. By the early hours of Sunday morning he was dead. On the outskirts of Bournemouth his BMW car had left the road at high speed. At the subsequent inquest it emerged he had been well over the drink-driving limit and was not wearing his seatbelt. Whatever the circumstances, Flahavan's death cut the club and their fans to the core. The death of one so young is rare enough; the death of a footballer in his prime, more shocking still. For a while, petty rivalries were forgotten. Flahavan's close friend, Saints striker Kevin Davies, came to Fratton to lay a floral tribute in a goalmouth.

Southampton-born Flavs was mourned with a minute's silence at St Mary's as respectful as that at Fratton Park. Like Bobby Stokes – who had died prematurely in May 1995 from broncho-pneumonia, his last job being to help out at his cousin's Harbour View café at The Hard in Portsmouth, and Steve Mills, who died of leukaemia in August 1988 – Flahavan's death was a salutary reminder that we are all equal in the end.

Flahavan's replacement, signed in time for the opening League fixture, at Wolves, was veteran ex-Saint, Chelsea and Wimbledon keeper Dave Beasant. As popular as a Saints player probably could be at Fratton Park, Beasant's good-natured giving and taking of stick at the Alan Knight testimonial stood him in good stead.

The attraction of St Mary's was underlined on 24th November when three further defeats failed to dissuade an all-time record Saints crowd of 31,198 to turn out. The night before that game with Charlton, a pagan priestess performed a ceremony to exorcise the stadium of the ghosts of an Anglo-Saxon burial ground local legend claimed lay beneath it. Hocus-pocus or not, it did the trick, Marian Pahars' header settling the game on the hour. Saints' improved fortunes were illustrated by a late Charlton shot which came back off the inside of the post: 'It's enough to make you start believing in religion again,' quipped Strachan to the *Guardian* afterwards (Holley and Chalk 2003). The win lifted Saints out of the bottom three and a run of five more victories in the next seven games transformed the landscape. Only a shock FA Cup third round exit at Second Division Rotherham partially curbed the surging optimism at St Mary's.

Many Portsmouth supporters failed fundamentally to grasp the significance of Saints' new home. Some have yet to. To spell it out, Saints were now a club geared for success in the modern football world, in which an ever-discerning public looked for best value in their leisure options, while the facility could generate revenue seven days a week. St Mary's provided a safe, comfortable environment to watch football and, whatever Pompey fans who have never visited the stadium might believe, it also could pack a punch in the atmosphere stakes. The *Observer* report of that momentous Charlton game recorded: 'The home fans remained vociferously behind their team. It was a classic example of how best to support a struggling team' (Holley and Chalk 2003).

Fratton Park, despite Terry Venables' not-to-be-forgotten cosmetics, was long past its sell-by date and now resembled, well, The Dell. The Archibald Leitch-designed South Stand always had much in common with the old Dell East Stand, and the concrete expanses of terracing, which could hold 50,000 in years gone by, simply could not be converted efficiently to accommodate seating.

On the pitch, too, Pompey were barren. Between December and March they won just three matches and were dumped out of the FA Cup third round at home by Third Division Leyton Orient. Conceding four second-half goals, after an own-goal had given Pompey the lead, was the last straw for Rix, although his reign limped on for another two months. The scapegoat was record signing, £1.7 million Japanese keeper Yoshi Kawaguchi, who had arrived amid a blaze of publicity in October. Whoever decided to sign the player, as anticipated merchandising revenues from the Far East failed to materialise, is as shrouded in mystery as ever.

Three years and several wasted million pounds later, Milan Mandaric was no nearer to finding the elusive Premiership formula. With car stickers popping up all over towns east of Southampton and west of Portsmouth proclaiming 'Saints is the South', the two clubs were probably as far apart as they'd ever been. Further even than Pompey's dark days in Division Four? True, Pompey were still only a division behind, as they had been for the best part of 35 years, but in terms of infrastructure and appeal, Pompey had little left with which to compete for the floating fan.

In fact, it looked like they were no longer 'floating'. Only once did Saints' gate drop below 30,000 in the second half of 2001-02, and on the final day a new record, 31,973, was set as Newcastle were beaten 3-1. 'Build it and they'll come,' so they say. At Southampton they'd come all right. Pompey's fans, with their 'you'll never fill it' jibes rammed back down their throats, were left with the single solace that, come what may, at least Saints were highly unlikely to win that coveted League title which had found its way south of London just twice, in 1949 and 1950. But like Proud Preston's 'double' in 1889 or Huddersfield's three consecutive titles in the 1920s, no matter how significant the achievement at the time, it had little to do with football 21st-century style.

For Southampton, though, fourth in the table was now the new first. Their plan was to move on to the next stage – that is to say join the Premiership's upper middle class, such as Aston Villa, Tottenham and Newcastle, who could realistically challenge for the cups and, in an exceptional year, maybe even Champions League qualification.

Portsmouth, on the other hand, looked doomed to perpetual living in their neighbour's long shadow. After the traumas of May 2001, 'mid-table mediocrity', promised pre-season by Graham Rix, was a realistic target, but it was to prove the rookie manager's epitaph. After the 0-0 home draw with Sheffield Wednesday on 23rd March, Pompey lay fifteenth with five matches to go.

It looked pretty much 'mission accomplished' for Rix, but he had fundamentally mis-read his employer's intentions. Mandaric was becoming increasingly frustrated that a substantial chunk of his personal fortune – knocked back, too, by the aftermath of the September 11th tragedies in the United States – looked like money down the drain. The promised Premiership land of untold riches, that's what they told him in 1999 anyway, seemed as far away as ever. Surely the last throw of his dice was to persuade Harry Redknapp out of semi-retirement as Director of Football and get back to managing again. However, the history of our rivalry surely tells us one thing. At the point when one club seems to have got the upper hand, like Pompey in the mid-1950s or Saints in the late-1970s, circumstances conspire to bring their orbits back into parallel. And so it came to pass.

The 2002-03 season is arguably the 'best' Hampshire has ever enjoyed. At Fratton Park, Redknapp set about dismembering Rix's squad, financed by the deadline-day sale of Peter Crouch to Aston Villa for £5 million. In a whirlwind summer it seemed like a player a week arrived at Fratton. The catalyst, however, arrived on the eve of the season. The 34-year-old Paul Merson, veteran of Arsenal glories past, not to mention a chequered list of clinical addictions, was persuaded to take a pay-cut to leave Villa Park. Immediately installed as captain, Merson's drive, determination and, above all, midfield class, transformed Portsmouth into title contenders. With Bulgarian Svetoslav Todorov also finding his range, the West Ham misfit striker, now signed twice by Redknapp, came into his own. Eight wins and a draw in the first nine games, with 22 goals scored, suggested this was no flash in the pan. Eight more wins in the next twelve games took Pompey beyond 50 points by the end of November 2002.

If nothing else, the relegation issue had been settled unseasonably early this year. From 26th August until 12th April Pompey led from the front. An injury-time home loss to relegation-bound Sheffield Wednesday, when a win would have clinched promotion, only delayed the inevitable by three days. Todorov scored the goal which beat Burnley before a sell-out – as it had been since January – 19,000 Fratton Park crowd. The result meant Pompey were back on top of the table and in the Premiership. At the final whistle some fans were on the pitch, although it wasn't quite over. The title arrived twelve days later, with a 3-2 win over Rotherham. As a champagne-soaked Paul Merson hoisted the very same championship trophy (or an exact replica) above his head that Reg Flewin had received more than 50 years previously, Portsmouth could start living the dream of a return to the big time.

After the promotion-clinching win over Burnley, Milan Mandaric – never shy of playing to the gallery – raised a banner which read: 'Step aside Saints, Pompey are in the Premiership!' For all the reasons already outlined, things weren't quite that simple.

Besides, Southampton were also doing a more than passable impression of a medium-large top-flight outfit these days. After an indifferent start, in which gates at St Mary's started drifting down towards that mid-20,000 mark, a run of eight wins and four draws in fourteen games saw Saints up to sixth. That elevated position was earned by a 1-0 win over Spurs, watched by close-on 32,000. The winning goal was scored by James Beattie, who was coming into his prime. Having failed to score in his first nine games, he now had thirteen to his name and was suddenly vying not only for the Premiership golden boot but an England call up too.

Three days later Beattie was at it again, as Saints sent the same opponents packing 4-0 in a televised Cup thrashing which confirmed that Saints were not in a false position. Earlier in the day, Pompey had also been televised in the third round, losing 1-4 at Manchester United. They had taken 9,000 supporters to Old Trafford, but with a swollen bank balance and the ability to now concentrate on promotion, there were few complaints. A gate of under 26,000 at St Mary's for the Cup-tie also served to illustrate the new reversal of priorities, that League football takes precedence in the modern football world. The season-ticket culture, well-established at The Dell, although not at Fratton, meant shelling out an extra £30 or so for every Cup-tie. Traditionally, FA Cup third round day meant a boost to average attendances, but no longer.

St Mary's was in fact booming. For twelve successive League matches from 9th November, more than 30,000 flocked to the stadium, a record that not even Pompey's championship-winning side could emulate. In October 2002, St Mary's was also full for the first international on the south coast for 100 years, as England drew 2-2 with Macedonia.

Gordon Strachan's side were soon packing them in for the Cup, too, as their run gathered momentum. For the fourth round against Millwall, however, the crowd was down to 24,000, partly due to restrictions on ticket sales. Steve Claridge, now with the Lions, put the First Division side ahead before wheeling off in delight, his name and number flaunted in the faces of the previously-taunting home fans. Saints had the last laugh though, as substitute Kevin Davies stabbed home an injury-time equaliser.

Saints' extra-time, 2-1 win at the New Den set up a fifth round tie with another First Division side, Norwich, the luck of the draw once again giving Southampton home advantage. Travelling Canaries ensured a gate of

31,000, but already there was a whiff that this might be Saints' year to get to, erm, 'Cardiff'. Wembley had been demolished eighteen months earlier, and until its resurrection – scheduled for 2006 – Cup finals would be held in the new Millennium Stadium. Anders Svensson and Jo Tessem scored the second-half goals against Norwich, which made the whiff a trifle stronger.

The quarter-final draw gave Saints yet another home tie, this time a delicate affair with First Division Wolves, managed now by Dave Jones. As befits an honourable man, he refused to play the media's attempted 'grudge match' game and concentrated on his own side's preparations. Another statistic which more blinkered Pompey fans might ponder upon was that when tickets went on sale to Saints members, the switchboard at St Mary's fielded 64,000 telephone calls in a day (Holley and Chalk 2003).

Southampton duly won 2-0 to reach the FA Cup semi-finals for the first time since 1986. Their luck held once again as they avoided 'Chelsea or Arsenal' and even Neil Warnock's grim-but-effective 'Sheffield United' and plucked First Division 'Number One, Watford' instead. A clash of dates with the London Marathon contributed to the two teams playing not in the capital, but at Villa Park. Southampton laid the ghost of their previous semi-final there in 1963 by winning 2-1. Brett Ormerod grabbed his first goal since October before half-time. The same player's cross with twelve minutes to go forced Paul Robinson to turn the ball into his own net, rendering Marcus Gayle's late reply meaningless.

Southampton were in the final! What better way to upstage their Pompey rivals' title march than by winning the FA Cup? That Saints did not is perhaps down to Gordon Strachan's fatal lack of conviction when it came to the crunch. In November, Saints had played a high-tempo, open style which had seen Arsenal (admittedly down to ten men) beaten 3-2 at St Mary's. Ten days before the 17th May final, playing a similar formation, Saints conceded five goals in the first 26 minutes at Highbury and eventually lost 1-6.

For the final, Strachan opted for young Chris Baird's defensive capabilities rather than Fabrice Fernandes' flair. Once Robert Pires gave Arsenal a first-half lead, it was too late to change the game plan and the Cup was lost. As a consolation prize, Saints found themselves back in European competition, earning the Cup 'winner's' UEFA Cup slot as second-placed Arsenal had already qualified for the Champions League. FA Cup runners-up or Division One champions? First rate 'nearly' men or second-class silverware? Even when both clubs do well, sorting out who has done better is far from clear-cut.

One thing certain was Portsmouth's right to be in the Premiership. With 98 points, 97 goals, six ahead of runners-up Leicester and eighteen of third-placed Sheffield United, predictions of a swift return from whence they had come defied the evidence. The previous two seasons had seen similarly emphatic First Division champions – Fulham and Manchester City – survive their first season with something to spare. But Redknapp knew he would have to shuffle his pack once more. Out went Paul Merson, joining Walsall as he continued to grapple with his addiction demons, while in came 'been there, done that, worn the tee-shirt' Teddy Sheringham.

After more than 40 years in Saints' shadow, Pompey were quick to take the opportunity to step out of it, going unbeaten in their first five matches and, for 24 hours on 26th August they were actually top of the Premiership, after a last-minute Sheringham penalty completed his hat-trick and a 4-0 win over Bolton. In more than ten years of trying, Saints had never managed to reach such an elevated position; Pompey had done it in what seemed like less than ten minutes. The bubble soon began to deflate and the 'natural', in Southampton at least, order was restored as Saints went back above Pompey on 20th September, winning 3-1 at Spurs, while Pompey lost 1-2 at home to Blackburn.

The first League derby for almost eight years was scheduled for Sunday, 21st December, another high noon shoot-out, this time at St Mary's. But like London buses, when the one fixture came along another quickly followed. The fourth round draw of the Carling Cup, the new name for the League Cup, pulled Saints and Pompey out of the hat in succession, scheduling a 2nd December dress rehearsal for the League clash. By then, both clubs were in the doldrums. Saints' 'European Tour' played just one date, Bucharest, where they lost 0-1 on the night to Steaua and 1-2 on aggregate. Around 2,000 Saints fans made the trip, but that impressive number was offset by anecdotal evidence by returning fans that it wasn't just the worst of Pompey's fans who could excel at boorishness. Similarly, the on-going legal proceedings over the so-called 'Battle of Maze Hill', a supposedly pre-arranged scrap between Saints and Charlton fans in April 2002, conceded more of the high moral ground.

The build up to the Carling Cup-tie was given a further twist by the death of 'Mr Southampton' Ted Bates a few days before the game. Arguably the greatest club servant English football has ever produced, in more than 60 years he had given his life to his beloved Saints as player, coach, manager, general manager and vice president. With hindsight, the decision to observe a minute's silence before the Cup-tie was ill-advised. When you have a jar of nitro-glycerine in your hand, the last thing you do is shake it. Before the kick-off, delayed by 30 minutes as traffic heading west on the M27 was held up by a serious accident which the driver of the Portsmouth team coach had skilfully avoided, the atmosphere was poisonous as anti-Pompey and anti-Saints taunts were traded. When referee Graham Poll sounded his whistle to commence the silence, a handful of the 4,500 Pompey fans present disgraced themselves by shouting out. Enraged by what they were hearing, the boos of Saints fans drowned out the cat-calls but rendered the 'silence' useless. Poll did the right thing in the circumstances and cut it short. Inevitably and understandably, the blame was heading the Pompey fans' way – 'you're the lot who booed Ted Bates' – but in reality it was an incident that did neither set of supporters any credit.

'The minute's silence was a shame. I never met a nicer man than Ted. I feared the worse and would rather they had left it until the weekend,' commented Redknapp afterwards. For the record, Saints fans did the right thing by their man the following Sunday, before the home game with Charlton. It is a genuine pity that the overwhelming majority of Pompey fans who would have liked to have done the same weren't allowed to by the moronic element amongst their own. It's also a shame the game wasn't as exciting as the pre-match shenanigans, but the two teams' lack of form, one win for Saints and two for Pompey in eight games respectively, made for an error-strewn affair. The difference was the class of James Beattie, who imperiously swept home the opening goal after 33 minutes, then stood his ground when it seemed easier to shoot in the final seconds to let Arjan De Zeeuw foul him in the box. He duly converted. Fighting outside the ground before and after the game led to sixteen arrests.

A little under three weeks later, the balance of power had firmly shifted back westwards. Saints had used their Carling Cup win as a launch pad, winning their next two League games, including the impressive scalp of Liverpool at Anfield, to sit in sixth place. Pompey could only draw and lose one in the same period and their slender squad, decimated by injuries and now suspension, as De Zeeuw served a ban for the red card incurred in fouling Beattie, were now in the thick of the relegation scrap. The cup-tie had been reasonably well contested, but the League affair was very one-sided. The Sunday lunchtime start drew some of the sting from the occasion, and the atmosphere was no better than lukewarm, but vitriol still took precedence over support. Once Saints' Jason Dodd's inswinging corner flew back off the far post and into the net off Sebastian Schemmel's head, there was only one winner. Marian Pahars made it 2-0 midway through the second half, and Beattie's plunging header completed the rout on the final whistle. 'Premier League? You're having a laugh,' sang the Saints fans. It was hard to argue. Meanwhile, Saints were up to fourth and ten points ahead. The prospect of qualification for the Champions' League was being openly discussed without prompting muffled laughter. Step aside Saints? Brush aside Pompey, more like.

The football season is, so clichéd wisdom tells us, a marathon, not a sprint. Southampton's first competitive visit to Fratton since 1987 was scheduled for 21st March and no doubt, after the December 'double', older Saints fans were licking their lips at the prospect of the treble, and, like in 1976, pitching Portsmouth closer to oblivion. Certainly, Pompey were staring down the barrel ahead of the game, delayed by 24 hours for Sky TV coverage. Leicester's last-minute point-saving goal against Everton the day before had ensured Pompey remained firmly lodged in the third relegation spot, with just nine games to play.

However, Saints' lofty ambitions had turned to dust. Two wins in eleven games had dumped them among the mid-table also-rans, while the Carling and FA Cup trails had gone cold, the latter at the first stage following a 0-3 battering at St Mary's by Newcastle for the benefit of the watching nation. Gordon Strachan had also departed at the end of January, citing the need of a break from football. In his place came Plymouth manager Paul Sturrock, who had taken the West Country club from the Third Division to the brink of the First in double-quick time. His start was good enough, a 2-0 win over Liverpool at St Mary's. A win at Fratton Park would go a pretty long way to proving that those sceptical of Sturrock's suitability were wrong.

The one thing in Pompey's favour was their decent home form – all their six Premiership wins to date, including the scalps of Liverpool and Spurs – had come at the old ground. Two weeks before, though, Arsenal had exposed the team's frailty, 5-1 in the FA Cup quarter-final, in another televised humiliation. Physical comparisons with The Dell of nine or ten years earlier were still apt. Fratton was down at heel, cramped and intimidating. In short, big-time Charlies, used to individual showers, personal toilets and dressing rooms the size of a small house, hated it. So did opposing fans. The Milton End, where the visitors were housed, didn't have a roof. Any atmosphere they tried to generate quickly dissipated, and when it rained …

Twenty minutes before kick-off it did more than rain. A violent hailstorm whipped in off the Solent causing the exposed Saints fans to scatter, fruitlessly scurrying for cover which didn't exist. And the Pompey fans started to laugh. To them it was funny. A portent? Proof that the Portsmouth city motto 'Heaven's Light Our Guide' perhaps had something in it after all? Or perhaps a demonstration that a club with such dilapidated facilities had no place in this League.

That inclement intervention somehow lifted much of the Pompey fan's burden of having to put up with being at least one step behind Saints for 40-odd years. Duly delivered, Fratton Park was at its noisiest and most intimidating throughout the 90 minutes, but as the game wore on Pompey's general dominance hadn't fashioned a truly decent chance. Saints were undeniably off-key, Beattie's speculative 40-yard free-kick ending with him kicking more turf than ball, causing more terrace hilarity. Then, in the 68th minute, Pompey's on-loan Russian midfielder Alexei Smertin found

Steve Stone breaking down the right. The former Forest and Villa winger's cross was true and Nigerian striker Yakubu guided home his first goal since January. But could Pompey hang onto their first proper victory over Saints at Fratton since 1963? In the final ten minutes Sturrock finally threw caution to the wind and the introduction of Pahars and Fernandes finally started to stretch Pompey. With time running out Beattie nodded down to Kevin Phillips, ten yards out. His angled volley looked a goal all over, but the football Gods were with Pompey and the ball hit the inside of the post and came out. Claus Lundekvam thumped a late header straight at Shaka Hislop and Pompey had done it. The course of the history of this particular derby had inevitably been changed. Serious disturbances after the match took some of the edge off the occasion, as baying Pompey 'fans' – although many had not even been at the game – fought pitched battles with police on Fratton Road. They took out their frustration after attempts to 'get at' the Saints contingent had been effectively thwarted. The ongoing police investigation has since seen scores of people convicted for their part in the disturbances.

Back on the field, Portsmouth were rejuvenated and seven unbeaten games later – among them a 1-0 win over defending champions Manchester United – a 1-1 home draw with Fulham ensured Pompey's Premiership survival, with three games to go. A fortnight later, with Saints winning just one and losing four of their last seven games, Pompey's 5-1 rout of Middlesbrough meant they had almost overhauled their rivals.

Now that Pompey have obtained planning permission to turn their stadium through 90 degrees, with the option of creating a 36,000-capacity arena, the battle for those floating fans may well soon be joined again in earnest. January 2005 is the latest reported starting date on the revamped stadium. Meanwhile, following Sturrock's departure after just six months, Saints have turned to former Pompey winger Steve Wigley to try to make that now overdue push for the upper reaches of the Premiership.

If you are reading this book in the hope of finding out just which club is the bigger, you will be disappointed. The best I can offer is that they are in fact pretty evenly matched. Unlike, say, the Manchester derby, which has been fought year-in, year-out and has seen one club comprehensively claim the ascendancy, this battle for south-coast supremacy is up for grabs once more. Saints' sound husbandry since the late 1950s contrasts starkly with the more chaotic boom and bust approach at Fratton Park, usually at the whim of a sugar-daddy chairman, but after more than 100 years we are back almost to where we started back in 1899: two clubs of similar stature who have got there by radically different means. The fact that there is no conclusive answer to the question 'who's better' should be seen as a positive, however. In consequence, this tale of two cities, of local passion, pride and prejudice, surely has many more chapters to run.

SOUTHERN LEAGUE

April 14, 1900	S 0	P 2	4,000
April 16, 1900	P 2	S 0	10,000
Sept, 20, 1900	P 0	S 0	12,000
April 6, 1901	S 2	P 0	4,000
Oct 12, 1901	P 2	S 2	10,000
Nov 2, 1901	S 3	P 4	14,000
Sept 27, 1902	S 1	P 1	16,000
Jan 10, 1903	P 0	S 3	20,447
Nov 28, 1903	P 0	S 1	12,152
Mar 26, 1904	S 2	P 0	15,000
Nov 26, 1904	S 1	P 0	15,000
Mar 25, 1905	P 1	S 2	12,000
Nov 25, 1905	P 1	S 0	16,000
Mar 31, 1906	S 1	P 2	unknown
Oct 20, 1906	S 2	P 0	12,000
Feb 23, 1907	P 1	S 2	12,000
Sept 28, 1907	P 3	S 0	18,000
Jan 25, 1908	S 1	P 0	6,000
Sept 26, 1908	S 2	P 0	16,000
Jan 30, 1909	P 3	S 0	12,000
Nov 6, 1909	P 1	S 1	12,000
Mar 19, 1910	S 1	P 2	unknown
Sept 10, 1910	S 3	P 0	unknown
Jan 7, 1911	P 0	S 1	9,000
Sept 28, 1912	S 2	P 3	unknown
Jan 25, 1913	P 2	S 0	14,000
Dec 25, 1913	P 2	S 0	14,000
Dec 26, 1913	S 4	P 3	19,291
Dec 25, 1914	P 0	S 1	9,494
Dec 26, 1914	S 4	P 3	7,000
Oct 18, 1919	P 5	S 1	20,000
Feb 28, 1920	S 0	P 0	18,000

FOOTBALL LEAGUE DIVISION THREE

Sept 11, 1920	S 2	P 0	18,000
Sept 18, 1920	P 0	S 1	20,585

FOOTBALL LEAGUE DIVISION THREE (SOUTH)

Mar 18, 1922	P 0	S 2	26,382
Mar 25, 1922	S 1	P 1	17,000

FOOTBALL LEAGUE DIVISION TWO

Sept 27, 1924	S 0	P 0	19,366
Nov 29, 1924	P 1	S 1	25,000
Sept 5, 1925	S 1	P 3	18,000
Jan 16, 1926	P 1	S 2	12,000
Aug 28, 1926	P 3	S 1	27,896
Jan 15, 1927	S 0	P 2	19,058
Aug 27, 1960	S 5	P 1	28,845
Dec 31, 1960	P 1	S 1	31,059
Oct 13, 1962	P 1	S 1	32,407
Mar 2, 1963	S 4	P 2	25,463
Sept 28, 1963	P 2	S 0	29,459
Feb 8, 1964	S 2	P 3	26,171
Sept 12, 1964	P 0	S 3	25,024
Jan 16, 1965	S 2	P 2	23,911
Aug 28, 1965	S 2	P 2	26,665
Feb 5, 1966	P 2	S 5	25,860
Sept 14, 1974	S 2	P 1	19,361
Dec 26, 1974	P 1	S 2	19,543
Sept 27, 1975	S 4	P 0	17,310
Apr 6, 1976	P 0	S 1	24,115

FOOTBALL LEAGUE DIVISION ONE

Aug 22, 1987	P 2	S 2	20,161
Jan 3, 1988	S 0	P 2	17,002

PREMIERSHIP

Dec 21, 2003	S 3	P 0	31,679
Mar 21, 2004	P 1	S 0	20,140

FA CUP

Jan 13, 1906 R1	S 5	P 1	14,000
Jan 28, 1984 R4	P 0	S 1	36,000
Jan 7, 1996 R3	S 3	P 0	15,236

FOOTBALL LEAGUE CUP

Dec 2, 2003 R4	S 2	P 0	29,201